LOVE AND THUNDER
Plays by Women in the Age of Queen Anne

The Adventures of Venice by Susanna Centlivre; *The Spanish Wives* by Mary Pix; *Love At A Loss* by Catharine Trotter; *Antiochus the Great* by Jane Wiseman. Edited and introduced by Kendall.

KENDALL grew up in a migrant working-class family in America's deep south, set out at sixteen to make her way in the world, and spent twenty-four years as a student and theatre worker. She acted for years and toured the States with her one-woman show called *Characters*; she started a feminist theatre company in New Orleans; and her plays and monologues have been performed on radio, in the streets, and in small theatres from Oregon to New York. She supported her artistic habits by working as waitress, shop clerk, secretary, counsellor for heroin addicts and juvenile delinquents, editor, English teacher, and itinerant typist. She also pours much of her life-energy into affairs of the heart, having, as Virginia Woolf scholar Jane Marcus says, 'a genius for passionate attachment.'

In 1983 she discovered a movement of eighteenth-century British women playwrights whose adventurous, poverty-stricken, eccentric and often desperate lives were not so different from her own. Her fascination with that group of women, and with the history of how people play, led her to take on a new identity as a scholar. She collected a Ph.D. in 1986 and now teaches theatre history and acting at Smith College in Northampton, Massachusetts.

LOVE AND THUNDER

Plays by Women in the Age of Queen Anne

THE ADVENTURES OF VENICE
Susanna Centlivre

THE SPANISH WIVES
Mary Pix

LOVE AT A LOSS
or
MOST VOTES CARRY IT
Catharine Trotter

ANTIOCHUS THE GREAT
or
THE FATAL RELAPSE
Jane Wiseman

Edited and introduced by
Kendall

Methuen Drama

A METHUEN PAPERBACK

This volume first published in Great Britain in 1988
by Methuen Drama, Michelin House, 81 Fulham Road, London SW3 6RB
Distributed in the USA by HEB Inc. 70 Cork Street, Portsmouth, New Hampshire
03801.

Selection and introduction copyright © 1988 Kendall.

Printed in Great Britain by Richard Clay Ltd, Bungay, Suffolk

British Library Cataloguing in Publication Data

Love and thunder: plays by women in the
age of Queen Anne. – (Methuen theatrescripts).
1. Drama in English. Women writers,
1702–1745. Anthologies
I. Kendall
822′.5′0809287

ISBN 0-413-17750-5

For Agnes Grinstead Anderson,
my mentor and genie,
and for
Margaret Richter Robison.

CONTENTS

ACKNOWLEDGEMENTS

This anthology exists because some amazing women lived and wrote and died in the time of Queen Anne; these women have peopled my dreams, thoughts, and fantasies for five years and are as lively to me as my own good friends. For bringing us together I thank the entire staff of the Humanities Research Center in Austin, Texas, especially Ken Craven and Pat Fox; Sarah Wimbush, of the National Portrait Gallery in London; and scholars Standish Meacham, Oscar Brockett, Jane Marcus, and Sue-Ellen Case, whose ideas and advice shaped, inspired, and guided me. I'm also grateful to Leslie Whitbread, for introducing me to the pleasures of irrelevancy; to Lillian Faderman, Dale Spender, Ruth Perry, Isobel Grundy, Lois Potter, and Constance Clark for advice and encouragement. Deborah Lubar stopped in the headlong rush to meet her own deadlines in order to read my introductions and save me from embarrassing excess, and the generosity of her friendship carries me on.

I thank Alice Walker for defining the word 'womanist'; and for helping me learn the womanist way of seeing which forms the basis of my analysis of history, theatre, and literature, and I thank certain friends who have been my models: Leif Anderson, Gloria Anzalduà, Moira Buckley Ambrose, Andrea Canaan, Mary Capps, Jyoti Hansa Cripps, Sylvia DeSwaan, Looie Drinkwater, Olga Francois, Ann Gallmeyer, Willie Mae Goolsby, Judy Grahn, Joan Lennox, Karyn London, Audre Lorde, Anne Lovell, Eddy Marshman, Donna Myhre, Darlene Hingle Olivo, Diana Panara, Elizabeth Rogers, Maryann Simpson, Patricia Sipe, and Sonny Wainwright.

I thank my Texas family, who saw this project take shape: Harriette Andreadis, who drove me to it; Mary Calk, who stood solidly with me in the first stages of discovery; Cate Cannon, whose presence sustained and delighted me during two years of the work; Brock, who celebrated all the 'family' birthdays with us and laughed when I took myself seriously; Paul Reinhardt, who taught me to curtsey and to curse with style; and Richard Runkel and Bill Stotts, my best buddies, who consistently advised me to lighten up.

I completed the project at Smith College, where John Hellweg and Chezia Thompson-Cager got me through icy winter and the mud-months of the soul; where I enjoyed the encouragement of the best of all possible deans, Fran Volkmann, and a thoroughly lovable chairperson, Len Berkman; and where I was bolstered by the immanent practicality of Sally Donohue.

I thank my teenage son, Seth, who surrendered use of the computer for four years, kept me in touch with rock and rap; and endured my obsessions with grace and charm. I thank Margaret Robison for the roadmap to my southern home and the splendour of the journey. I thank Dale and Lynn Spender for a high-spirited breakfast in Oxford, and for telling Methuen about this work. And finally but by no means least, I thank Nick Hern, Pamela Edwardes and Peggy Butcher for thoughtful editing, tact, and patience.

INTRODUCTION

1694, London. A tense coquette flirts with a squire old enough to be her grandfather. She hides the moth holes in her overskirt with a flitting fan, disguises her desperation with well-turned phrases, hopes for a marriage offer from the jowled frog whose snuff-stained fingers reek of mildew and power. She has known better times. Her father was a favourite of King Charles II; she spent her childhood writing poems and reading leather-bound volumes on velvet cushions by mullioned windows. But now her father is dead at sea, which leaves her dependent on city relatives who ridicule her bookish airs and whisper about her meetings with a certain Lady in town. She is Catharine Trotter, fifteen and without a dowry.

This gifted teenager finds Mary Pix, a ruddy-cheeked widow in her thirties who has an idea and calls in Delariviere Manley, another bookish girl seduced and abandoned by her guardian and left to fend for herself in the streets of London. Pix knows that the local theatre company is in turmoil, desperate for new scripts; Aphra Behn is six years in the grave and no woman playwright has come to claim her following.

With Trotter, Pix, and Manley a movement is born: a movement of women playwrights, conscious of themselves as women working in a man's field, proud to call themselves the successors of Aphra Behn, determined to survive financially without male sponsorship, politically aware of themselves as women with an alternative vision to offer theatregoers, a vision which would later be called feminist. Including plays by a runaway named Susanna Centlivre and a mysterious serving woman named Jane Wiseman, over forty women's plays were actually produced on London's stages between 1695 and 1723. Some plays bore their authors' names; others their initials; some were published 'By a Young Lady.' But all offered a new view of women and women's relationships.

The most immediate questions, to those of us now steeped in the history of the silencing of women's voices, are: How was this phenomenon possible? How did these women get the nerve to impose themselves on the British public? Who were their models? Who believed in and encouraged them? Who attended their plays? Who risked producing them?

The easy and quick answers lie right in the prologues and prefaces the women wrote to their plays. Their models were Aphra Behn, Katherine Philips, and Sappho, whom they invoked again and again as proof that women were capable of writing literature. They were helped by the presence of a woman who was heir apparent to the throne in 1695 and monarch between 1702 and 1714: during the time of Anne, outright misogyny was tantamount to treason. They were also helped by the existence of a women's movement in their time. The friends and contemporaries of this group of playwrights in London's tiny literary world included pioneers of feminist theory: Mary Astell, Sarah Fyge Fields Egerton, Judith Drake, Elizabeth Rowe, Lady Mary Chudleigh.[1]

Both women and men supported the playwrights; both women and men attended their plays. But women's support was particularly vital. Female playwrights dedicated over a third of their plays to women, and they begged 'the ladies' for approval, or thanked 'the ladies' for support in one preface after another. Their nerve came from the (often desperate) need to earn money, the lure of the well-packed third night,[2] the personal chutzpah that led them to dare to compete with men in the play-market. In brief, they wrote to earn money.

It took more than models, a female monarch, a feminist movement, and nerve or desperation, however, to make the movement of women playwrights possible. London's theatre world was in spectacular disarray in the season of 1695–96, the 'annus mirabilis' in which half the new plays produced in London were by women. There was an unusual demand for new plays, for different plays, for sensational plays or plays by sensational authors.

In 1694, the theatre in Drury Lane was the only one licensed to perform. Its unpopular manager, attempting to pressure the mature stars to retire, reassigned their starring roles to young hopefuls. The elder stars and their loyal supporters approached patrons and the British bureaucracy with their grievances and ultimately left in a flurry of heated words and legal documents in the season of 1695–96, establishing a rival theatre in the tennis courts at Lincoln's Inn Fields. Bombast, internecine feuds, and desperate heroics made theatre life as dramatic offstage as on.

When the dust settled, the Drury Lane company was left with the old manager, two well-fitted houses, a large and elaborate stock of scenery and props, a collection of glamorous costumes, and a gaggle of second-string, largely untried, undisciplined, or alcoholic actors. Lincoln's Inn Fields, managed by two women and a man, had the finest actors in the English-speaking world, and little else. Neither house had exclusive rights to plays written before 1695, which meant that on occasion both might stage the same play at the same time, and both plays might fail.

It had been difficult for one theatre to sustain itself; it seemed impossible for two.[3] Between 1695 and 1702, both houses flirted with bankruptcy and were often unable to pay actors and stagehands. Audience composition and taste had been changing over the past fifteen years and had become nearly impossible to predict. The bawdy, stomping comedies of the Restoration still titillated some but revolted others. Ribaldry worked one day then faltered; mellifluous grandiosity followed the same course. Shakespeare was judged a rude and unlettered fellow, his plays acceptable only with much editing and adaptation.

Preachers issued pamphlets, inveighed in their pulpits against the evils of the theatre, and enjoined the faithful not to attend. Fops made flamboyant entrances at each theatre of an evening but escaped ticket sellers at both. Italian singers, rope dancers, jugglers, even trained swans and monkeys were hired to perform between the acts, in the hope of pleasing all the people. Show-time was postponed to early evening, so that businessmen, shopkeepers and apprentices might attend in larger numbers. Managers and playwrights cultivated the approval of 'the ladies,' who might fill the boxes with parties of their well-dressed friends. An evening's entertainment, including inter-act variety numbers, lengthened to five hours or more, while purveyors of oranges, nuts, and sex plied their trade in the aisles and the pit.

By the time the two London companies reunited in 1708, the movement of women writers had begun to wane. Pix was on her deathbed; Trotter had married a clergyman and moved to the provinces; Manley had turned to novel-writing; Wiseman had purchased a tavern and quit writing. Only Centlivre, by then married to Queen Anne's Yeoman of the Mouth, continued writing plays until after the Queen's death; and in 1716 *The Northern Heiress*, an intriguing comedy by an Irish widow, Mary Davys, was successful enough to earn Davys the purchasing price of a Cambridge coffeehouse. It was set in York, where Davys had been living for some years and had likely seen local productions of the other women's comedies, for it is similar in tone, spirit, and theme to many of them.

While not all of the plays by women which appeared on London stages between 1695 and 1716 differ in every respect from contemporaneous men's plays, it is generally possible to distinguish a woman's play of the era from a man's without an author's name. Since the only standard of playwriting was the male one, it is surprising that women's plays differ as much as they do. The most apparent distinctions are in female characterization and theme.[4]

The women's plays usually feature female protagonists who are intelligent, independent, and personally forceful. While women's tragedies adhere to class conventions of the time (all principals are 'nobly' born), significant supporting roles are often given to the noblewomen's female attendants, who may be lower-class. Women's comedies often feature ingenious heroines who marry above their class or acquire enough money to establish themselves independently by the end of the play (Susanna Centlivre's *The Beau's Duel* [1702] is one good example). Women playwrights of Queen Anne's time seldom created standard men's heroines who were 'feminine' in the sense of passive and helpless, whose only desires were to be loved and protected by a strong man. Rather, the women's heroines are active and sly in seeking out financially advantageous matches; they object to misogyny and men's abuse of power, challenge sexual hypocrisy, and are remarkably tolerant and forgiving of 'fallen' women in their midst. Like men's plays of the time, the women's plays decry forced marriage and have good fun with cross-dressing of both sexes, yet with a twist: in women's plays, clever women frequently outwit boorish fathers or would-be suitors and may choose single life over marriage; and in women's plays, men who dress like women are merely ridiculous, while women who dress like men take on men's privileges and power.[5]

Another theme common to many of the women's plays is particularly significant to the study of women's history. It is the depiction of female friendships of primary, sometimes romantic, intensity. Trotter's *Agnes de Castro* (performed 1695, printed 1696), based on Aphra Behn's novel of the same title, may be called the first lesbian play in English stage history.[6] Written when Trotter was sixteen, in a style imitative of Dryden's heroic tragedies, it lacks the rapid repartee of her later works and would be difficult to stage with conviction, though it rewards study. Similarly eroticized relationships between women occur in Pix's tragedies, *Queen Catherine* (1698) and *Double Distress* (1701); and women's friendships are central in Pix's *Czar of Muscovy* (1701), and *Conquest of Spain* (1705).

In addition, Pix and Trotter both feature reliable, trustworthy female friendships in their comedies (the plays in this volume are typical in that respect). Jane Wiseman features friendships of considerable importance and intensity between the ladies and their female companions in her *Antiochus* (performed 1701, printed 1702); some of Susanna Centlivre's heroines risk losing male lovers to preserve their own relationships, as in *The Wonder* (1714); and the complicitous friendship of the female principals in Mary Davy's *Northern Heiress* (1716) provides a refreshing complement to the more simple-minded and conventional friendship of the two men. The only playwright of the era who does not emphasize female friendship in her plays is Delariviere Manley, though she creates trusting relationships between her noble divas and their loyal female attendants.

Male playwrights customarily created female principals who abused their attendants and related to each other as rivals for the love of the male star. (See Vanbrugh's *The Relapse* [1696] and *Provok'd Wife* [1697], Congreve's *The Old Batchelour* and *The Double-Dealer* [both 1693], and his *The Way of the World* [1700], and many more by Cibber, Lee, Shadwell, and others.) Most men's plays focused on men's activities and featured male protagonists, and all depicted men's activities, friendships, or disputes with each other as central to dramatic action. Men usually portrayed women only in relation to men or in competition with each other, and their heroines' highest goals were male approval and matrimony.

There were good reasons, in the age of Anne, why men's characterizations of women were so limited. Men and women of the upper and middle classes were reared separately and educated differently; courted each other formally; and even within marriage, typically interacted with each other in highly structured ways, which did not lead to much depth of understanding.[7] Thus male playwrights were simply unable to write knowledgably about the nature of women's lives, the concerns of women's hearts, or the ways women related to each other when no men were present. Yet all literature provided a textbook that women might read, if they sought understanding of male psychology.

Female playwrights, therefore, had a much richer conception of the character of woman than did their brothers; and they had considerable insight into the character of man, as well. To the hundreds of married women in the boxes and middle galleries whose oldest and deepest friendships were with other women, and who found that indeed most of life's dramas took place after the wedding dance with which so many men's plays conclude, the women's plays must have seemed uniquely 'right.' Men in the audience, trained not to expect much from the minds and pens of women, were pleasantly surprised as well.

The women playwrights were hailed as 'immortals of the age.' Great poets. Masters of their craft. Yet most of their plays fell into obscurity by mid-eighteenth century. (A few of Centlivre's, which remained popular long enough to be exported to the colonies, proved the exception.) There are many reasons for the disappearance of the women's plays from the literary and dramatic canon: fashion, backlash against the feminism inherent in many of the plays, and institutionalized misogyny that led gentleman scholars, librarians, and anthologists of succeeding decades to ignore the works of 'scribbling women' are just a few.[8] Not every one of the women's plays of the Queen Anne era is worthy of being remembered. Some are no better than plays by lesser male playwrights whose belaboured works have also dropped from view. Yet some are real jewels, remarkable plays of dramatic force and poetry. This volume brings a handful of those to light again.

Forgotten and unexamined until the 1970s, and since then available only in obscure dissertations, costly multi-volume facsimiles, or decaying and mottled first editions in rare book collections,[9] the best of the women's comedies are rollicking, action-packed, and stageworthy; as fit for the polyglot tastes of twentieth-century theatregoers as they were for audiences of their own time. Like the comedies of Congreve, Vanbrugh, and Farquhar, they're a bit verbose for modern taste. Yet many are well worth staging again, with some cutting.

The tragedies are, at worst, ponderous and unlikely; at best, poetic and still deeply affecting. Most don't accord with modern tastes; nor, for that matter, do the tragedies of Congreve and Dryden. Yet Congreve and Dryden are upheld by the canon, and the best women's tragedies are similar to theirs in plot, style, and language. And while the feminism inherent in the women's plays was ahead of its time in Queen Anne's day, and was simply confusing to critics of the last two centuries, it now has a startlingly contemporary ring, and with that a depth of characterization in female roles unheard of in 'period' plays by men.

The comedies in this volume have been chosen for their stageworthiness; the tragedy, for its literary value. No attempt has been made to restrict their use, for the recovery of these plays and the movement which served as their context is merely the opening of a door on an era in theatrical and literary history which has been closed to scrutiny too long. There is room for a great deal of scholarship, speculation, and study, here. There is room for more discovery, for reading aloud, and for jubilation and whooping, at the reclamation of so much good theatre, such thigh-slapping hilarity, such pretty love. There is reason for producers, directors, actors, and audiences to celebrate the availability of love and thunder written by women in a colourful idiom which resonates with philosophical issues as current as the latest news, and with well-drawn roles for both women and men.

About the time I discovered these plays, I came across a rather interesting recipe for the success of women playwrights in the introduction to the first of Michelene Wandor's anthologies of modern women's plays. She writes,

> . . . women surface as playwrights when the conditions are right: when there are changes in the dominant sexual morality which benefit the social position of women, when a movement for political change includes a feminist component, or when revolutions in the theatre itself make it possible for women to seize the time and make their own mark.[10]

All these conditions were present in 1696. I would add to Wandor's statement: Women surface as playwrights when there is a market for new plays; when there are people hungry for women's voices and women's vision, willing to support women's plays by attendance; when there are women in theatre management who make a particular effort to produce women's plays; when there are capable actresses looking for representations of women which demand and reflect the truth of women's experience; when those who decide which plays will be produced have women's plays to choose from; and when women writers are confident they are capable of writing plays, can draw strength from the tradition and heritage of women as playwrights, and can expect financial rewards for their work.

Kendall, 1988

[1] *The works of many of these writers have recently been made available in Moira Ferguson's* First Feminists: British Women Writers 1578–1799 *(Bloomington: Indiana University Press, 1985); Hilda Smith's* Reason's Disciples: Seventeenth-century English Feminists *(Urbana: University of Illinois Press, 1982), is also helpful.*

[2] *Playwrights in this period earned the profits from the third night of the run of their play. Many plays failed to survive three nights, in which case their authors made no money at all. But a full house on the third night could yield a playwright enough money to set herself up in a regular business, and if the play were a complete runaway success, the author would receive proceeds from the sixth night, or even the ninth. Seldom did any play run longer than nine nights, though Centlivre's* Gamester *(1705) ran twelve.*

[3] *Judith Milhous'* Thomas Betterton and the Management of Lincoln's Inn Fields 1695–1708 *(Southern Illinois University Press, 1979) is particularly useful for details of these difficulties.*

[4] *See Richard Levin's article, 'Some Second Thoughts on Central Themes,' in the* Modern Language Review 67 *(1972) 1–10, for an amusing perspective on thematic analyses of drama.*

[5] *For extensive discussions of these themes in the women's plays, see Edna Steeves' introductions to the Garland facsimile edition of* The Plays of Mary Pix *and* Catharine Trotter *(1982), and three American doctoral dissertations: Paula Louise Barbour's* A Critical Edition of Mary Pix's The Spanish Wives *(1696), with Introduction and Notes (Yale, 1975, UMI 76–13,695); Constance Clark's* The Female Wits: Catharine Trotter, Delariviere Manley, and Mary Pix – Three Women Playwrights Who Made Their Debuts in the London Season of 1695–96 *(City University of New York, 1984, UMI 8409389); and Kathryn Kendall's* Theatre, Society, and Women Playwrights in London from 1695 through the Queen Anne Era *(University of Texas, 1986, UMI 8618505).*

[6] *See 'From Lesbian Heroine to Devoted Wife: or, What the Stage Would Allow,' by Kathryn Kendall, in* Journal of Homosexuality *(May 1986), pp. 9–22.*

[7] *The journal kept by a travelling gentlewoman,* The Journey of Celia Fiennes *(1696), available in several modern reprints, vividly describes this homosocial world, and the extreme superficiality and formality of relations between the sexes. So too do the memoirs of foreign visitors to England in this era:* Mr. Misson's Memoirs and Observations, *by Henri Misson, translated by John Ozell and published in London in 1719; and Zacharias Konrad von Uffenbach's* London in 1710, *translated by William H. Quarrell and Margaret More and published in London by Faber and Faber in 1934.* The Wentworth Papers, 1705–1739 *(edited by James Joel Cartwright and published in London by Wyman & Sons in 1883) are particularly effective in documenting how separate were the lives of upper class men and women. More recent analyses include that by Lawrence Stone,* The Family, Sex and Marriage in England 1500–1800, *Harper, 1977.*

[8] *Joanna Russ, in* How to Suppress Women's Writing *(Austin: University of Texas Press, 1982), deals in depth with this issue, as does Dale Spender's* Women of Ideas and What Men Have Done to Them *(London: Routledge & Kegan Paul, 1982).*

[9] *Fidelis Morgan's* The Female Wits: Women Playwrights on The London Stage 1660–1720 *(Virago, 1981), is the exception; it made four of the plays available in popular form, along with a model play by the pioneer who led the generation of women writers before them, Aphra Behn.*

[10] *In the introduction to* Plays by Women, Vol. 1 *(London: Methuen, 1982), p. 8.*

EDITING OF THE TEXTS

Audiences in Queen Anne's time delighted in extended word-play and felt cheated if a theatrical evening ran less than four to five hours. Obviously, plays created then are over-long by contemporary standards. In all the comedies I have inserted brackets [] around text which may be cut to suit twentieth-century audiences. Suggestions for major cuts (a half-page or more of the original) are indicated by bold brackets **[]**. I have also bracketed incidental verbosity, references to then-current events now forgotten, puns that no longer work, and a few archaic expressions. Occasionally I have inserted a word or two to clarify meaning, and braces {} are used to indicate these insertions.

Wherever parentheses are used (), they were present in the original; the same is true for dashes. Spellings used by the authors to indicate dialect are followed by (sic) when this use is not instantly apparent. It should be noted that the authors' use of second person pronouns (your, thy, you, thee) is inconsistent and has been left so in this edition, as have other inconsistencies, such as use of contractions and spellings of expletives.

I have regularised the use of capital letters and punctuation and have altered spellings to conform with modern practice in all the comedies, in order to enhance their producibility.

I have not altered anything in the tragedy. As it has not been reprinted in any form since 1702, and because in my estimation its value for our time is literary rather than theatrical, I present it exactly as it first appeared, save in typography.

THE ADVENTURES
OF VENICE

Susanna Centlivre

Tales of the life and perils of Susanna Centlivre are the stuff of a young girl's dreams. She was the most successful of the early women playwrights, the one who has been most thoroughly studied and written about.[1] Nancy Cotton neatly encapsulates conflicting stories about Centlivre as follows:

> Susanna Centlivre was a gentlewoman, daughter of a Mr. Freeman of Holbeach, Lincolnshire, a zealous Parliamentarian who lost his estate at the Restoration. (Alternatively, her maiden name was Rawkins and her birth was mean.) She was precocious, composing a song before she was seven, and self-educated, with a flair for languages, mastering French before she was twelve. She was orphaned young, her father dying; nonetheless, she had a wicked stepmother [or stepfather] who drove her at the age of fourteen to run away from home with a company of strolling players or, alternatively, with Anthony Hammond, who dressed her in boy's clothes and took her with him to Cambridge for several months as his lover. At the same time, or shortly thereafter, she married, 'or something like it,' a nephew of Sir Stephen Fox and was widowed in a year. She then married an army officer named Carroll, who was killed in a duel eighteen months later. Destitute and beautiful, she turned (or returned) to provincial acting (winning the heart of Joseph Centlivre by playing in breeches) and then to playwriting.[2]

Whatever else she may have been, she proved herself a protofeminist in the prefaces and dedications to her works. One of the most vehement is the dedication of *The Platonick Lady* (1707) to 'All the Generous Encouragers of Female Ingenuity.' In it she inveighs against 'the Carping Malice of the Vulgar World; who think it a proof of their Sense, to dislike every thing that is writ by Women.' She complains of gender-specific criticism, of outright misogyny, of specific injustices done to her and her works, and of the disloyalty of some women who are 'often backward to encourage a Female Pen.' She closes this dedication with a hymn of praise to Queen Anne and notes, 'After naming this Miracle, the Glory of our Sex, sure none will spitefully cavil at the following Scenes, purely because a Woman writ 'em.'

Though she wrote to suit her market, and was less self-expressive in her plays than in her prefaces, Centlivre often depicted working-class heroines of startling independence and personal ingenuity. In one early play, *The Beau's Duel* (1702) she not only vindicates a fallen woman, but she rewards her with an independent income at the end of the play and sets her up as indifferent to male approval or affection.

In *The Adventures of Venice* (1700), the sub-plot of her first play produced in London, the serving-woman moves the plot forward, and, like other Centlivre heroines who were to follow, secures an independent fortune for herself and brings down the curtain with a philosophical acceptance of the pleasures of her single life. The play features most of the stock comic devices of its time: cross-dressing, wig-snatching, nearly-consummated adultery, disguise, and a plot full of suspense. This play-within-a-play, which can be staged as a one-act or an afterpiece, with or without major additions of music and dance, offers more farce and bawdry than either love or thunder. But it crackles with the humour of its author and possesses an economy unlike other pieces of the era, which may certainly recommend it to ours.

[1] *For detailed treatment of Centlivre's life, see John Wilson Bowyer's* The Celebrated Mrs. Centlivre *(1952, reprinted New York: Greenwood, 1968); the introduction to* A Bold Stroke for a Wife *(Lincoln: University of Nebraska Press, 1968), by Thalia Stathas; Henry ten Hoor's dissertation, 'A Re-examination of Susanna Centlivre as a Comic Dramatist' (University of Michigan, 1963); and a sketch in Fidelis Morgan's* The Female Wits *(London: Virago, 1981).*
[2] Women Playwrights in England c. 1363–1750 *(Lewisburg: Bucknell University Press, 1980), p. 123.*

Characters

PIZALTO, *a noble Venetian*
LUDOVICO, *a Frenchman*
MOUNTAINE, *Ludovico's servant*
LADY PIZALTA, *Pizalto's Wife*
LUCY, *her Woman*
MASKERS, DANCERS, SINGERS, *and* ATTENDANTS
Scene: *Venice, in Carnival Time*

Scene One

The Curtains fly up and discover a Mask in PIZALTO's *house.* PIZALTO, LADY PIZALTA, LUCY; LUDOVICO *talking to* LADY PIZALTA; *other maskers.*

A Spanish Entry.

While the dance is performing, LADY PIZALTA *and* LUCY *advance to the front of the stage.*

LADY PIZALTA:
    Oh! Lucy, I'm undone –
    That stranger there has charm'd my
            heart: I feel
    the pow'r of conquering love; quick,
            quickly tell me,
    What shall I do to ease this racking
            passion?

LUCY: Nay, madam, I fancy your passion has little occasion for lenitives; it blazes so violently at first, 'tis like to be soon extinguish'd.

LADY PIZALTA: Dear Lucy, don't trifle with me; but contrive, imagine, do anything, to bless thy love-sick mistress with the sight of that dear man. And as an earnest of further rewards, here, take this – (*Gives her a ring.*)

LUCY: Madam, I receive your commands with much joy, (*Aside.*) but your present with more. (*To her.*) I'll try what this projecting brain can do, and if you step into the next room, I'll soon give you an account of my proceedings.

    Exit LADY PIZALTA.
    LUCY *pulling* LUDOVICO *by the sleeve.*

LUCY: Sir, sir, one word with you.

LUDOVICO: Your business –

LUCY: May one ask you a civil question and be resolv'd?

LUDOVICO: Hum – A civil question, say'st thou? What's it, prithee, a night's lodging? If so, pull off thy mask, and I'll resolve thee instantly – But I never strike bargains in the dark.

LUCY: [I don't know, sir, but it may tend to that, by way of proxy, at the long-run. But] At present my commission reaches no further than to know your lodgings; if anything comes on't, I fancy 'twill not displease you.

LUDOVICO (*aside*): Hum – This is but a pettifogger in intrigues, I find. Egad, I'm like to be pretty well employ'd during the carnival. Well, considering I am a stranger here, this hit may be a lucky one, and the lady handsome. I'll fancy her so at least, wer't but for the pleasure of expectation.

LUCY: What are you studying, sir? Are you so long resolving whether you shall accept a lady's favour, or no?

LUDOVICO: No, faith, child: I am not over-scrupulous in those matters. Let her be but woman, and we shan't disagree – and so thou may'st tell her. (*Tears the Superscription of a letter and gives it to her.*) There's a direction for thee.

Exit LUDOVICO.

LUCY: Frank and easy, *a la mode de Paris* – Well, these indifferent sparks charm more than all your cringing fops. Now for my business. Let me see – I'll to my lady, she'll write; I'll carry the letter, and the devil will turn saint, if I don't bring 'em together and merit a further recompence.

    By coupling many have their fortunes
            made;
    I only want preferment, not my trade.

    Exit LUCY.

Scene Two

LUDOVICO's *Lodgings.*

LUDOVICO *solus.*

LUDOVICO: Who waits?

Enter MOUNTAINE.

MOUNTAINE: Did you call, sir?

LUDOVICO: Mountaine, run to Signiora Ronquilla and tell her I have done with her for ever, if she does not send this evening the hundred ducats she promised to lend me. And harkee, as you come back, acquaint Signiora Cornara I shall be busy tomorrow and desire she put off her visit till another day.

Knocking at the door.

MOUNTAINE: Sir, there's somebody at the door.

LUDOVICO: See who 'tis.

MOUNTAINE: Sir, a Gentlewoman desires to speak with you.

LUDOVICO: A Gentlewoman! admit her – well, 'tis a great fatigue to oblige the whole sex.

Enter LUCY.

Oh! what news from your lady?

LUCY: This will inform you, sir. (*Gives him a letter.*)

LUDOVICO (*reads*): Hum, hum, a letter – 'Tho' it may seem improper for one of my sex to make the first step in an *amour*, yet you ought to consider that the rigorous confinement we are under all the year round, may, in some measure, excuse the liberties we take during the carnival. If you have the courage to meet me, I shall be at four in the afternoon in the Piazza d'Espagna, invisible to all but yourself.' Well, I believe all women in Venice are wild for gallants.

LUCY: Sir, what answer shall I return to my lady?

LUDOVICO (*aside*): Egad – I am in doubt whether I shall throw my time away on this intrigue or no. (*To her.*) Harkee child, step into the next chamber, and I'll answer your message instantly.

Exit LUCY.

Let me see – (*Reads in his Table-book.*) Monday, at two in the afternoon, I am to see Signiora Belleza at her nurse's. She's a pretty rogue, and so I'll go. At three of the clock, Signiora Dorinda, the Senator's wife, at the Indian House. Pshaw, she's an old acquaintance; I shan't go. At half an hour past three, the Countess Wrinkle, who presented me with a gold-hilted sword. Silly fool! does she think I'll bestow one of my visits on an old shrivelled piece of antiquity for a trifling present, not worth above three-score pistoles? At a quarter past four, my seamstress Dorothy Steenkirk, who supplies me with linen. Oh! this visit

may be put off for a new intrigue, and so I'll acquaint the messenger.

Exit LUDOVICO.

Scene Three

A Chamber in SIGNIOR PIZALTO's *House.*

Enter LADY PIZALTA, LUCY.

LADY PIZALTA: Did you deliver my Letter to Ludovico, Lucy?

LUCY: Madam, I did. [I found him in his study, reading the Lover's Watch, which he swears does not at all agree with his constitution. He hates injunctions of love, like those of penance: for the one, says he, is no more pleasurable to the body, than the other beneficial to the soul.]

LADY PIZALTA: [What a fine gallant I'm like to have with these principles!] Well – what did he say to a summons from a woman of my quality? Did it not make him wish the time of assignation were sooner than the appointment in the letter?

LUCY: He first hummed over your *billet*; and pausing a while, he desired me to stay for an answer in a next room; then coming to me, he ask'd me what countrywoman you were. 'For,' said he, 'if she should prove an old acquaintance, I would use her damnably.' But when I had assured him you never saw the outside of these walls, he began to have that desire which all men have to a new face.

LADY PIZALTA: Very well; and what then?

LUCY: He strait enquir'd whether you were black, brown, fair, old, young, maid, wife, or widow. I told him you was a wretched wife to an old, impotent, rich, covetous, noble Venetian; beautiful, young, generous, and of a fair complexion. He hugg'd me at these words, seemed transported with the news, and swore that in intrigues a wife was most suitable to his temper. 'For,' said he, 'there's neither children to father, nor honour to repair.' And where his pocket and liberty are safe, he is contented to venture his body and soul.

LADY PIZALTA: Excellent maxims!

LUCY: In short, madam, he says he has had several bills of this nature drawn upon him of late, and how much his stock may be exhausted, he knows not; but however he'll meet you, and if he cannot answer your expectation, he'll give you earnest.

LADY PIZALTA: You talk merrily, girl; I hope you did not tell my name. I should be loath to trust a man of his character with my reputation at first dash.

LUCY: No, madam, I only told your quality.

LADY PIZALTA: That's well. Oh, reputation, what several sorts of slavery do we undergo to preserve thee! for to be thought virtuous, we are forced to be constantly railing against vice, tho' our tongues and maxims seldom agree.

LUCY: Alas! Madam, that pretence is grown too common. For the men now take it for granted that a lady is very near surrendering when once she holds out that flag of defiance.

LADY PIZALTA: Well – Men use us very barbarously: they will neither suffer us to be honest, nor allow us to be thought so. Here, take this key and secure everything that concerns my reputation; and if my husband wakes ere I come back, you may easily find some excuse to prevent his enquiries: for the carnival allows us more liberty than at other times we dare pretend to. I know thy honesty and will rely upon't.

LUCY: Yes indeed, madam, I am honest at the bottom.

LADY PIZALTA: Well, I'll be gone; 'tis about the hour.

Exit LADY PIZALTA.

Enter PIZALTO.

LUCY: Good luck attend you, madam. Oh! Heavens! here's my lord – Madam, madam, madam – Oh lord, what shall I say, now she's gone?

PIZALTO: Hist, hist, Lucy. Don't, don't, don't call your lady, for I have a word or two to say to thee in private, and have waited for this lucky opportunity a great while –

LUCY (*aside*): Now Venus be praised. I hope he has found some business of his own, that may give my lady an opportunity to mind hers.

PIZALTO: Well, Lucy, well, – canst thou guess my business now?

LUCY: No indeed, sir – (*Aside.*) But I'm certain an old man's business can't be great.

PIZALTO (*gives her a looking-glass*): Here, child, this will tell thee. Look in't, look in't, I say – Ah! ah! thou hast a pretty pouting lip, a delicate roguish eye, such an ogle, such a cast. Ah! Rogue, faith, thou'rt very pretty; and, in short, if anyone rival thy lady, it will be thee, Lucy. Egad, I have fire in me yet.

LUCY (*aside*): O' my conscience, and little too, I believe. Yet I wish he has enough to serve my ends. I'll make my fortune. (*To him.*) Lord, sir, what do you mean? I rival my lady! Heaven forbid; I would not injure so good a woman for the world –

PIZALTO: Pshaw, pshaw – Where's the injury done to her, child? Adod, I'll give thee a hundred crowns.

LUCY: No injury, say you, my lord? Why, I wonder you should be so jealous of my lady, and preach such religious maxims to her, when your own principles are quite opposite.

PIZALTO: Look ye, child, a man may do that which would look abominable in a wife. A woman's reputation is a nice thing –

LUCY: 'Tis so – and therefore 'tis but reason I should take care of mine.

PIZALTO: Prithee, no more of that. Thy reputation shall be safe; I'll marry thee to my gentleman.

LUCY: Gentleman – Valet! Faugh – And what good will a hundred crowns do me, when my virginity is gone? Indeed, if you lov'd me as much as you say, and would make my fortune (for I should love extremely to be a lady), I cannot tell how far you might persuade me. I know my reputation would be safe in your hands.

PIZALTO: Make thy fortune! Why, I've known some of our nobles marry a wife with less than a hundred crowns. But adod, thou'rt a charming girl, and therefore I'll make it a hundred pistoles. What say'st thou now, Lucy? Ah! Adod, I must buss thee. (*Kisses her.*) Ah! Rogue, methinks I'm a young, lusty, vigorous fellow again. Thou shalt find I am, girl.

LUCY (*aside*): I believe I shall fail you, old Gentleman. (*To him.*) Well, my lord, make it up a thousand pistoles, and I am yours; else I'll die a maid, I'm resolv'd.

PIZALTO: A thousand pistoles? Why, thou art the most unconscionable wench in Italy! Why, 'tis a price for a Duchess in some countries. Come, come, prithee be reasonable, Lucy.

LUCY: Reasonable! why, you don't ask a reasonable thing. Look you, you know my mind, I'll not bate a penny. I'll warrant my lady will give me two hundred at least for my discovery. (*Going.*)

PIZALTO (*aside*): Udslife! she won't tell my wife, sure, I'm ruin'd if she does; I'd rather give her two thousand. (*To her.*) Hold, hold, Lucy, sweet Lucy, prithee come back. Faith, thou'rt so charming, I can deny thee nothing. Come, it shall be what thou wilt. Come now, rogue, let's retire to thy chamber –

LUCY: Nay, nay, no ent'ring the premises till you have paid the purchase –

PIZALTO: Adod, thou'rt a wag. Come in then, and I'll discharge the debt: thou'rt a cunning gipsy.

Exit PIZALTO.

LUCY: You shall have reason to say so, ere I have done with you, old Gentleman. For I am resolv'd to show you a trick, and preserve my virtue.

For did base men within my power fall,
T'avenge my injured sex, I'd jilt 'em all.
And would but women follow my advice,
They should be glad at last to pay our price.

Exit LUCY.

Scene Four

The Piazza d'Espagna in Venice.

Enter LADY PIZALTA sola.

LADY PIZALTA:
Not come yet! ungrateful man! must a Woman of my quality wait?
[How have we lost our pow'r since the creation?
When the whole world had but one single Lord,
Whom every creature readily obey'd?
Yet he, that mighty he, caught with a smile,
Flew to th'embraces of the tempting fair.
But now each puny sinner dares to cross
A woman's inclinations.]

Enter LUDOVICO.

Oh! are you come Signior? I suppose you have
Some other assignation, that made you miss
My hour. Pursue it pray – I'll not interrupt you –
Your Servant – (*Going, then aside.*) I hope he'll not take me at my word.

LUDOVICO: Nay, nay, Signiora, why this passion? (*Stops her.*) You sent me a challenge, and I, like a man of courage, am come to answer it. Pray don't let a quarter of an hour break squares. I own it was a fault to make a lady wait; but friends, madam, friends and good wine are the devil. Come, I'll make you amends.

LADY PIZALTA: Friends and good wine! I suppose those friends were female ones –

LUDOVICO: No, faith. You shall judge of that – but suppose they were? Why should you be angry that I did not fly with the desired haste, as long as I am come time enough to give you satisfaction? Besides, I han't seen your face yet, and for aught I know, it mayn't reward my compliment in coming now. Prithee, child, unmask, and then I'll tell thee more of my mind.

LADY PIZALTA (*aside*): The devil take this fellow – and yet methinks I love him for his indifferency. (*To him.*) You talk as if you were unskill'd in the art of love. Don't you know that expectation feeds more than twenty tasted pleasures?

LUDOVICO: Hum – some sort of fops it may: but I'm none of those. I never give my opinion of a dish till I've tasted; neither do I care to dine often on one sort of meat without changing the sauce. But when that cloud's withdrawn, how long I shall keep my resolution I know not.

LADY PIZALTA: Say you so! Why then the only way to preserve your appetite is to feed you slenderly; or only let you see the food, but not to taste.

LUDOVICO: Faith, madam, I'm no chameleon, but flesh and blood. Therefore these prescriptions are of no use. One sight of that dear charming face of yours would be more obliging to your humble servant.

LADY PIZALTA (*unmasks*): Well, sir, what think you? Is there anything in this face worth your regard?

LUDOVICO: Ah! by Heaven, an angel. Oh! Madam, now blame yourself for my neglect, for had you sent the picture of her, in whom all those beauties centre, I had in this place waited the coming of my goddess, or rather flown on the wings of eager love, to meet my fair, tho' in the arms of ten thousand dangers. Say, my charming angel, do you forgive me? But why do I ask? Your eyes assure me you do; at least I'll force a pardon from these dear, soft, ruby lips. (*Kisses her in ecstasy.*)

LADY PIZALTA: Hold, hold! been't so lavish – a sparing gamester is the likeliest to keep in stock, whilst a profuse hand at one cast throws all he has away.

LUDOVICO: To fear that, were to doubt your charms, in which a lover is sure to find constant supplies. But we lose time. Let's retire to my lodgings, where I'll give thee the best proofs of my love I can.

LADY PIZALTA (*aside*): Well! He's a charming fellow. How happy are the wives in France and England, where such as he swarm!

LUDOVICO: Come, madam, come – Why, what do you mean by this delay? Consider I'm a man, a mortal, wishing, amorous man –

LADY PIZALTA: And consider I'm a woman –

LUDOVICO (*aside*): Ay, ay, that I know. At least I hope to find you such – or I would not be in such haste –

LADY PIZALTA: And have a reputation to preserve.

LUDOVICO (*aside*): Oh lord, what a damn'd turn's here? (*To her.*) Reputation, say you? (*Aside.*) Egad, I find all women make pretence to that mysterious word. (*To her.*) What! Are not you married, madam?

LADY PIZALTA: Yes, what then?

LUDOVICO: Why then you have a reputation to preserve. That's all.

LADY PIZALTA: All, sir, yes, and all in all to me. Do you consider what country you're in, sir?

LUDOVICO: Yes, faith, madam, and what constitution I am of too. I know murder is as venial a sin here, as adultery is in some countries. And I am all too apprehensive of my mortal part not to avoid danger. Therefore, madam, you have an infallible security – if I should betray you, I bring myself into jeopardy, and of all pleasures, self-preservation is the dearest.

LADY PIZALTA: A very open speaker, I vow.

LUDOVICO: Ay, madam, that's best. Hang your creeping, cringing, whining, sighing, dying, lying lovers. Pugh! Their flames are not more durable than mine, tho' they make more noise in the blaze.

Sings.

Hang the whining way of wooing, Loving was design'd a sport.

LADY PIZALTA (*aside*): The deuce take me if this fellow has not charmed me strangely. Well, the carnival is almost over, and then I must be shut up like a nun again. (*To him.*) Hey! hoa! This time will be so short –

LUDOVICO: Let's make the better use on't then, my dear. We will consider when we have nothing else to do, but at present there's a matter of the greatest moment which I must impart to you. Therefore, come dear rogue, come –

LADY PIZALTA (*looking at her watch*): Hold – I have outstaid my time, and must return home instantly, to prevent discoveries.

LUDOVICO: Faith, madam, this is not fair – to raise a man's expectation, and then disappoint him! Would you be serv'd so yourself now?

LADY PIZALTA: I'll endeavour to disengage myself from my jealous husband, and contrive another meeting.

LUDOVICO: But will you be sure to meet me again?

LADY PIZALTA: I give you my hand as a pledge –

LUDOVICO (*kisses it*): And I this kiss in return – Adieu, my charmer.

LADY PIZALTA: Signior, farewell.

Exeunt severally.

Scene Five

LADY PIZALTA's *Lodgings.*

Enter LADY PIZALTA, LUCY.

LADY PIZALTA: Well, thou'rt an admirable girl! What would half the ladies in Venice give for such a servant?

LUCY (*aside*): Truly you have reason to say so, for 'tis not the first intrigue I have manag'd for you. (*To her.*) Oh! dear madam, your ladyship does me too much honour. But how do you like your new servant, madam?

LADY PIZALTA: Oh! above all men living, Lucy. He has the most bewitching conversation I ever met with. Say, is there no way to contrive a second meeting? For I'm impatient till I see the dear man again. The end of the carnival draws near, which is indeed the end of life to me. For then I must be coop'd up with age: condemned to an eternal coughing, spitting, snoring, and ill-nature. Then let me make the best of life, since hell cannot have a worse plague in store than I have felt already.

LUCY: Indeed, madam, I pity you, and wish 'twere in my power to free you from this old wither'd log, but tho' that's impossible, yet I may do you some little services to make life's tedious journey pleasant. Let me see, I have it – What would you say now, madam, if I should contrive a way to have your lover in your own chamber?

LADY PIZALTA: That were worth a king's revenue – Speak, quickly, how, how, good Lucy?

LUCY: Why, thus: he shall put on my clothes, and in my place attend you.

LADY PIZALTA: Rare contrivance! but my husband, Lucy?

LUCY: Oh! let me alone, madam, to manage him. He is defective in sight, you know; and not mistrusting anything, will not be over curious. If he should, I have a way to bring you off. My life on't – (*Aside.*) This plot may be of use to my design; I'll manage it with care.

LADY PIZALTA: Oh! the pleasure of hearing my husband lie coughing and calling me to bed. And my answering him, 'I'm coming, dear'; and while he imagines me in the next room undressing, I'm happy in the arms of my Ludovico. [Certainly there's as much satisfaction in deceiving a dull jealous husband, as in getting a new gallant, were it not grown so common. Each tradesman's wife must have her gallant too, and sometimes makes a journeyman of the apprentice e'er his indentures be half out. 'Tis an insufferable fault, that quality can have no pleasure above the vulgar, except it be in not paying their debts.] Well, dear Lucy, I admire your contrivance. About it instantly –

LUCY (*aside*): About it instantly! Is that all? I must have my fee first. (*To her.*) I will, madam; and you may expect your lover instantly. But, madam, what's to be done with your brocade night-gown you tore last night? it can ne'er be mended handsomely.

LADY PIZALTA: Nothing to be done without a bribe I find, in love as well as law. Well, Lucy, if you manage this intrigue with care and secrecy, the gown is yours.

Enter PAGE.

PAGE: Madam, my Lord desires to speak with you.

LUCY: Madam, I'll go about your business. Your ladyship's very humble servant.

Exit LUCY.

LADY PIZALTA: Tell him I'm coming –

Exit PAGE.

Now by way of mortification, I must go entertain my old jealous husband.

Exit LADY PIZALTA.

Scene Six

The Piazza.

Enter LUDOVICO singing.

Give me but wine, that liquor of life,
And a girl that is wholesome and clean,
Two or three friends, but the devil a wife,
And I'd not change state with a king.

Enter LUCY.

LUCY: What singing, Signior! Well you're a pleasant Gentleman –

LUDOVICO: Ah! My little female Mercury, what message bring'st thou? Ha – will thy lady bless me with another sight? Ha – how – when? Where? I am all in a flame.

LUCY: Come along with me, sir; I'll help you to an extinguisher presently.

LUDOVICO: If thou meanest thy lady, with all my heart. But I can tell thee, she'll rather prove oil, than what you speak of. But, say, where am I to see my lovely charmer?

LUCY: In her chamber –

LUDOVICO: Good! But how the devil can that be done?

LUCY: Nay, without the help of a conjuror, I assure you. If you dare take me for your pilot, I'll warrant you success in your voyage. I'll set you safe in the island of love. 'Tis your business to improve the soil.

LUDOVICO: I'll warrant thee, girl. Do you but bring me there once, and if I play not my part, may I never more know the pleasure of an intrigue.

LUCY: Which, if I mistake not, is the strictest curse can fall on you. Well, you must suffer a small metamorphosis: what think you of personating me a little? That is, dressing in my clothes, and waiting on your mistress in her bed-chamber – Ha?

LUDOVICO: Egad, I'm afraid I shall make but an awkward chambermaid; I'm undisciplined in dressing a lady's head –

LUCY: Oh! Sir, your commission won't reach so high as the head. I believe my lady will excuse little matters. You can undress, I suppose.

LUDOVICO: Oh! the best and the quickest of any man in Venice. But a pox on't – Can'st find no other way? – I, I, I, – I like petticoats in their proper places, but I don't care to have my legs in 'em.

LUCY: And so you resolve against it? Ha – (*Going.*)

LUDOVICO: No, not absolutely resolve, child: But – a –

LUCY: But what, sir!

LUDOVICO: Nothing – I will follow thy directions, whatever comes on't. Now lead the way, for nothing suits better with my humour than a friend, a bottle, a new mistress, and a convenient place.

Exit LUCY, LUDOVICO.

Scene Seven

PIZALTO's *Lodgings.*

Enter PIZALTO with a bond in his hand.

PIZALTO: Well – My wife's a fine woman! a very fine woman! But a pox she's a wife still, and this young jade runs in my head plaguily. Well – here 'tis under my hand: a thousand pistoles. A great sum for a maidenhead, as maidenheads go now-a-days. Ah, had I been young now.

Sings.

A fiddle and a treat had bore the prize away,
But when we old fools dote, they make us pay.

Enter LUCY.

Oh! are you come! Here, here, Lucy: here's a fortune for thee, worth twenty maidenheads, adod! I have not so much money by me at present, but there's security. (*Gives her the bond.*)

LUCY: Your lordship's bond's sufficient. Well, but that I am satisfied my reputation is safe with your lordship, or twice the sum should not have prevailed. Go to my chamber, my lord; I'll but step and see if my lady wants anything, and I'll be with you instantly.

PIZALTO: You won't stay, Lucy? Ah, girl, buss thy lady's Chucky, now, do now.

LUCY: Oh! Lord! not here, we shall be discovered.

PIZALTO: Well, thou art a cunning sinner. Make haste, Lucy, dost hear?

Exit PIZALTO.

LUCY: You're in mighty haste, old Gentleman! but I shall deceive you,

My end is gained; I have my fortune made,
Man has not me, but I have man betrayed.

Scene Eight

PIZALTO's *Lodgings.*

Enter PIZALTO *solus.*

PIZALTO: Why, what makes this young jade stay so long? Adod, this it is to pay before hand. Ha – methinks I hear a laughing and giggling in my wife's apartment. I must know whence their mirth proceeds. Ho! here's Lucy coming – Harkee you, pray, why did you make me wait so long? Nay, I'm resolved you shan't escape me now – (*Goes to the door, and pulls in* LUDOVICO *in* LUCY's *clothes, whose commode falls off in the struggle, and discovers his bald head.*) Oh! Benedicite! What have we here? A man disguis'd in my wife's chamber! and I unarm'd! Oh! curst minute! Speak, thou wicked prophet, thou son of iniquity, what camest thou here for? Ha – thou priest of Baal, to offer sacrifices on the altar of my wife? Oh! my head! my horns weigh it down to the ground already! Within there, bring me my sword and pistols!

LUDOVICO: A pox on all petticoats – What the devil shall I say now? Oh! for a sword! that would be of more use to me now than my tongue.

Enter LADY PIZALTA.

PIZALTO: Oh! thou wicked fallacious woman!

LADY PIZALTA: What ails my dear Chucky? Why dost thou call for arms, deary?

PIZALTO: To cut down that vile creeper which over-runs thy garden of virtue –

LADY PIZALTA (*aside*): Now impudence assist me. (*To him.*) Ah! Heavens! What's here? A man in disguise? A thief it must be – raise the servants – Oh! Heaven! we might have had all our throats cut in our beds. (*Aside.*) Now for Lucy, for I am at a loss to come off.

PIZALTO: No, no, I warrant, you know he is more gentle in bed.

LUDOVICO (*aside*): Oh! the devil, what does she mean? Death, hell and furies! If I come off now, catch me at this sport again, and hang me –

Enter LUCY.

LADY PIZALTA: Oh! are you there, Mistress? How came this man here in your clothes? Ha! Gentlewoman –

LUCY (*aside*): How confidently she asks the question, poor lady, as if she knew nothing of it! Now must I bring her off – (*To her.*) For reasons you must not know, madam.

PIZALTO: Ah! Thou wicked pair of bellows to blow the fire of iniquity! Why thou art the very casement through which thy mistress sucks the air of abomination. Tell me, I say, how he came here, and for what – and be sure it be a substantial lie, or 'twill not pass.

LUCY (aside): All my hopes are in her impudence. (To him, taking him away from the others' earshot.) Sir, one word with you – Do you remember our agreement tonight?

PIZALTO: Why, what of that? Ha –

LUCY: Then imagine what I design'd that gentleman for; I'm honest, sir, that's all –

PIZALTO (mimicking her tone): I'm honest, sir, that's all – Honest! with a pox – What! and so you honestly provided a companion for my wife in my absence, ha?

LUCY: No, sir, I design'd him for your companion in my absence. This is the business he was dressed for. Therefore no more words, but believe my lady honest, or all shall out.

PIZALTO: Oh! the Devil! this shan't pass, hussy. Do you think I'll be cuckolded, jilted, bubbled, and let it pass for a Christmas gambol? Adod, give me my bond again, or – or – (Holds up his cane.)

LUCY: No! hold there, sir. Women and lawyers never refund a fee. But 'tis your best way to be patient now. I'll not take blows.

LADY PIZALTA: Why all this whispering? Why mayn't I know the business?

PIZALTO: I am mistaken if you have not known too much business already. But I am right enough serv'd. I had more ground before than I could manage; I had no need of my neighbour's.

LUCY: Right, my lord. [Ground that lies fallow will breed weeds in time; but yours is clear yet.]

PIZALTO: Damn your jests; I shall expect a better account, do you hear?

(To LUDOVICO.) I'll find a servant to see you out of doors.

Exeunt PIZALTO *and* LADY PIZALTA.

LUDOVICO: Well, this was an admirable lift at a pinch. She has brought me off now. And if e'er they catch me at this music again, I'll give 'em leave to make an Italian singer of me. No more intrigues in disguise – if it had not been for the waiting-woman now, I might have been hang'd for a thief.

LUCY: What all amort, Signior, no courage left?

LUDOVICO: Faith, not much. I think I have lost my manhood with my breeches. This transformation may suit with gods, but not with mortals of my humour. Come, prithee, good Mistress Lucy, help me to my proper shape again; for tho' I have a natural inclination to petticoats, I hate 'em upon my own back.

A flourish of music within.

LUCY: Hark! I hear Count Bassino's music. He gives a Mask tonight; you are already dressed for masquerade; won't you stay and take a dance?

LUDOVICO: Egad, I'd rather dance a jig with thee elsewhere. Faith, thou'rt a pretty girl, and hast a good deal of wit too. But then, pox on't, thou'rt honest, thou sayest; you cannot swallow a pill, except 'tis gilded over with matrimony.

LUCY: And that turns your stomach, I warrant.

LUDOVICO: Why, ay. Faith, my stomach is damn'd squeamish in these matters. Yet, egad, if I could find one with half as much money as thou hast wit and beauty, I'd marry and live honest.

LUCY: That is, you'd marry her money –

LUDOVICO: One with the other, child. There's no living on love thou knowest. Tho' faith, I could live well enough too.

LUCY: Well, suppose I help you to a lady with a round sum; you'd keep your word, and marry her?

LUDOVICO: I am a gentleman; I scorn

to break my word.

LUCY: Well, sir, come to the Mask, and I'll engage you a mistress, if you are not over-curious.

LUDOVICO: With all my heart.

I'm now resolv'd to leave this
     wenching-trade;
For no man's safe upon a hackney
     jade;
Th'allay of danger makes the pleasure
     pain,
A virtuous wife will always be fame.

Scene Nine

A Mask in BASSINO's *Lodgings.*

A company in disguise; SIGNIOR PIZALTO, LADY PIZALTA, LUCY, *etc. An entry of three men and three women of several nations. Enter* LUDOVICO, *singing.*

LUDOVICO: Ah! Mistress Lucy! I'm come thou see'st. I expect thou shalt be as good as thy word, child. Is the lady here?

LUCY: The lady is forthcoming, if you are still in the same mind.

LADY PIZALTA: My lover here! Harkee, Lucy.

LUCY: By and by, madam, I am catering for myself now. Well, sir, will two thousand pistoles do?

LUDOVICO (*aside*): I must humour her – (*To her.*) Ay child.

LUCY: Why then I take you at your word, sir, and can produce the aforesaid sum – (*To* PIZALTO.) with a little of your assistance, my lord.

LUDOVICO (*aside*): Hum – a pretty wife I am like to have. Catch me there if you can –

PIZALTO: Ha – How's that?

LUDOVICO: How! Mistress Lucy, worth two thousand pistoles?

LUCY: Ay, and I have a very good paymaster for one half of it too – (*To* PIZALTO.) Do you know this hand, my lord? (*Shows him the bond.*)

PIZALTO (*aside*): Confound your jilting sneer.

LUDOVICO: Ha, ha, ha – What, a thousand pistoles a dish, my lord? I hope you don't change often, ha – ha –

PIZALTO: Hussy, I'll be reveng'd – 'Tis all false, 'tis counterfeit.

LUCY: Ha – ha – But it had been current coin, if I had suffered you to put your stamp upon't – in my bedchamber, my lord.

LADY PIZALTA: How, mistress, have you trick'd my husband out of a thousand pistoles, and never told me of it?

LUCY: Nay, madam, don't frown. Remember you have tricked him out of something too, which I never told him of – Don't urge me to more discoveries.

LUDOVICO (*aside*): So – Here's trick upon trick: But, faith, you shall never trick me out of my liberty. I'm not so fond of a wife to marry a chambermaid, though with ten times as much money. And so, sweet mistress [Abigail], your humble servant.

Exit LUDOVICO.

LADY PIZALTA (*aside*): The jade has me upon the hip – I must be silent.

She who has her husband's bed
     abused,
Can ne'er expect she should be better
     used.

Exeunt all but LUCY.

LUCY: Ha – What! my lover gone, with all my heart. Better now than after; for whilst I have my fortune in my own hands, I shall have no need to sue for a separate maintenance, and get nothing for it neither.

A flourish of music
Song.

When the winds rage, and the seas
     grow high,
They bid mankind beware,
But when they smooth and calm the
     sky,
'Tis then they would ensnare.

So the bright Thais kindness shows,
By frowning on her lovers,
For ruin only from her flows,
When she her charms discovers.

THE SPANISH WIVES

Mary Pix

There is something kindly, good-humoured, and ample about images of Mary Pix. They suggest a summery English meadow or a cabbage rose. The statistics of her life are spare and simple ones.[1] She was a country girl, a minister's daughter, born in Nettlebed, Oxfordshire, in 1666. She must have educated herself in her father's library, perhaps with the approval of her mother, Lucy Berriman. At eighteen she married George Pix, a merchant tailor about whom we know nothing more. She moved to London and gave birth to a daughter who died in infancy and was buried in 1690; she may have had other children. Her husband may have died young. One source suggests he was a gambler and ran the family into debt. Between 1695 and 1708 she wrote frantically and earned what must have been a respectable income from her writing. By 1709 she was dead.

In her forty-three years, Mary Pix wrote prolifically: poems, a novel, and at least thirteen plays. Several more anonymous plays were probably hers, and her habit of collaborating with or assisting other women playwrights makes counting seem silly. Though newspapers were not the most reliable sources of information about women writers, the *London Gazette* and the *Post Boy* both declared that Pix wrote 'the greatest part' of Susanna Centlivre's two most successful plays, *The Gamester* (1705) and *The Busy Body* (1709), and when Pix died the theatre offered a benefit performance of the latter play for her bereaved family (which at least raises the possibility that she had surviving children).

Mary Pix made a wide acquaintance with the intellectual and literary set in London, especially those involved in theatre and in the burgeoning feminist movement. Aphra Behn was writing plays when Pix reached London, and Pix would have seen productions of Behn's plays and may have known Behn herself. Somehow Pix became friends with Elizabeth Barry, the leading actress of the era, and Pix counted among her friends other theatre regulars such as Pierre Motteux, who wrote songs for her plays, and William Congreve, of whom she was said to be a 'favourite.'

In 1688 an anonymous feminist tract called *Sylvia's Revenge* appeared in London. It was prefaced by a poem signed 'M.P.,' which was probably Pix's first published piece. By 1696 Pix had made acquaintance with Mary Astell's bookseller, Richard Wilkin, for two of Pix's works are advertised on the back page of the 1697 printing of Astell's best-selling work, *A Serious Proposal to the Ladies for the Advancement of Their True and Greatest Interest* (published successively in 1694, 1697, and 1701). Pix was associated with the poet Sarah Fyge Field Egerton, and she dedicated a play to a woman popular at Queen Anne's court, Cary Coke, whose gallivanting husband was ridiculed in Delariviere Manley's novel, *The New Atalantis* (1709).

The more one learns about this period, the more incestuous the relationships appear. One almost thinks there were but ten people in all London, and the opulent social scene was all done with mirrors. If this were so, Mary Pix was certainly one of the ten. She seems to have ignored all class lines – to have consorted with servants as well as counts, actors as well as clergy, orange-sellers, poets, and clowns. And yet she was, at least on paper, the most humble and self-effacing of the women playwrights of her time.

In the dedication of her first tragedy, *Ibrahim, the Thirteenth Emperour of the Turks* (1696) she writes, 'I am often told, and always pleased when I hear it, that the Works not mine; but oh I fear your Closet view will too soon find out the Woman, the imperfect Woman there.'[2] Two pages later she writes, 'I am very sensible those that will be so unkind to Criticize upon what falls from a Womans Pen, may soon find more faults than I am ever able to answer.' None the less she begs pardon and concludes with a hope that 'the Good-Natur'd World' will excuse any errors 'in a thing only design'd for their Diversion.'

For all their gusto, most of Mary Pix's plays are either too long, too bombastic, or too thickly plotted to work on today's stage. Her *Innocent Mistress*, with a cast of twenty-one, was part of the York Festival in 1984. The production, skilfully directed and beautifully staged in the Merchant Taylor's Hall, where travelling companies actually did perform in the eighteenth century, was a hit with festival-goers; but it was difficult to follow, awkward to stage, and costly to produce. Even with cuts it ran three hours, but its statement never fully came across. A more demanding audience would have been less kind.

None of these problems beset *The Spanish Wives*, however, which is brisk enough to stand as is, with a few optional but unnecessary cuts. In addition, it has only ten speaking parts, six of which are brilliant characterizations, showpieces for fine comedians. The most tightly plotted play Mary Pix ever wrote, it offers a devasting critique of marriage; it pokes outrageous fun at the clergy; and finally it blows apart the coveted notion that cuckoldom is the worst fate that can befall a man.

In many ways, *The Spanish Wives* is atypical of Pix's work and unlike other women's plays of its time. It does not feature a female protagonist, and the women in the play are relatively passive. While the role of the Governor's lady is well-developed and relatively complex, demanding split-second timing from a talented actress, 'Tittup' is not quite so memorable as the gallery of male buffoons who blunder, huff, pine, and chase each other into trees and over park palings, shoot at each other with pistols, lose each other in the dark, and steal each other's wigs. What is most remarkable about the play is its ridicule of the kind of misogyny which so blighted the lives of women in Pix's time and which, I hear, is still alive in some quarters.

Pix pits a kindly and reasonable old Governor against a mean-spirited and violent Marquess, both married to women much younger than themselves. The Governor views his wife as a responsible individual. He doesn't mind that she entertains gentleman serenaders beneath her window, dances with other men at official functions, and disports herself pretty much at will. The Marquess treats his wife as a chattel. He keeps her under lock and key and threatens to have her bled fifty ounces for daydreaming at her window, but then he decides not to let her see a doctor, for fear of 'a surgeon quiddling her white arm, and looking babies in her eyes'. Pix put the words of some anti-feminist pamphlets of her day directly into the mouth of the absurd Marquess, who rants and carries on as follows: 'Oh Women! Women! Women! They are Crocodiles; they are painted Serpents, gilded Toys, disguis'd Fiends, – But why name I these? They are woman'.

At one point this play makes history. When the Marquess warns the Governor that he should assert more authority over his spirited wife, lest he be cuckolded, the Governor answers him, 'Lord! Lord! your Head is always upon Cuckolding. All the Cuckolds may be hang'd, for what I care'. While perhaps in some musty corner there may be another play in which a sympathetic male character jovially debunks the male terror of being cuckolded, I haven't seen it. As if to emphasize her point, Pix gives the Governor a second, even more explicit speech, much to the same point. He tells the Marquess, who has warned him of the 'evil' his wife means to do him, 'Evil! What Evil? The evil is my knowing it; if I had not 't had been none. – Yet how am I convinc'd you have not abus'd my Tittup: By the Honour of Spain, I'll Fight for Tittup: *Guilty or not Guilty'* (italics mine).

Since Pix had pretty much staked the honour of women on the behaviour of the Governor's wife, the obvious and politically correct course (and the one suggested in the works of staunch feminists like Astell *et al.*) would have been to show that the young wife was unwaveringly faithful to the husband who treated her so fairly. Good politics, perhaps; but bad theatre. Pix took her plot through a more delicate, humane, and amusing turn. She created a Tittup who was achingly, sweetly tempted and *was* planning a sexual encounter with the foppish and highly-perfumed English Colonel. This gave suspense to the play, humour to the bedroom confrontation between the Governor and his lady, and believability to the resolution. As the old Governor lovably decides to forgive all, he scores a more effective blow at the myth of cuckoldry than could have been done if his pretty Tittup had never considered a transgression.

There is so much literature already on the significance of cuckoldom in the male imagination that I need add little to it, though the most exciting recent analysis appears in Eve Kosofsky Sedgwick's *Between Men: English Literature and Male Homosocial Desire.*[3] Sedgwick emphasises that a man cuckolds another man; the woman is scarcely more than a tool in a show of power between men. Without the other man, the activity loses its potency. This is particularly obvious in Wycherley's *The Country Wife* (1675), whose rake-hero is named 'Horner,' because his real interest is in putting horns on other men; women are simply a means to his end. It is interesting, therefore, if not surprising, that a woman playwright should execute an elaborate and clearly intentional turn on the stock comic conventions regarding cuckoldry. She does not stop there.

She creates Camillus, overall a rather dull romantic fellow, chasing his beloved from Italy to Spain to retrieve her from the clutches of the old Marquess. What is revolutionary about Camillus, though, is that he still wants to marry Elenora, even though she has been forced to marry the Marquess and has presumably consummated that union. In men's comedies it is customary to want to sleep with another man's wife, but it is unheard of to want to marry her. Camillus is clear about this. He tells the Colonel who is pursuing the Governor's wife,

> Ah Colonel! our Cases are very different, – You hunt but for Enjoyment, the huddl'd Raptures of a few tumultous moments: – But I am in quest of Virgin-Beauty, made mine by Holy Vows; constrain'd by Fiends, instead of Friends, to break the sacred Contract, and follow the *Capricio* of a mad Old Man. – Virgin did I call her? – By Heaven, I dare believe she is one, at least her Mind is such; – and were she in my power, I'd soon convince the World of the Justice of my Cause.

A hero who worships the virgin *mind* of his beloved, disregarding her other parts, is clearly the product of a woman's fancy. This is one of the light-hearted benefits to posterity of having access to the products of women's imaginations as well as men's.

Pix had a source for her play. It was the novel by Gabriel de Brémond which appeared in English as *The Pilgrim* in 1680 and was also the source for Dryden's *The Spanish Friar* (1681). Pix knew both the play and the novel, but that did not restrain her from taking delicious liberties with both. The novel is a dry thing, the play is certainly not one of Dryden's best, and both were woman-hating pieces that ridiculed the Governor's wife as a lust-driven hag. Barbour reports, 'The only detail of plot common to de Brémond, Dryden and Pix, is that all three have their Friars threaten to excommunicate either the men whose cuckolding they are abetting or their agents. . .' Barbour offers a detailed and thoughtful comparison of the three works, emphasizing that the charming character of 'Tittup' is entirely Pix's creation; that while Dryden and de Brémond concentrated dramatic attention on the male characters, Pix greatly expanded the roles of the females; and that while the men aimed their ridicule at women and at the Roman Catholic Friar, Pix softened the anti-Catholicism, eradicated the woman-hating, and created a whole new focus by ridiculing misogyny itself. Pix's work is the only one that examines the nature of marriage, questions male prerogative and power, or offers happy endings for the various couples.[4]

Though the play was not published with a cast list, there is good evidence that the role of the Friar was created by the great William Bullock, widely known and loved for his interpretations of Falstaff and Dogberry; that Hidewell was played by William Penkethman, also much-loved by audiences of his time; and that 'Tittup' was written for the talents of Susanna Verbruggen, whose skill and beauty so dazzled Colley Cibber that he wrote she was 'Mistress of more variety of Humour than I ever knew in any one Woman Actress' and particularly admired her '*Je ne scay quois*' (sic).[5] The farce opened to success at Dorset Gardens, the large stage usually reserved for Opera but operated as a subsidiary of the Drury Lane company, and it was revived in 1699, 1703, and 1711, making it by far the most popular of the plays included in this volume.

For a modern company it offers roaring comedy, superbly crafted roles for a gallery of character actors, politics without polemics, and social commentary without tedium. It is the essential eighteenth-century farce, a madcap circus complete with antique expletives and oaths, without the sexism and classism which make so many such farces offensive to modern taste. *The Spanish Wives* is a model of what a feminist farce is, and how pleasant it can be.

[1] *I have culled facts about Pix principally from three sources: Edna Steeves'*
introduction to the facsimile edition of The Plays of Mary Pix and Catharine Trotter, *in 2 vols. (New York: Garland, 1982); Constance Clark's dissertation,* The Female Wits: Catharine Trotter, Delariviere Manley, and Mary Pix – Three Women Playwrights Who Made Their Debuts in the London Season of 1695–96 *(Ann Arbor: University Microfilms International, 1984, No. 8409389); and Paula Louise Barbour's superb and meticulously researched dissertation,* A Critical Edition of Mary Pix's The Spanish Wives (1696), with Introduction and Notes *(Ann Arbor: University Microfilms International, 1976, No. 76–13,695).*
[2] *Quotations from the plays, including* The Spanish Wives, *are from first editions located in the Humanities Research Center in Austin, Texas. Front-matter, including prefaces, dedications, and prologues, is not paginated.*
[3] *New York: Columbia University Press, 1985.*
[4] *See Barbour, pp. 24–44.*
[5] *Discussed at length in Barbour, pp. 18–24; Cibber qtd. in Barbour, p. 23.*

Characters:

Men
GOVERNOR OF BARCELONA, *A merry old lord that has travel'd and gives his wife more liberty than is usual in Spain.*
MARQUESSA OF MONCADA, *A jealous lord, guest to the Governor.*
CAMILLUS, *A Roman Count, following the Marquess's lady, as contracted to her before.*
COLONEL PEREGRINE, *An English Colonel.*
FRIAR ANDREW, *One that attends the Count.*
HIDEWELL, *Retained by the Count.*
DIEGO, *Servant to the Governor.*

(THREE SERVING MEN *of the Marquess;* SENTINEL, SERVANTS, GENTLEMEN, MUSICIANS, SINGERS *and* DANCERS.)

Women
THE GOVERNOR'S LADY ('TITTUP'), *A brisk and airy lady.*
ELENORA, *Wife to the Marquess.*
SPYWELL, *Woman to the Governor's lady*
ORADA, *Woman to Elenora.*

(MAIDS, LADIES, SINGERS *and* DANCERS.)

ACT ONE

Scene One

Hall in the Governor's Palace.

Enter the GOVERNOR OF
BARCELONA *and the* MARQUESS.

GOVERNOR: Prithee, my Lord
Marquess, don't trouble me with thy
jealous whims. You say there was
masqueraders last night under the
windows; – why let 'em be a God's
name! I am sorry 'twas such a cold
raw night for the honest lads. By the
honour of Spain, if I had heard 'em, I
wou'd ha' sent the rogues a glass of
Malaga to warm 'em.

MARQUESS: O Lard! O Lard! I shall
run mad! Sure, my Lord Governor,
your horns will exceed the largest in
the palace hall. – Oh! that my wife
were out of your house, and
Barcelona! Methinks I am not secure,
tho' she's under eleven locks.

GOVERNOR: By my Holy Dame, I am
of your mind: I don't think you are
secure.

MARQUESS: How! Do you know
anything to the contrary?

GOVERNOR: Why, by th' Mass, this I
believe: her head's at work; and I dare
say she has made ye a cuckold in
imagination, with every don she has
thro' any peephole seen, since your
first marriage.

GOVERNOR: Oh! dam' her! dam' her!

GOVERNOR: You'll never take my
advice! (*Sings.*)

Give but a woman her freedom still,
Then she'll never act what's ill.
'Tis crossing her, makes her have the
will.

[– Phough! I have been in England.
There they are the happiest husbands.
if a man does happen to be a cuckold,
which, by the way, is almost as rare as
in Spain; but, I say, if it does fall out.

all his wife's friends are his; and he's
caress'd – nay, godszooks, many times
rises to his preferment by it.]

MARQUESS: Oh, insufferable! I am not
able to hear your discourse.

*Enter {*HIDEWELL, *disguised as} a
country fellow.*

– A man coming from my wife's
apartments! – Oh, the Devil! the
Devil!

GOVERNOR: I see no cloven foot he has.

MARQUESS: No, but he is one of his
imps, a letter carrier. I read it in his face.

GOVERNOR {*scrutinizing*
HIDEWELL}: Ph! I begin to perceive
it now; here's the superscription writ in
his forehead: 'To the beauteous Donna
Elenora, Marchioness of, &c.' Ay, 'tis
very plain.

MARQUESS: Well, Governor, these
jeers won't be put up so.

HIDEWELL: What a wannion ails ye,
trow? What do ye mean by letters? Ich
am no schollard; my calling is to zell
fruit; and zum o' the meads o' this
hause (meads ich think 'em) beckon'd
me in; – I zould 'em zum; and that's
all I knaw.[1]

GOVERNOR: Ay, honest fellow, I dare
swear 'tis. Why if thou wert a monkey,
he'd be jealous on thee.

MARQUESS: You may think what you
please, but I fear other things.
Therefore, if, as a guest, you will let
me have the freedom of your house,
I'll take this fellow in, and search him.

GOVERNOR: Ay, with all my heart.
(*Aside.*) Oh these jealous fools!

MARQUESS: Come along, sirrah; I'll
look as much as in thy mouth.

GOVERNOR: Ay, for fear there should
be a note in a hollow tooth.

HIDEWELL: Why, do ye zee, as for
matter o' that, – ye ma look in my a –

---

[1] Barbour notes in her critical edition of this play, 'whenever Hidewell plays the country
bumpkin for the benefit of the Marquess (II.vi, III.iii, III,v), he affects a broad southern dialect.
Besides adopting obsolete words and ungrammatical constructions, Hidewell freely mixes vowels
and changes "s" to "z," "f" to "v," "you" to "ye," "I" to "Ich," and "I am" and "I would" to
"ch'am" and "chould" (p. 185a). Mary Pix took care to represent Hidewell's country bumpkin
accent orthographically, in dialect apparently current in her day. In a modern revival of this
play, any rustic dialect recognizable as such to the audience might be substituted.

GOVERNOR: Hold, Beast, 'tis a man of quality you speak to.

HIDEWELL: Zooks, I think 'tis a madman.

MARQUESS: Come your ways, impudence!

[HIDEWELL: But, sir, sir, – must the meads zerch me, or the men?

MARQUESS: I'll tell you presently, ye wanton rogue.]

Exit {MARQUESS,} driving {HIDEWELL} before him.
Exit the GOVERNOR's LADY.

GOVERNOR: How now, Tittup?

LADY: Morrow, Deary.

GOVERNOR: Why, Tittup, [here the Marquess has been fretting, fuming, swearing, raging: he is just horn-mad. Hark-ye, Tittup,] did you hear any serenading last night?

LADY: Yes, Deary, 'twas the English Colonel to me – You are not angry, Deary.

GOVERNOR: Not I. (*Sings.*)
He that has a handsome buxom wife,
Must surely be always pleased;
Blest with a pleasant quiet life,
And never, never teased.

But hark ye, Tittup, that English Colonel has such a leer, such a tongue, such a nose, such a – Have a care on him, Tittup.

LADY: I warrant ye, Deary, the honest freedom you allow is sufficient; I'll never go farther. You know he dines here today, and brings his music to entertain us in the afternoon.

GOVERNOR: Yes, yes; I must dispatch some business, to be ready to receive him. B'w'ye,[2] Tittup!

LADY: B'w'ye, Deary; buss, before ye go.

GOVERNOR (*kisses her*): A pies! a pies! Your kisses glow! Fie, fie! I don't love ye.

Exit laughing.

LADY: 'Tis my Colonel, my Peregrine, sets my heart on fire and gives that

[2] A contraction of "God be with ye."

warmth my old husband found upon my lips. – But then such a husband, – so good, so honest, preventing every wish. – Then such a Colonel, so handsome, so young, so charming. Where's the harm to give a worthy begging stranger a little charity from love's store, when the kind old Governor can never miss it?

Exit.

Scene Two

{COUNT CAMILLUS's *Lodgings.*}

Enter COUNT CAMILLUS *and* FRIAR ANDREW.

FRIAR: Well, my lord, now we are come to Barcelona, I fear this devil of a Marquess will be too hard for us.

CAMILLUS: How, Father Andrew, desponding? 'Twas but this morning, over your Malaga, you swore by the eleven thousand virgins and all your catalogue of saints, you'd bring my Elenora to my arms.

FRIAR: And by fifty thousand more, so I will, if it be possible. If not, my oath is void. You know the Marquess hates me heartily, as I do him, because once he caught me carrying your letter to his wife.

CAMILLUS: For the good office, I think, us'd ye most scurvily.

FRIAR: Scurvily! Basely, barbarously; without respect to these sacred robes: toss'd me in a blanket, cover'd me with filth and dust, and so sent me by force to our convent. For which, and my natural inclination to cuckoldom, I have joined in your attempts and waited on you to Barcelona, to be revenged.

CAMILLUS: You know there's justice in my cause. Elenora was, by contract, mine at Rome, before this old Marquess had her. And cou'd I again recover her, I don't question but to get leave of his Holiness for a divorce, and marry her myself.

FRIAR: Nay, that's as you please; when she's in your possession, marry or not, 'tis all one to Father Andrew. It never shall trouble my conscience. I must own, were I in your condition, I should not marry; because daily experience shows a wife's a cloy, and a mistress a pleasure.

CAMILLUS: Well, we'll discourse that when we have the lady; and in the meantime, good Father, be diligent.

FRIAR: I think I am diligent. I am sure, I am worn to mere skin and bone in your service. This morning I found ye a Mercury, a letter carrier that can slip thro' a keyhole to deliver a *billet doux* to a fair lady.

CAMILLUS: I wish he were return'd; I fear some misfortune has befallen him.

FRIAR: Oh! here he comes, sound wind and limb!

Enter HIDEWELL (*the Country Fellow before*) {*no longer disguised*}

So, my dear tool of gallantry, how hast thou sped?

HIDEWELL {*no longer affecting rustic speech*}: Gad, the hardest task I ever undertook. Sir, you gave me five ducats; as I hope for preferment, and to be made pimp-master general, it deserves double the sum.

CAMILLUS: Nor shalt thou fail of it, boy, if thou hast succeeded.

HIDEWELL: First then, the damn'd old jealous Marquess caught me, and notwithstanding my counterfeit speech and simplicity, had me amongst his varlets, to be search'd. They knew his custom, and no sooner enter'd, but they flew upon me like so many Furies. I fear'd it had been to tear me limb from limb; but prov'd only to tear my clothes off, which was done in a twinkling, and I left as naked as my mother bore me, whilst the old Marquess grovel'd all over my habiliments, and run pins in 'em so thick that a poor louse would not have 'scaped spitting. The only thing which pleas'd me was to observe a peephole the maids (knowing this to be their master's searching-room) had made; and sometimes one eye, sometimes another, viewing my proportions.

CAMILLUS: But had you any letter? Was that safe? Satisfy me there.

HIDEWELL: Pray let me take my own method. – Nothing being found, they gave me again my clothes, and the Marquess a ducat for my trouble. Yet I had a letter –

CAMILLUS: Which thou ingeniously swallow'dst.

HIDEWELL: No, which I more ingeniously brought.

CAMILLUS: What, in thy hat?

HIDEWELL: My hat had the same severe trial.

CAMILLUS: Thy shoes –

HIDEWELL: They passed the same scrutiny – impossible in any of them to hide a scrip, the least shred of paper.

CAMILLUS: How then?

HIDEWELL: My lord, do ye observe this stick?

CAMILLUS (*viewing it*): Yes, 'tis an honest crabtree stick. I see no more in it.

FRIAR (*taking the stick and putting on his spectacles to view it*): Come, come, let me see it; I can smell out a note that comes from a fair hand. By St. Dominic, here's neither paper nor writing upon it.

HIDEWELL: Give it me. (*He unscrews the ferrule at the bottom, takes out the letter, and gives it to* CAMILLUS.)

FRIAR: Thou dear abstract of invention, let me kiss thee.

CAMILLUS: Excellent Hidewell! If thou wilt stay with me whilst I am in Barcelona, I'll satisfy thy utmost wishes.

HIDEWELL: Most willingly.

CAMILLUS (*skims letter*): Here Father, here dear confident! Orada writes that the tormented Marquess has removed {Elenora.} from those apartments that were next the streets, to some that overlook the gardens. Thither, she says, my Elenora would have me come this night; and if they can find a place to 'scape at, before the lodgings are better secur'd, they will. If not, we shall hear of them; – a gentle whistle is the sign. Hidewell, you shan't appear in this, because if seen, you'd be known again.

FRIAR: Pray let me go; [gad, if the business shou'd be done without my help, I shou'd take it very ill].

CAMILLUS: Well, well, we'll in, and consider on't.

Exeunt.

Scene Three

{*Ballroom in the* GOVERNOR's *Palace.*}

The GOVERNOR, *his* LADY, COLONEL PEREGRINE, *several gentlemen and ladies,* {*musicians*}.

A Song.

[I]
Alas, when charming Sylvia's gone,
I sigh, and think myself undone!
But when the lovely nymph is here,
I'm pleas'd, yet grieve and hope, yet fear,
Thoughtless of all but her I rove;
Ah! tell me, is not this to love?

[II]
Ah me! what power can move me so?
I die with grief when she must go;
But I revive at her return;
I smile, I freeze, I pant, I burn:
Transports so sweet, so strong, so new,
Say, can they be to friendship due?

[III]
Ah! no, 'tis love, 'tis now too plain,
I feel, I feel the pleasing pain:
For, who e'er saw bright Sylvia's eyes,
But wish'd, and long'd, and was her prize?
Gods! if the truest must be blest,
Oh! let her be by me possest.

COLONEL PEREGRINE *and the* GOVERNOR's LADY *dance; all the time the* GOVERNOR *cries,* 'Ha boy, Tittup! Well done, Tittup! Ha boy, Tittup!'

GOVERNOR (*the dance done, he goes to* {*his lady*}): You are hot; you are hot, child.

LADY: A little warm.

[GOVERNOR: Well, Tittup, do but carry thy body swimmingly, without tripping, and we'll begin a reformation

in Barcelona, shall thou go thro' Spain. The ladies shall live like Cherubims. But have a care, Tittup; have a care of a *faux pas.*

LADY: Fear not, Deary.]

GOVERNOR: Come, now let's sit down, and see the rest perform. Let me have some lively songs. (COLONEL PEREGRINE goes to sit next {to} the GOVERNOR's LADY.) Hold, friend hold! I have not learnt so much of your English fashion yet, to let another man sit by me with my wife, and I decently keep at a distance.

COLONEL: I beg your pardon, sir.

GOVERNOR: Nay, no harm. (*Sings.*)
If an old man has a beauteous treasure,
Let her sing, and dance, and laugh without measure,
And then she'll think of no other pleasure.

COLONEL: Your own, sir?

GOVERNOR: Ay, ay, boy; I have a thousand of 'em in a day, *extempore.*

COLONEL: Is't possible?

GOVERNOR {*to musicians*}: Come, now I ha' done, do you strike up.

Songs and dances.
The music ended, enter a SERVANT.

SERVANT: My lord, there is to wait on your honor, His Excellency the Duke Gonsalvo de Medina, de Sidoni, de –

GOVERNOR: Hold, hold, enough, enough. Where is he?

SERVANT: In the Hall of Ceremonies.

GOVERNOR: Gadso! I must go to him. Sit you merry; I'll be with you presently.

Exit all but COLONEL PEREGRINE, *the* LADY, *and* SPYWELL.

LADY: Spywell, stand at yonder door, and give me information as soon as ever my lord comes up the great stairs.

SPYWELL: I will, madam.

Exit SPYWELL.

COLONEL {*practising his elevated style*}: My angel! By Heaven I am raging mad, burnt up with violent love. Thy shape – thy every motion fires me.

But thy eyes – they set me in a blaze. Oh! I must die, unless the cordial of returning kindness save me.

LADY: Can you be so ungenerous to wrong this noble Governor, who is so fond of you, and even dotes on me?

COLONEL: He wrong'd thee more, when he condemn'd thy lovely youth to wither'd sapless arms. Can little foolish tricks of fondness make amends for ecstasies, pantings, the joys unutterable of vigorous love?

LADY: I must not hear ye.

COLONEL: You must, you must! I'll, kneeling, fix ten thousand burning kisses on thy beauteous hand, and the little wanton god swims and revels in thy sprightly eyes.

LADY: Why am I fastened here! Too rigorous Heaven! Take from this wondrous stranger his conquering charms, or give me more insensibility!

Enter SPYWELL.

SPYWELL: Madam, my lord's upon the stairs.

LADY (*to* COLONEL): Away, away! Mark what I say, and keep up the discourse.

COLONEL: This is but living upon the rack; you might contrive a better opportunity.

LADY: Peace, and observe. {*Raising her voice.*} But are your ladies then so free and yet so innocent in England?

GOVERNOR (*peeping*): Gadso, they are together. Tho' I am not jealous, 'tis convenient to hear a little what their conversation is.

COLONEL: Chaster in their thoughts than your nuns, yet merrier; more frolicsome than your carnivals.

LADY: Very pleasant! Just so I wou'd live, yet if a bold encourag'd wretch once offer'd at my honour, I wou'd not stay to use my husband's sword, – but with my own hands stab the vile presumer.

COLONEL: You need not, madam, talk

of weapons. Your eyes, tho' they roll in fire, yet shoot chaste beams, and show your heart as cold as ice.

GOVERNOR (*entering*): [So, so; very, very well, by th'Mass! How is't my Ganymede o' the war, who look'st fitter to storm hearts than towns? Yet, igad, you English boys fear not their pretty faces, but fight like rugged Romans, or the old rough Gauls.

COLONEL: You compliment us, my lord.

GOVERNOR: No, faith, I hate 'em.] – Well, Tittup, are ye almost ready for your dinner?

LADY: When you please, Deary.

GOVERNOR: I warrant the Marquess would not let his wife dine with us for the King of Spain's next plate fleet.[3]

LADY: He has let me see her but once. When I offered it again, he plainly told me my company was unfit for her. Rude brute!

COLONEL: To us who have been bred otherwise it seems a miracle that men can be so barbarous to the fair sex.

GOVERNOR: But I'll set 'em an example, if Tittup holds her ground. Come along.

(*Sings.*)
Merrily, merrily let's pass our time,
In freedom, joy, and plenty;
At sixty appear but in our prime,
Whilst the thinking sot is old at twenty.

They exit.

---

[3] plate fleet: ships that carried silver to Spain from the colonies.

ACT TWO

Scene One

A Chamber {in the Governor's Palace}.

Enter ELENORA, *Marchioness of Moncada, and* ORADA.

ELENORA: Dost think the messenger got off, Orada?

ORADA: Faith, I know not, madam. I thought I heard the Marquess's voice as he went out. The fellow seem'd very cunning.

ELENORA: All his policy but little would avail him if my husband met him. By Heaven, 'tis kindly done of Count Camillus to leave his wealth, his palaces, and all the pleasures of delightful Rome, to follow wretched me to Barcelona. I am a thing accurs'd by cruel guardians [for my parents died when I was young. They would not else sure have forc'd me, condemn'd to an old jealous madman. – I saw his follies and his humours, and I begged, like a poor slave, who views the rack before him – all in vain. They were inexorable. So may just heaven prove to them in their greatest need!]

ORADA: This is a melancholy thought; complaints won't break locks. We must set our wits at work to free ourselves. I have search'd the lodgings round, but there's no passage. An imprisoned mouse could scarce escape.

ELENORA: But prithee, dear Orada, how got you in favour with my lord? He us'd to hate ye abominably.

ORADA: True; and whilst he did so, it was impossible for me to serve your ladyship. So I wheeled about, rail'd at you and all your ways most heartily, and immediately obtain'd his grace.

ELENORA: Wou'd that do?

ORADA: Yes. [With a bantering letter I show'd him, pretending I had got it from you, and a long harangue how wives ought to hear with their husband's ears, see with their eyes, and make use of no sense without permission. In fine,] I ravish'd him with my discourse, till he threw those withered sticks, his arms, about me,

and swore I shou'd remain his heart's joy.

ELENORA: 'Tis a great point gain'd. You must wheedle him this night with some story, and keep him in the closet whilst I watch for Camillus or his agent.

ORADA: I warrant you, madam.

ELENORA: Orada, get me the song I love; [the succeeding tedious,] imprisoned wretches thus count the succeeding hours, and groan the melancholy time away.

Be gone, be gone, thou hag despair;
Be gone, back to thy native hell;
Leave the bosom of the fair,
Where only joy shou'd dwell.

Or else, with misers, willing revels keep;
And stretch thy wretched lids from sleep.
But hence be gone, and in thy hated room
Let's hope, with all its gentle blessings, come.

A noise of unlocking doors.

So! now my jailor comes.

ORADA: Then I'll observe my cue. {*Louder.*} Come, come, madam, you must not complain. Suppose your husband kept you in an oven, or a cellar; you ought to be content. I say, wives must submit.

ELENORA: Hold thy tongue, Impertinence! [When you were good for anything, my husband wou'd not let ye come at me. Now he has brought you to his turn,] I must be perpetually plagu'd with you.

Enter the MARQUESS.

MARQUESS: You are a perpetual plague to me, I'm sure. You hate everybody that tells you your duty.

ELENORA: Inhuman Spaniard! What wouldst thou have? Am I not immur'd, buried alive?

MARQUESS: Yes, yes, I have your body, but your heart is with the young Count Camillus. D'ye blush, ye strumpet, in imagination? Ye Eve! Dalilan Devil! I'll let out that bounding blood. Orada, get a surgeon to take away fifty ounces.

ORADA: My lord, you are not mad!

What! have a surgeon quiddling her white arm, and looking babies in her eyes!

ELENORA: Monster! be thyself the butcher, and let my heart's blood out. That gentleman you named has honour, truth, and virtue.

MARQUESS: Thou li'st, false woman! He's a rake, a hellhound, and wallowing now in Rome's brothels.

ORADA (*aside*): I could contradict him if I durst.

ELENORA (*laughing*): Perhaps so.

MARQUESS: D'ye fleer[4], poisonous witch? I am going to dispatch the last business that brought me to Barcelona. Then, minion, thou shalt be immur'd in a remote castle, where thou sha't not see the face of humankind, except thy women, and when I design to visit thee.

ELENORA: Know this, and let it gnaw thy jealous heart: thy visits will be my severest punishment.

MARQUESS: Watch her, Orada; preach those maxims thy zeal for me suggests; let her not have liberty to think.

ORADA: Fear not; let me alone to tease her.

Exit MARQUESS, locking the doors after him.

ELENORA: Ay, make all fast – insufferable tyrant! Come, Orada, let's go view the place, which at wish'd-for night brings my dear Camillus to me.

Exeunt.

Scene Two

A Hall {in the Governor's Palace}.

Enter the MARQUESS.

MARQUESS: Where's this plaguy Governor? [I must have him with me, because 'tis about the King's business; tho' I hate him for breaking our Spanish customs, in letting his jilting wife have such liberty.] Ha! Here she comes, {his wife} and a spark with her. I'll abscond, and see how virtuously she carries herself.

Enter COLONEL PEREGRINE and the GOVERNOR's LADY.

LADY: I dare not stay; my husband thinks I am gone into my chamber. If by any chance he should come this way, all our hopes are ruin'd.

COLONEL: Were he by, I'd seal my vows upon thy melting lips. – Oh! receive my heart; it flutters near thee and struggles for passage.

LADY: I am cover'd o'er with blushes!

MARQUESS (*aside, peeping*): Confound your modesty! Were you mine, you should be cover'd o'er with blood.

COLONEL: My life! Can't ye contrive some way to bless me? Your sex were ever most ingenious lucky at invention.

LADY: Suppose you pretended a quarrel in England, for which you were pursu'd, and begg'd leave to hide here. If you were in the house, I might get an opportunity to visit ye. – But sure you would not be such a naughty man to ruin me, if I did.

COLONEL: Not for the world!

[LADY: I wou'd fain love ye and preserve my honour.

COLONEL: That is preserv'd whilst 'tis conceal'd. The roses in your cheeks will only wear a fresher dye, and those dear eyes are no tell-tales. Love will make 'em shine and sparkle more.] I'll put your advice in execution.

LADY: I must not venture on another moment. Farewell.

COLONEL: Farewell, my blessing.

Exeunt severally.
Enter MARQUESS.

MARQUESS: Oh women! women! women! They are crocodiles; they are painted serpents, gilded toys, disguis'd fiends. But why name I these? They are women. Just such another is my damsel of darkness, if fortune wou'd but throw a handsome fellow in her way. Here comes the Governor, singing, I warrant ye. Poor credulous fool, I cannot but laugh – ha, ha, he!

Enter the GOVERNOR singing.

[4] *Laugh.*

GOVERNOR: 'Let her have her will'
&c. Hey da! I am glad to find you so
merry. 'Tis as great a wonder to see
you laugh, as 'twou'd be to see me cry
– and that I han't done these fifty
years, old boy.

MARQUESS: My lord, which is best, for
a man's wife to cuckold him in
imagination or reality?

GOVERNOR: Lord, Lord! Your head is
always upon cuckolding. All the
cuckolds may be hanged for what I
care.

MARQUESS: Oh fie, no! Hanging
would be a scurvy death for a man of
your quality.

GOVERNOR: Why – what d'ye mean
by that, now, ha? Don't provoke me, I
say, do not. [I shall make old Toledo⁵
walk if you do, for all 'tis in my own
house.]

MARQUESS (*aside*): I must not tell him
now; it will put him so out of humour,
he won't go with me. {*To him.*}
'Twas only a jest, my lord. I wou'd beg
the honour of your company to the
Duke of Sidonia's.

GOVERNOR: With all my heart; come,
come: (*Sings.*)
Tormented still's the jealous fool,
Himself, nor bosom wife can never
rest:
Yet he often proves the woman's tool,
Whilst the contented man is ever blest.

Exeunt.

Scene Three

*A Chamber {in CAMILLUS's
Lodgings}.*

Enter CAMILLUS, FRIAR ANDREW,
and HIDEWELL, *with a ladder of
ropes.*

CAMILLUS: So, Hidewell, hast thou got
the ladder of ropes?

HIDEWELL: Yes, my lord, here's all
the tackling.

FRIAR: Is it strong? for I am something
weighty.

⁵ *sword*

CAMILLUS: How Father! just now you
said you were worn to skin and bone.

FRIAR: Ay, my lord; but you know
bones ill-cover'd will soonest be
broken.

CAMILLUS: True; take care of yourself,
be sure. Hidewell, I have alter'd my
mind. Thou shalt {go} along with us;
watch [on the] outside the wall, and
give us notice when the coast is clear.

HIDEWELL: With all my heart.

[FRIAR: Let me see; have I got my holy
water about me?

CAMILLUS: Holy water! For what?

FRIAR: Oh! I always love to say my
prayers and have those trinkets when I
undertake a dangerous design.

CAMILLUS: Don't be so profane,
Domine; you'll never thrive. Yet if
your devotion's strong, you've time
enough. We shan't go this hour or two.

FRIAR: Nay, I won't hinder ye'; an
ejaculation as I go along does the
business.]

Enter a SERVANT.

SERVANT: My lord, the English
Colonel [that lodges in the house]
sends to know if you are at leisure.

CAMILLUS: Tell him I am, and long to
kiss his hands.

Exit SERVANT.

I like that gentleman; he appears
brave and bold. Should our designs
grow desperate, I dare believe he
would not scruple his assistance.

FRIAR: Faith and troth I like him too.
He treats like an emperor; I dined with
him today, and he so agreeably forc'd
flesh upon me, that by St. Dominic, I
cou'd not refuse him, tho' 'tis a strict
fast, a horrible strict fast, as I hope to
be an abbot. Then the obliging toad
has such a waggish eye, I'll pawn my
beads {he's} a plaguy dog for the
women, and they are ever good-
natured. By his Holiness's toe, I love
the sex myself, for all this dangling
robe, and my foolish vow of chastity.

CAMILLUS: 'Tis a pity you were not a
knight errant. The Church has robb'd
the ladies of a famous adorer.

FRIAR: No, faith, my lord, I do 'em more service in these weeds; I have sav'd many a desperate soul.

CAMILLUS: How?

FRIAR: Thus: in procuring them the full possession of their desires, [and that surely brought 'em to repentance; and you know what repentance brings 'em to].

HIDEWELL: Truly, Father, I shall grow angry with you. For if [once the] priests take up the office of procuring, there will be no business for a lay-pimp.

CAMILLUS: Peace, the Colonel comes.

Enter COLONEL PEREGRINE.

COLONEL: I am your lordship's humble servant. I have just had some music to complement me. I am a great lover of {music}; if your lordship is so, we'll have the entertainment there.

CAMILLUS: Nothing can oblige me more. Some chairs there!

{Enter singers and dancers.}
A dialogue-song and dances. At the time of the dances CAMILLUS *and* PEREGRINE *seem in discourse.*

HIDEWELL: If your lordship pleases, being in this dress, I will aim at a jig. I danc'd thus once in a masquerade.

CAMILLUS: Prithee do.

A jig by HIDEWELL.
A song betwixt a Spaniard and an English lady[6]

HE:
Fairest nymph that ever bless'd our shore,
Let me those charming eyes adore,
And fly no more, and fly no more.

SHE:
Spaniard, thy suit is all in vain;
I was born where women reign,
And cannot brook the laws of Spain.

HE:
For thee my native customs I'll forego,
Cut my black locks, and turn a beau.

SHE:
Ere I submit to be your wife,

Listen to an English husband's life:
With sparks abroad I'm every day,
Gracing the gardens, park, or play,
Hearing all the pretty things they say,
Give and take presents, and when that's done,
You thank the beaux when I come home.

HE:
Oh! I now my temper fear.

SHE:
Oh! sigh not yet; there's more to hear:
At my levy crowding adorers stand,
Fix'd on my eyes, and grasping my white hand;
All their courts and oglings bent on me,
Not one regardful look towards thee:
At this thou must be pleas'd, or else not see.

HE:
Then we must part, and I must die.

SHE:
If thou art such a fool, what care I?

HE:
I cannot share thee, so I am undone.

SHE:
A wiser will supply thy room.

CHORUS:
Then we must part, &c.
If thou art such a fool, &c.
I cannot share thee, &c.
A wiser will supply, &c.

COLONEL (*to the singers and dancers*):
So, well performed. Return to my apartments; I'll be with ye presently.

Exeunt {singers and dancers}.

CAMILLUS: The oddness of our adventures surprises me: both our mistresses in the same house! I hope 'twill further our designs.

COLONEL: It must. My lord, I have a favour to beg: that you wou'd lend me one of your implements tomorrow, to manage a plot I have in agitation.

CAMILLUS: Most willingly, take your choice.

FRIAR: I am at your service.

HIDEWELL: You are so forward,

---

[6] *The original reads: 'A SONG. Betwixt Mr. Leveridge a Spaniard, and Mrs. Cross an English lady.' Leveridge and Cross were members of the acting company.*

canonical fornication-broker. I believe I am fittest for the gentleman's service.

[FRIAR: Goodlack, upstart! I help'd ye to my lord, and now ye are for engrossing all bus'ness to yourself.

COLONEL: Nay, I must have the most expert, because the case is difficult.

FRIAR: Well! I'll not say much! – but here stands little Andrew, who has undertook to bring a smock-fac'd Cardinal to a madonna secur'd with a guard more numerous than Argus's eyes, and more dreadful than the dragon you wot of; yet spite of massy doors, impenetrable bolts, and Italian padlocks, effected it.

HIDEWELL: Phough! what's that! I have carried on an amour for the Queen of Spain; convey'd her letters made up in wax candles, love-complaints writ in the inside of her glove, besides a thousand other contrivances you never dreamt of. 'Tis true, at last the fate of all court-pimps was mine: I fell into disgrace. As that had rais'd me, so it ruin'd me. I lost a coach and six by my profession, and shall you pretend to rival me?

FRIAR: You lost! Why, sirrah, sirrah! I tell thee, if I had employ'd my parts in church politics, in tricks of priestcraft, by this time I had been Pope. But the bringing kind loving things together, was dearer to me than the Triple Crown. And shall a varlet contend with me?]

COLONEL: Gentlemen! dispute no more, I find either of you is qualified for my purpose. My noble lord, good night. If you want me, on the least notice, I am ready.

CAMILLUS: I thank you, dear neighbour; good night.

Exit COLONEL.

Hidewell, take up the ropes, and come away.

FRIAR: Along, blunderbuss.

[HIDEWELL: I hope, Father Peremptory, before tomorrow morning you'll stand in need of cunning, to deliver that lov'd carcass from some imminent danger.

FRIAR: I defy thee, and all thy shallow imaginations.

CAMILLUS: Leave jangling, and make haste.]

Exeunt.

Scene Four

{*A Passageway in the Governor's*} *Palace.*

Enter the MARQUESS, ORADA *following him.*

ORADA: My lord, I have a thousand things of greater consequence to say. Pray return.

MARQUESS: Dear Orada, by and by; I must see where my devil of a wife is.

ORADA: You know she cannot {leave} her lodgings; perhaps she's at her devotions.

MARQUESS: No, she's too foul to pray.

ORADA (*taking him by the arm*): But, my lord, – as I was saying –

MARQUESS (*flinging from her*): I'll return immediately.

Exit.

ORADA: There's no keeping this mad fool out of his wife's sight. [They must e'en to bed, whilst I parle with the lover.]

Enter MARQUESS, *pulling in* ELENORA.

MARQUESS: So, gentlewoman! I have caught ye! How? With your head out at window, making your amorous complaints!

ELENORA: I was almost stifled for want of {air}. Sure you are not jealous of the trees and stars; they were my only objects.

MARQUESS: Oh impudence! Did I not hear you say, 'When will he come: my light, my life? break thro' this veil of darkness, and shoot with rays of comfort on me'?

ORADA (*aside*): A deuce of these thinking minds! So brimful of cogitations, they must run over.

ELENORA: I knew you behind me, and therefore did it to torment ye.

MARQUESS: It may be so, but I shan't trust ye. Come, into the bedchamber. Orada, do you school her. I'll watch for your light and life myself.

ORADA: My lord, you had better go to bed with her, and then you'll be secure.

MARQUESS: No, no. In, in. (*Shuts 'em in and locks the door.*) Now for my pistols, that I may give this midnight guest the welcome he deserves.

Exit.

Scene Five

The orchard outside the Governor's palace.

COUNT CAMILLUS *and* FRIAR ANDREW *come down the wall by a ladder of ropes.*

FRIAR: So! We are got well in; heaven send us safe out again!

CAMILLUS: Father, Father! don't trouble heaven in this affair; [you'll never prosper].

FRIAR: Bless me, my lord! Prayers are natural to me; if you are so wicked to neglect 'em, I can't help that.

CAMILLUS: Come, mind your bus'ness. Where's the whistle?

FRIAR: Here, here. Now for a delicious vision of a peeping angel!

(Whistles.)

MARQUESS (*above*): The signal's given, and here's the answer. (*Shoots off a pistol.* FRIAR ANDREW *falls flat.*)

CAMILLUS: We are discover'd, and if I stay, all other opportunities are left forever. (*A cry within of* 'Thieves! Thieves!') Why, Friar! Friar! Father! You are not hurt; the bullets went over our heads.

FRIAR: Are ye sure I am not hurt? I did conceive I was kill'd.

CAMILLUS: No, no, but [I know not what] you may be if you stay. Follow me, with speed.

(CAMILLUS *gets over the ladder. When the* FRIAR *is halfway up, the ladder breaks, and he falls down.*)

FRIAR: Oh pox! The devil of all ill luck! Ruin'd, hang'd, drawn, and quarter'd! No possibility of escaping without a miracle, – and I can't have the impudence to expect a miracle. (*Noise within:* 'Where! Where! Thieves follow.') Oh! They come! They come! And now at my greatest extremity I cannot pray. Godso! Here's a tree! I'll try to mount it.

Gets up the tree.
Enter the MARQUESS. *and several* SERVANTS.

MARQUESS: Search well, boys! Leave not a shrub or tuft of grass unexamin'd. Five {gold coins} to him who finds one.

FIRST SERVANT: I warrant ye, my lord! Let us alone for ferreting 'em. Soho! what have we here? A pox, 'tis a stub of a dead tree. 'T has broke my nose.

SECOND SERVANT (*looking up in the tree, where the* FRIAR *is*): Oh rogue! are ye there? I'll be with ye presently. (FRIAR ANDREW, *as the fellow gets up, throws his bottle of holy water full in his eyes, pulls his cowl over his face, and roars out. They both fall from the tree together.*) The Devil, the Devil! Oh, my eyes are {put} out!

The rest cry, 'The Devil!' *They drive the* MARQUESS *in, who often turns and cries,* 'Let me see him! Let me see him!' *The* FRIAR *follows 'em, roaring.*

Scene Six

Scene changes to the inner part of the house. Several servants enter in confusion. A great knocking at the door, and cry of 'Fire, Fire!' *One of the servants opens the door. Enter* HIDEWELL, *men and maids, as from their beds, some crying* 'Fire' *and some crying* 'Murder, Treason,' *&c. After them, enter* FRIAR ANDREW, *driving several servants, who run out, crying,* 'The Devil! The Devil!' {*leaving* FRIAR

ANDREW *and* HIDEWELL *alone for the moment}.*

HIDEWELL: Make haste, unlucky devil! 'Twas I cried, 'Fire' – open'd the door for your deliverance. Fly, and own me for the master of your art for ever.

FRIAR: I cannot stay to thank ye, but –. I yield, I yield.

Exits, running.
Enter the GOVERNOR *in his nightcap, sword drawn.*

GOVERNOR: *Benedicta Maria!* What! fire, murder, and treason all abroach at once! A horrible plot! [By the honour of Spain, a terrible one, as I hope to be a grandee!]

Enter the GOVERNOR's LADY, *attended {by Spywell}.*

LADY (*aside*): Spywell, what can be the meaning of this? My Colonel would not come in such a way. (*To him.*) My lord! My Deary! the matter, the cause of this disturbance!

GOVERNOR (*to a* SERVANT): Here, sirrah! raise all the guards. Oh Tittup! We're like to be murder'd, drown'd, and blown up, nobody knows how, nor which way. A damnable plot! by his Majesty's mustachoes, I swear!

LADY: Sure 'tis a false alarm. The house has been searched by some servants discreeter than the rest, and they find nothing.

Enter MARQUESS, {*whipping*} *his* SERVANTS.

MARQUESS: Villains! Dogs! Under the notion of the Devil, these sheep-lookt rogues, these dastard whelps, have let the robber of my honour escape; whilst I but just examin'd if my wife was safe, the wolf, the goat is gone.

GOVERNOR: Hey da! My Lord Marquess, are we then alarm'd only with a jealous whim of yours? By the peace and pleasure of my life, I'll suffer it no longer. Any other of my palaces are at your service, but such a wasp shall molest my honey-hive no more.

MARQUESS: Uncivil lord! Thy palaces, nor all thy wealth shou'd bribe my stay. Tomorrow I've resolv'd for my departure. In the interim, I desire an hour's conference.

GOVERNOR: Soon as you please, I am free.

Enter a SERVANT *with* HIDEWELL.

SERVANT: My lord, here we've found a man that nobody knows.

GOVERNOR: Ha! Who are ye, sirrah? your name? From whence d'ye come? Whither d'ye go? What's your business? Answer me all at once.

HIDEWELL (*pretending to be a country rustic*): I daut I caunt; but I'll do no more than monny a mon: I will tell ye the truth. Coming to morket with my fruit, d'ye zee, ich heard the noise of 'Fire, fire! thieves,' ond such-like. Zo che thought good Crabtree-stick might walk amongst the rogues; zo ich have left the fruit with our Margery, and come with main vorce to help ye, d'ye zee.

GOVERNOR: An honest lad! And, d'ye hear, you may sell your fruit to my family.

HIDEWELL: O Lard, O Lard! Ch'am a made mon, and my wife and children. What! Zell my fruit to my Lord Governor – made forever! Henceforth I'll scorn my neighbours, and despise my betters.

MARQUESS: I like this fellow, because I search'd him thoroughly, and found him no go-between. Here, sirrah! Here's something for ye. (*Gives him money.*) [And were I to stay, ye shou'd ha' my custom.]

HIDEWELL: I thank your honours.

GOVERNOR (*to a sentinel*): Let him out.

Exit HIDEWELL.

MARQUESS: You'll remember tomorrow morning early.

GOVERNOR: Most certainly.

MARQUESS (*aside*): Then I'll convince this credulous easy man what need there is of watching one's wife. Good night.

Exit.

GOVERNOR: Farewell. Go thy ways for a troublesome, maggot-pated,

jealous-crown'd simpleton, as thou art.
Hey boy, Tittup! How is't, Tittup?
How shall you and I get to sleep
again, Tittup? Ha!

LADY: I know not.

GOVERNOR: What, moody, Tittup?
(*Sings.*)
I'll rouse ye, and mouse ye, and touse
   ye as long as I can,
Till squeaking I make ye confess:
There's heat in a vigorous old man,
When he loves to excess, when he
   loves to excess.

Exeunt.

ACT THREE

Scene One

A Chamber {in Camillus's lodgings}.

Enter CAMILLUS *and* FRIAR
ANDREW.

CAMILLUS: Curst be my disappointing
stars, that thus have cross'd me! Whilst
I but aim at Elenora's freedom, she,
for my attempts, suffers from her
tyrant-husband worse usage.

FRIAR: You may curse your stars if you
please; but for my part, I bless the
pretty twinkling gentlemen, that is if
they had a hand in my deliverance. I
am sure if I had been caught, my
usage would have been bad enough. I
long to know what has become of that
hangdog Hidewell. – Oh! talk of the
Devil, and he appears.

Enter HIDEWELL.

HIDEWELL: Down on your
marrowbones, Domine, and thank my
ingenuity, else your brittle thread had
been cut, and you left in a dark way
by this time.

FRIAR: Come, come; don't be so
triumphant: for had not my own
roaring preaching voice –

HIDEWELL: Ay, ay; much used to
preaching, I believe – unless it was
indulgence to a yielding female.

FRIAR: Well, as I was saying, had not
my own almighty voice struck terror
thro' 'em, I had been in limbo long
before your ingenuity came to my
assistance. Not but you did me a
kindness, and I acknowledge it. That's
enough for a man of my qualifications.

CAMILLUS: Oh Hidewell! All my hopes
are ruined, and poor Elenora must
remain a slave forever.

HIDEWELL: My lord, you are
mistaken. Our expectations now stand
fairer. The Governor and Marquess
both take me for a very silly honest
fellow and have order'd I shall have
full and free access. Then let me alone
for a contrivance. I'll get the lady for
you, and the {serving} woman for
myself, [following the example of all
noble knights and trusty squires].

FRIAR: I find you are providing for yourselves; but what must I have for my painstaking in this affair?

HIDEWELL: You know you cannot marry; I'll give you leave to tempt my damsel, when I have her. [D'ye conceive – if she loves spiritual food, I'll not be your hindrance.]

CAMILLUS: Dear Hidewell! thou sha't go immediately, learn when they remove; fathom their designs. I'll force her from him on the public road. He forc'd her from her plighted faith, her vows, and all her wishes: my force is just.

HIDEWELL: Trust to me, my lord, and fear not.

Enter COLONEL PEREGRINE.

COLONEL: My lord! your humble servant! I ha'nt rested tonight, since I heard of your disappointment, reflecting how my own affair may prove.

CAMILLUS: Ah Colonel! our cases are very different. You hunt but for enjoyment, the huddled raptures of a few tumultuous moments. But I am in quest of virgin beauty, made mine by holy vows, constrain'd by fiends, instead of friends, to break the sacred contract, and follow the capriccio of a mad old man. Virgin did I call her? By heaven, I dare believe she is one; at least her mind is such. And were she in my power, I'd soon convince the world of the justice of my cause.

COLONEL: My lord, [you shall command my sword and interest in Barcelona, yet you must give me leave to mind my own affairs.] I grant your passion more heroic, for I shou'd scarce accept the Governor's wife for mine, if he wou'd give her. But I am amorous and eager, as love and beauty can inspire hot and vigorous youth.

FRIAR: By St. Dominic, well said, old boy! I'll stick to thee. I hate these whining romantic lovers. Nor wou'd I have trudged to Barcelona, had I thought the Count only fix'd on honora – psha, I can get it out, – honorable love.

COLONEL: Since you are so willing, sir, I have employment for you. Can you [play the hector well,] pursue with a fiery countenance, swear without intermission, make noise enough, no matter what you say?

FRIAR: I'll try, I'll try. hum! hum! – by St. Dominic, by St. Patrick, St. –

COLONEL: Hold! hold! What d'ye mean? you must swear by Jupiter, Rhadamanthus, Mars, and those blustering sparks, not such puny passive saints.

FRIAR: [Well, sir, I shall be soon instructed.] But what must I swear all this for? [Or like the bullies of the age, must it be all for nothing?]

COLONEL: No, no, there is a cause. Come along with me, and I'll give ye clothes and full directions.

HIDEWELL: If I might advise ye, sir, he should not undertake it. He has something in that unlucky phy's[7] shows him unfit, [tho' coveting intrigues: plaguy unfortunate lines, I swear].

FRIAR: Peace, envy! Screech owl! Raven! Bat! Devil! When did I ever fail before last night? nor then neither, sirrah, ha!

[HIDEWELL: Rage on, Spite! I say but this: have a care, when in all your gallantry, you don't forget, and make a Friar-like salutation.

FRIAR: Pox take ye for putting me in mind on't, for I always do a thing I am forbid.]

Enter a SERVANT.

SERVANT (*to* CAMILLUS): Please your honour, a lady desires to speak with you.

CAMILLUS: I'll wait on her.

COLONEL: I'll leave you this apartment free, my lord, my business being in haste. Come, Father!

CAMILLUS: Farewell; may your desires be fulfilled, or you cur'd of 'em.

COLONEL: Your servant.

FRIAR: B'w'ye Hidewell! I don't question but to top you in my

---

[7] *physique*

performance when we meet next.

HIDEWELL: Heaven help the weak, I say.

Exeunt COLONEL *and* FRIAR.
Enter ORADA.

CAMILLUS: Ha, my dear Orada! What miracle got thee this liberty?

ORADA: My lady was so thoroughly frighted at the noise of the pistols and the confusion she heard (for you, I suppose), that she has since been ill. The jealous Marquess cou'd not find in's heart to trust a doctor with her, but sent me for a cordial.

CAMILLUS: I hope her sickness has no danger in it.

ORADA: No, no, 'tis over now, – scarce enough left for a pretext for my coming.

CAMILLUS: But what hopes? What shall be our next design? Speak comfort, my best friend!

ORADA: [Faith, I know not well.] Suppose the Marquess were some way informed you are in Barcelona; 'twou'd fright him out of his wits. I'd back it and persuade him to send Elenora away in the night privately, lest you attempt her on the road. Then you may seize the unguarded fair. Methinks something like this might be done.

CAMILLUS: We'll in and consider farther on't.

HIDEWELL: Hark ye, donna, if your lady falls to my lord, you prove my natural perquisite, by the example of a thousand years.

ORADA: What means the fellow?

CAMILLUS: Despise him not, Orada. He has prodigious parts under that russet coat.

ORADA: I care not for him, nor his parts; I shall ne'er examine 'em.

HIDEWELL: You and I shall be better acquainted for all this.

ORADA: Away, bumpkin!

CAMILLUS: I tell ye, he's a beau in disguise.

ORADA: I believe so.

CAMILLUS: Come to this inner room, Orada, lest we are interrupted.

Exeunt.

Scene Two

A Hall (in the Governor's Palace).

Enter the GOVERNOR, MARQUESS, *and* DIEGO.

GOVERNOR: A pox, a pox! Was this your conference? If I had guess'd at it, the Devil should have conferr'd with ye for me.

MARQUESS: I would ha' thank'd a friend that forewarn'd me of an approaching evil.

GOVERNOR: Evil! What evil? The evil is my knowing it; if I had not, 't had been none. Yet how am I convinc'd you have not abus'd my Tittup? By the honour of Spain, I'll fight for Tittup: guilty or not guilty. My lord! what you have said is a scandalous, contagious, outrageous –

MARQUESS: Hold! If you say one word more, I draw.

GOVERNOR: Well, well! I will have patience. But if this Colonel doth not come with the sham plot you have buzz'd into my head, by King Philip's beard –

MARQUESS: Threaten not; I'll meet you when and where you please, ill-manner'd fool!

Exit.

GOVERNOR: Diego! I have borne up, yet, igad, to own the truth, I am damnably afraid there's something in it. That English Colonel is a plaguy dog. [He looks as if he were made to enter all breaches, conquer every way.] I'll try if I can sing after this news. (*Sings.*)
Lock up a woman, or let her alone;
Keep her in private, or let her be known;
'Tis all one, 'tis e'en all one.

A scurvy tune, as I hope to be a grandee. Nay, if my voice is broke, my heart will quickly follow. Diego!

DIEGO: My lord.

GOVERNOR: I ever found thee faithful.

If the spark does come, follow exactly my directions, and all shall be well yet.

DIEGO: [Fear not me, my lord.] I'd lose a leg or an arm at any time in your honour's service, and never cry, 'Oh!' for't.

GOVERNOR: Hark, hark! I think I hear a noise.

Cry of 'fire' here. Without a cry of 'Murder,' and shutting doors. Enter COLONEL PEREGRINE, *his sword drawn, leaning upon his servant.*

COLONEL: Oh, my noble lord! I'm ruin'd, unless your pity save me. In England I, in a duel, killed a gentleman, and his friends have pursu'd me hither, setting upon me four at once.

GOVERNOR: Alas and welladay! 'Tis sad indeed. And you, I warrant, are wounded desperately.

COLONEL: I fear, to death. Oh! oh!

GOVERNOR (*aside*): Ah, the dissembling rogue! It grieves me almost to disappoint him, the smock-faced dog does it so cunningly. Diego!

DIEGO: Sir.

GOVERNOR: Diego, get one of my able surgeons to search the wound.

COLONEL: I thank you, my lord; my own servant has great skill in surgery. I'll trust him.

GOVERNOR: Diego, carry this gentleman to an apartment near the garden, free from noise. I'll send Tittup to visit ye by and by.

COLONEL: Your lordship's all goodness.

Exit {COLONEL. DIEGO, and SERVANT}.

GOVERNOR: And thou all treachery. Oh! the English whining dog. How shall I punish him? By the honour of Spain, he deserves to be utterly disabl'd, rendered wholly incapable. But I'll have mercy in my anger: hang't, I have lov'd the handsome whipster, [and he shall find it].

Enter DIEGO.

So, have ye dispos'd of him as I ordered?

DIEGO: Yes, my lord, and whilst I was in the chamber, he groan'd as if his heart were breaking. But I had the curiosity to stay a little at the door and heard both laugh ready to burst, an't please your honour.

GOVERNOR: Please me! Not much, in faith, Diego; but – let me tell 'em, had they fell into the hands of any other of our nation, their mirth wou'd quickly ha' been spoil'd, and their whoring too, adod.

Enter SERVANTS, hauling in FRIAR ANDREW (disguised and wearing false whiskers).

SERVANT: My lord, we have took the ringleader that pursu'd the noble English Colonel.

COLONEL: Good boys! good boys! Well, sir, and what are you?

FRIAR: If you are a man of authority, as by your house and port I guess you are, I charge you do me justice. For by yonder blue firmament, and all those hated stars that twinkl'd at my brother's murder, I'll flay that cursed Colonel.

GOVERNOR: Thou hangdog, begot in lewdness and born in some sink of sin, son of a thousand fathers, and maker and contriver of cuckolds without number: I know thee for a pimp. Here, Diego! Fasten upon one whisker whilst I take t'other. If they are fast, I may alter my opinion. [They are reverend whiskers, I confess.] If not, I proclaim thee a pimp. (*They pull, and the whiskers come off between 'em.*)

FRIAR: Oh mercy, mercy! I do own my profession. But good my lord, forgive me.

GOVERNOR: Aye, that I will, but I'll punish thee first. Here, carry him to the red tower, and let him have two hundred lashes, till all thoughts of concupiscence, either for himself or others, be thoroughly mortified.

FRIAR: Hear me, my lord!

GOVERNOR: No, away with him.

FRIAR: You must hear me; I am a priest. I excommunicate ye else.

GOVERNOR: A priest, and a pimp! Oh Lord!

DIEGO: Look, my lord! Here hang his heads under his clothes.

FRIAR: Now my lord, [you are satisfied the secular arm can't punish me. Pray] give me a release.

GOVERNOR: Hold, hold; not so fast. Take him, and carry him to the next abbey just as he is, and tell the fathers what ye know.

FRIAR: 'Tis well 'tis no worse. [To deal with the tribe, let me alone;] they'll judge my frailties by their own.

[GOVERNOR: Say ye so, Beelzebub, in his own clothing! But I'll be a thorn in thy side, I'll warrant thee, old Father Iniquity.

SERVANT: My lord, we'll set the mob upon him; that's worse than all the justices in quorum.

FRIAR: I'll curse, excommunicate, purgatory ye, hang ye, damn ye.]

Exit, forced off.
Enter GOVERNOR's LADY.

LADY: My Deary, Spywell tells me our dear Colonel's wounded.

GOVERNOR: Oh, most dangerously, Tittup. [He has as many holes thro' him as a Jew's cake.[8]]

LADY: Alas, then I fear he's dead.

GOVERNOR: No, no, nature has fram'd his body for the purpose. A sword passes and repasses like a juggler's ball, and no harm done.

LADY: Cruel Deary! You make a jest on't, but I'll visit and comfort him.

GOVERNOR: Hold, hold. His wounds are dressing. You would see him naked, would ye?

LADY: Oh gad! Not for the world.

GOVERNOR: Retire to your chamber. I'll send for you when 'tis convenient.

LADY: I will, Dear; but pray take care of him.

GOVERNOR: Yes, there shall be care

taken of him, I promise ye.

Exit LADY.

A hopeful young gentleman, by the honour of Spain. – Diego, follow to my closet; there I'll make thee sensible of my design.

Exeunt.

Scene Three

(ELENORA's *Apartment in the Governor's Palace*).

Enter the MARCHIONESS ELENORA, meeting ORADA.

ELENORA: Dear Orada! Bring'st thou comfort, or must I remove from Barcelona to wilds and unfrequented deserts, impenetrable castles, and all the melancholy mischiefs spritely youth can fear?

ORADA: I hope not, madam. The Lord Camillus employs his brain and all his busy instruments for your deliverance.

ELENORA: Give me the scheme of his design, [that I may guess at the success] –

ORADA: Madam, my lord.

Enter the MARQUESS.

ELENORA: Take that, (*strikes ORADA*) thou impudent performer of my tyrant's will.

ORADA: My lord, you see what I suffer for your service.

MARQUESS: But we'll be so reveng'd, Orada. When we have her wholly to ourselves, by Heaven, I'll bring that pamper'd carcass down. The roses shall wither in her wanton cheeks; her eyes, whose hot beams dart fire, {will} grow dull and languid. [By all my pangs of jealousy, I'd rather clasp a fiend than, doubting, sleep by such an angel.]

ELENORA: And 'tis thy doubts, old man, not I, torment thee. Our sex, like water, glides along pleasant and useful; but if grasp'd by a too-violent

---

[8] *Barbour suggests this is a reference to matzoh, which 'contains regular rows of perforations'* (238a).

hand, unseen we slip away [and prove the fruitless labour vain].

MARQUESS: To waters, waves, and rocks most justly may you be compar'd. But I want time to hold an argument. Prepare this night for your remove. I am fix'd. Your jewels, equipage and all, put up.

ELENORA: Let my slaves take care of that. What need have I of jewels, ornaments, or dress, condemn'd to cells and everlasting solitudes?

Enter a SERVANT.

SERVANT: My lord, a country fellow is very importunate to speak with you.

MARQUESS: Bring him in.

Exit SERVANT.

Mistress, you to your chamber. You hear the man's business is with me.

ELENORA: May it prove a vexatious one, I beseech heaven.

Exit {ELENORA}.
Enter HIDEWELL *{in rustic disguise}.*

MARQUESS: Oh, my honest fruiterer, what brought you hither?

HIDEWELL: Why, an't shall please ye, a marvelous thing has hap't since I see ye last. A parlous contrivance, by th'Mess; as I hope for Margery, I ne'er see the like.

MARQUESS: The matter, friend!

HIDEWELL: Nay, gadsores, 'tis zo strange, I can't tell whether I was asleep or dreamt, or no.

MARQUESS: Prithee tell me quickly. What wonder hast thou met with, fellow?

HIDEWELL: Zir, I'm but a poor fellow; but, as neighbor Touch has it, I can zee into a millstone, as var as another man.

MARQUESS: Talk to the purpose, or I shall grow tired. Is it anything concerning me or my honour?

HIDEWELL: Ay, ay, zir, you don't know the bottom of this plot.

MARQUESS: Nor the top on't neither. Dallying fool, proceed.

HIDEWELL: Nay, you'll know it soon enough. han't you a very handsome wife, buxom and free, as the saying is?

MARQUESS: Oh the devil, lies it there? Well! What follows?

HIDEWELL: Ifags, cuckoldom, ch'am afraid, zir. For coming out of this hause, there meets me a waundy handsome fellow, gadsores. He had the swingin'st what d'ye call't –

MARQUESS: Peruke, d'ye mean?

HIDEWELL: Ay, udslid! Our biggest bushel, that's kept on purpose for the masters of the measures to zee, wou'd not – no, i'facks, ch'um zure – it wou'd not cover it.

MARQUESS: Did he inquire after my wife?

HIDEWELL: By my troth he did. 'Friend,' says he, 'do you go often to that house?' 'Mahap I do, mahap I do not,' said I, 'what's that to you?' 'Nay, no harm,' quoth he, and thereupon slipped a piece of gold into my hand. I must confess that softened me, and he went on, 'Dost thou not know an old jealous, freakish, confounded Marquess lives there?' Pray ye now dan't be angry, sir; I use but his own words.

MARQUESS: No, no, go on.

HIDEWELL: 'And has he not,' quoth he, 'a young lovely wife?' – And then he run on with hard words I cou'd not conceive for above a quarter of an hour, tho' I was wise enough to pick it out that he was amour'd on her.

MARQUESS: Confound him; confound him!

HIDEWELL: Quoth he, 'Canst thou convey a letter to her?' 'Why how now mon,' zed I, 'who dost take me for, a pimp? No, no, ch'am no pimp; an I war, chou'd ha' better cloas o' my back. By the Mess, chall do none o' your bawdy messages, not I. Do't yourself, an you will, for Tim.' With that he drew his sword, and I very vairly took up heels and run away, for ch'am very veard of a naked sword.

MARQUESS: Couldst thou not discover his name?

HIDEWELL: His servants call'd him Count a, Cam – Cam – Cam – ch'am zure 'twas zummot about Cam.

MARQUESS (*starting*): What, – Camillus!

HIDEWELL: Ay, ay, that's it. That's it in troth.

MARQUESS: Oh, I am ruin'd, blown up, undone! Camillus has his pockets cramm'd with gold. He'll bribe the world to take his part. Then that contract, so firm and sure. I lose her, and what I value more, her large fortune. Orada, what shall I do?

ORADA: Suppose ye remove my lady in a litter, without any of your own attendants, for indeed I fear he'll waylay all the roads. My lord, she may be got many leagues this night, and when in safety, you may send back for your equipage.

MARQUESS: Many leagues! We'll go a thousand, for I'll be with her, and force her speed.

ORADA (*aside*): That I suspected.

HIDEWELL: Zir, zir, here che may serve ye, for I keep a litter, as well as zell fruit.

MARQUESS: Oh! Thou'rt an honest fellow! And fear not, you shall be rewarded beyond your wishes. Come in, I'll give thee an order for one of my best horses, [because my servants shall not suspect 'tis for myself]. Orada! get your lady ready. 'Tis now near night, and it shall be done with speed.

Exit MARQUESS.

ORADA: Be sure you lame the horse now, for as soon as the litter has lost sight of the Marquess, we return into the city, and towards the morning escape [in a felucca already ordered], whilst the disappointed Marquess is hunting the roads in vain.

HIDEWELL: Madam, I desire none of your directions. I am perfect master of my trade. I cannot but think how bravely I shall maintain thee, girl; for money comes rolling in.

ORADA: Mind your business, and think of fooling afterwards.

Exeunt.

Scene Four

Chamber {in the Governor's Palace}.

The scene draws and discovers
COLONEL PEREGRINE *upon a bed, and his man by him.*

COLONEL: I begin to grow damnable weary of nursing up this no-wound. I wish the dear angel wou'd but come, and heal the real wound my heart endures.

SERVANT: Truly, sir, I shou'd have but little stomach to a mistress, if I were in your circumstances. What! Attempt to cuckold a Spanish Governor in his own house!

COLONEL: Peace, coward, and see who's coming.

SERVANT: Sir, sir, 'tis my Lord Governor.

COLONEL: Well, well. Oh! oh! oh!

Enter GOVERNOR and DIEGO.

GOVERNOR (*aside to* DIEGO): Diego! unobserv'd secure that sword, hat, and peruke. I shall have use for't.

DIEGO (*aside to* GOVERNOR): Yes, my lord.

COLONEL: Oh, oh, oh!

GOVERNOR: How d'ye, sir?

COLONEL: Oh, very bad. Just, just fainting.

SERVANT: Please ye to have some cordial, sir?

COLONEL: A little, if ye will.

GOVERNOR: And are not you a damn'd dissembling handsome toad? Answer me that now, answer me that. What! Corrupt the wife of my bosom, my darling Tittup! Break the laws of hospitality! Well, thou'rt a desperate fellow, I protest. Design to cuckold one that hopes to be a grandee of Spain! Abominable, by St. Jacques! Come, come, get up; your wound's not mortal, I'll engage.

COLONEL: I'm so confounded, I know not what to say.

SERVANT: Ay, I thought 'twould come to this; now shall I be toss'd in a blanket, burnt, drown'd, hang'd!

COLONEL: Be quiet, rascal, and be damn'd!

GOVERNOR: What, you're out of humour, sir! I must confess, 'tis a plaguy disappointment. Come, in short, I'll use ye much better than you ought to expect. Go with haste and privacy to your lodgings, and the town shall know nothing of the matter. Your wig and other accoutrements shall be sent after ye; but I must use 'em first.

COLONEL: My lord, I beg your pardon for this attempt; you know 't has been no more.

GOVERNOR: Your good will was not wanting, thanks to your whoring stars.

COLONEL: Tho' unarm'd, I will not stir from hence, if you practice a thousand cruelties upon me, unless I have your promise that you will not hurt your wife. I have honour, tho' the rules are now transgress'd. Nor can I leave a lady (whom my love has entic'd) to the resentments of a Spanish husband.

GOVERNOR: An honourable dog, as I hope to be sav'd! By all that's sacred, I will not hurt her. Only she must remain depriv'd of that liberty, which, against our country's custom, I had given her.

COLONEL: That I'm sorry for but cannot ask more.

GOVERNOR: But I shall ask you to be gone. Diego, [get one of my closest chairs, and] let him be convey'd home, as sick.

Exit DIEGO.

COLONEL: Oh, I cou'd tear my flesh.

GOVERNOR: No, no, fast and mortify it.

COLONEL: I own you generous, but have not the heart to thank you.

GOVERNOR: I tell ye once again, your absence will best express your acknowledgment.

COLONEL: Your servant.

Exit COLONEL.

GOVERNOR: Oh, your very humble servant, [sweet friend in a corner!] – Now Diego! help to equip me.

{*Enter DIEGO, with COLONEL's wig*}

DIEGO: My lord.

GOVERNOR: The peruke, [the peruke block]. Oh, how the amorous rogue has perfumed it; the [pulvil,] essence and powder o'ercomes me. {GOVERNOR *puts on the wig.*}

DIEGO: My lord, may I presume to tell ye, your black beard and that white peruke look very disagreeable.

GOVERNOR: No matter, the curtains will hide that. Now go to my wife, and tell her I am gone to the castle to see the guards reliev'd, and shall sup there. Tell her also I desire she would visit the wounded Colonel in my absence.

Exit DIEGO.

Now I shall find if Tittup knew the bottom on't and were consenting to this roguery. (*Throws himself on the bed.*)

Enter his LADY and SPYWELL, her woman.

LADY: Oh, we are happy beyond what we cou'd expect. My husband sups at the castle tonight. Yet I tremble every limb of me; I swear I love this old Governor, and nothing but this charming Englishman cou'd have tempted me to break my vows.

SPYWELL: Madam, you walk and talk you know not where. You are in his chamber.

LADY (*goes towards his bed*): My love, my life, wilt thou not meet me? There is no further need of counterfeiting.

GOVERNOR (*leaps up and snatches her hand*): Ungrateful Tittup!

LADY (*shrieking*): Ah!

GOVERNOR: How couldst thou serve me so?

LADY: Phogh, I knew 'twas you, and did it on purpose to make you jealous.

GOVERNOR: A-pies, a-pies, no, no. you did not know 'twas I. I wou'd be deceiv'd, but cannot.

LADY: Oh, what must I expect?

GOVERNOR: Diego! First turn this

baggage {Spywell} out o' doors, and d've hear mistress, if ye tattle of these affairs, I'll have ye poisoned. Else ye are free and safe.

SPYWELL: Madam, farewell; I can't excuse myself.

Exit DIEGO, SPYWELL.

LADY: Now my turn's a-coming.

GOVERNOR: Ah, Tittup! whither, whither art thou fallen?

LADY (*crying*): No, Deary, not fallen; I was but staggering, and you caught me, Deary.

GOVERNOR: For which I humbly conceive you wish me hang'd, Deary.

LADY: Indeed, indeed, Deary, I'm glad my honour's safe. I never had an inclination before, and never will again, if you forgive me.

GOVERNOR: You shall never have another opportunity. Your back apartments must be your prison, and an old duenna your companion, till time and age have wrought off your loose desires. No more hoity-toity, no more appearing at windows, dining at Deary's table, and dancing after it for digestion. I say, Tittup, all these vanities must be forgotten.

LADY: Oh, stab me first! [Let me not be a May-game to all my servants, who by my confinement wou'd guess at my disgrace.] You us'd to swear you lov'd your Tittup. I never did a fault before, but what a frown might punish. Now let me experience your boasted fondness, and take me to your heart, with kind relenting smiles; else leave me distracted on the earth in endless fears bemoaning my indiscretion and your cruelty.

GOVERNOR (*aside*): I feel I begin to mollify. (*To her.*) Oh, Tittup, Tittup! thou hast been a baggage! a very baggage, by the honour of Spain.

LADY: I confess I have been frail, but I will be forgiven, so I will. I'll hang about thy neck, nor leave the dear place till my pardon's sign'd.

GOVERNOR: What! Give you again your freedom to see another Colonel, and be again betray'd?

LADY: No, there is not such another Colonel.

GOVERNOR: How, Tittup!

LADY: Not such a tempter, such a seducer, I meant.

GOVERNOR: Thou pretty epitome of woman's weakness – I dare not trust thee. Tittup, you must retire.

LADY: Do, lock me up; and next moment you are gone, I'll hang myself in my own garters, so I will. Can you behold your Tittup hanged? Her eyes goggling, her mouth you have bussed so often, gaping; and her legs dangling three yards above ground? This is the sight you must expect.

GOVERNOR: Oh! I can't bear the thoughts on't. Stand farther off. Farther yet – that I may rush upon thee with all the vigour of sixteen, and clasp thee from such a danger. Thou resistless ruler of a doting, fond, old fool! Here – I forgive thee, but if after this I catch ye staggering, expect no mercy.

LADY: By the new joys your returning kindness brings me, I'll die first.

GOVERNOR: The world may blame my conduct; but then, they know not Tittup's charms, the power of her eyes, the pleasure of her arms. I cannot raise my voice to sing yet – hum! no, gad, zooks, 'twon't do.

LADY: Henceforth 'Good humour shall supply thy want of youth;
You shall be always kind, I full of truth.'

Exeunt, hugging.

Scene Five

A Hall {in the Governor's Palace}.

Enter ELENORA *and* ORADA.

ELENORA: Do we succeed, my dear Orada?

ORADA: Beyond expectation, madam! Within some moments, you are in Camillus's arms. [Hidewell is gone for a well-appointed litter, which wheels but round whilst Hidewell plays tricks with my lord and then carries you to the English Ambassador's.]

ELENORA: Now my desires are so near fulfilling, I begin to fear 'em. Yet I know Camillus is honourable.

ORADA: All's honourable. The house is honourable, the lady honourable. Fear nothing, but in, and pray for our success. I think I hear my lord; you must be sure to seem very unwilling.

ELENORA: I'll warrant ye.

Exit ELENORA.
Enter the MARQUESS.

MARQUESS: Is your lady ready?

ORADA: Yes, my lord. But, good Lord! What a life have I had with her. I believe she has thrown fifty things at my head. She swears she won't go like a thief in the night.

MARQUESS: Oh, when the litter comes we'll do well enough for that. I'll make her go, or leave her dead upon the place. Do any of the servants perceive our preparations at this back door?

ORADA: My lord, there's no danger. ['Tis so far through the gardens; and now we have these apartments, their people never come at 'em.]

Enter HIDEWELL.

MARQUESS: Here comes my trusty fellow. Well! hast got a litter?

HIDEWELL: Aye; and by th'Mess, an able one too. [I worn ye mon, afore day, we be past whistling after.

ORADA: Friend, you never talk'd to a lord in your life, I suppose.

MARQUESS: Pho, pho! 'tis all well.] Is the horse for me ready too?

HIDEWELL: Just by the litter, my lord. [My lord, i'fackens it saunds rarely.]

MARQUESS: Call Elenora.

ORADA: I will venture, but Heavens! how I shall be used! (*Exit, and re-enter with* ELENORA.) Nay, madam, it's in vain disputing it; for you must and shall.

HIDEWELL: A vine dame, by th'Mess.

ELENORA: Commanded by my slave! Monster! Whither dost thou intend to have me at this dead hour of night? To death, I hope.

MARQUESS: To death, if you resist. Orada, haul her along.

ORADA: [I think I do pull her.] I believe her arm will come off.

HIDEWELL: Why, law ye, mistress – dan't be so veard; ye shall come to no hort. I have had vine volks in my litter 'vore now.

ELENORA: Away, fool! Leave hauling me; I will go – thou cruel devil!

MARQUESS: Come, I'll see her in the litter and then take horse.

Exeunt.
Re-enter MARQUESS *and* HIDEWELL.

MARQUESS: Sirrah! Sirrah! Where's my horse?

HIDEWELL: My lord! My lord!

MARQUESS: Sot! Dunce! My horse!

HIDEWELL: I'm gone, I'm gone – ({*Exits and} comes back.*) My lord, must I bring him hither?

MARQUESS: Fly and search! Bid the litter go softly; I'll o'ertake 'em.

HIDEWELL: I'm gone, I'm gone – ((*Exits and*)) *comes back.*) My lord, must I bring him hither?

MARQUESS: Eternal fool! Call to me, and I'll come out.

HIDEWELL (*stopping*): Udsookers! 'Ch'am zummat aveard.

MARQUESS: This fellow will make me mad. Beast! Will ye stir!

HIDEWELL: Ch'ave heard volks talk of ghosts, zo I have, about the park pales.

MARQUESS: Rascal! I'll make a ghost o' thee, if thou dost not go, or direct me, where my horse is.

HIDEWELL: I run; I run! (*Exit, the* MARQUESS *following him.* HIDEWELL *crosses the stage running. The* MARQUESS *within cries, 'Where are ye?'*) I'll lead him a dance. Here, here! (*Exits, within.*) Here, here!

MARQUESS: A pox, where? (*Entering.*) Oh! the devil! I can't wag a step further. I have lost sight of him and the litter, and am lam'd into the bargain. I hope Orada observ'd my directions for the road. [The pass I gave 'em, lets 'em through the city gates.] If this fool wou'd come once, I should soon overtake 'em. Numps, fool! Are you coming?

HIDEWELL (*within*): O Lard! O Lard! Ch'am an undone mon! Ch'am an undone mon!

MARQUESS: What's the matter?

Enter HIDEWELL leaning on his stick; as soon as he comes in, he falls down and roars out.

HIDEWELL: Oh! Oh! Oh!

MARQUESS: What ails the fellow? Where's my horse?

HIDEWELL: A murrain, a plague take your horse. Ch'am maim'd forever. For getting up to make haste, he has thrown me, and broke my leg. Oh, my poor wife and children! [They must to the parish.] Then Margery – how she'll take on! For, to zay truth, I loved her better than my wife. Oh! Oh! Oh!

MARQUESS: The Devil take thee, and all thy family, for an unlucky dog! I see I must call up my servants at last.

Exit.

HIDEWELL (*getting up*): Farewell, sweet Señor! For by this time, your lady's in safe hands.

HIDEWELL exits hastily, singing. Enter the MARQUESS.

MARQUESS: Pedro! Olonzo! Valasco!

{*Enter PEDRO, OLONZO, VALASCO.*}

PEDRO: Did you call, my lord?

MARQUESS: Yes. A fellow has broke his leg. You must wake Monsieur Cureclap, my French surgeon – and Olonzo, give orders to my grooms this moment to prepare two horses; Valasco shall go with me.

PEDRO: My lord! What fellow? Where is he? Why, here's nobody.

MARQUESS (*looking about*): Gone! Hell and furies! A plot upon my honour, my life, my wife, my estate! Murder! Murder! Saddle all my horses; get what friends money will purchase; search every road. My estate! My wife! Hell and damnation!

Enter GOVERNOR, with a letter in his hand; his lady, DIEGO, and SERVANTS.

GOVERNOR: So! The cry's up again; but Heaven to be thanked, 'tis almost over now. What's the matter, my Lord Marquess?

MARQUESS: Ruin'd, undone forever! My wife's run away!

LADY: How! Run away! That's worse than I, Deary.

GOVERNOR: I know not; 'tis according as you prove, Tittup. A bad wife's better lost than found.

LADY: Unkind, Deary.

MARQUESS: My lord, burying all animosities, I beg you wou'd assist me now. I shall run mad; my wife, nay more, a great estate, lost! lost!

GOVERNOR: My lord, you must be pacified. I've ill news to tell you. There's a letter sent me from Rome, by the Cardinal Patron of Spain, that you stole a young lady firmly contracted to a noble Roman Count; also His Majesty's order to put the lady in a monastery till your cause is tried.

MARQUESS: I'll hang myself! I'll drown myself! I'll bury myself alive! Dogs! Whelps! Get me cords, knives, poison, sword, and fire.

Exit raving.

GOVERNOR: The man's distracted. Diego, after, and persuade him.

Exit DIEGO.

LADY: 'Tis a just judgment on him, Deary, for being so jealous.

GOVERNOR: Ay, Tittup, when women never give any cause, you know, Tittup.

LADY: Hump!

Enter a GENTLEMAN.

GENTLEMAN: Sir, my Lord Camillus sends to give you an account that he expects the Lady Elenora at the English Ambassador's. He hears by an express, your honour has orders from the King relating to her, to which he willingly submits.

GOVERNOR: An honest lad, by the honour of Spain. Tell him, friend, I'll wait on him immediately at the Ambassador's.

Exit GENTLEMAN.

LADY: Deary.

GOVERNOR: What now! That begging look's put on for something.

LADY: Let me go with you, and see the Ambassador's Lady, and the Marchioness, and –

GOVERNOR: – And the English Colonel. Ha! Why, Tittup, canst thou look me in the face and ask this? [By the honour of Spain, I believe this hoity-toity will desire me to admit him for her gallant.]

LADY: Truly, Deary, if the Colonel is there, you shall hear me charge him never to see me more.

GOVERNOR: A new way, Tittup! To go into a man's company, to forbid him your sight! Come, thou shalt along, and – (*Sings.*)

If with horns my kindness thou dost repay,
I'll punish thee some unknown, uncommon way,
Nor hear whate'er thy charming tongue can say.

Exeunt.

Scene Six

Changes to the English Ambassador's.

CAMILLUS *meeting* ELENORA *and* ORADA; *runs and embraces* ELENORA.

CAMILLUS: My Elenora! Art thou here! Do I hold thee fast, thou choicest blessing of my youth!

ELENORA: Witness my heart, which strongly beats, how much I'm pleas'd in my Camillus's arms! But oh, I blush when I remember I am another's wife.

CAMILLUS: No more o' that; the Cardinal's my friend and has promis'd a divorce immediately. Therefore crown my joys with smiles, and forget past dangers.

ELENORA: I can only say this: I love ye –

CAMILLUS: And not descending angels, with all their heavenly tunes, cou'd charm like that dear sound! [Safe in a monastery thou shalt remain till the dispute is ended. And then, oh! thou blest charmer, then all my sufferings shall be liberally paid, and longing love revel in feasts of unutterable delight.] Nor art thou forgot, dear Orada, but whilst I have life shalt be used like a friend and mistress of my fortunes.

ORADA: I thank your honour and rejoice at my lady's happiness.

CAMILLUS: Poor Hidewell! I hope he is in safety –

Enter HIDEWELL.

HIDEWELL: Yes, and here at your honour's service, tho' I have had a broken leg and two or three other misfortunes. But all's well now, and I can dance for joy.

CAMILLUS: Thou art a witty rogue, and [henceforward shalt ha' no occasion to expose thyself.] I'll provide for thee like a gentleman.

HIDEWELL: I'm your ready slave. (*To* ORADA.) D'ye hear that, Mrs. Scornful? How d'ye like my parts and person now?

ORADA: Troth I've seen so much between my lady and the Count, that my mouth almost waters.

HIDEWELL: We shall soon agree, I find.

[*A lady enters and whispers {to}* CAMILLUS.

CAMILLUS: My dear Elenora, the Ambassador's lady sends word her husband is gone for a few days to hunt. She is very ill, but that all things in her house are at your service.

ELENORA: Tomorrow I'll wait on her.]

Enter COLONEL PEREGRINE.

CAMILLUS: Oh, my dear friend! Here's the lovely prize, which so well deserves the pains I have taken.

COLONEL: A charming lady! My lord, you are a happy man.

CAMILLUS: How goes your affair, and what's become of the obliging Friar?

COLONEL: Nay, heaven knows! The story is too long to tell; only I found the old lord generous, and resolve to attempt the wife no more.

[CAMILLUS: I'm glad on't. In your age you never will repent an uncommitted sin.

ELENORA: That Governor's Lady seem'd a pretty good-humour'd creature; therefore, my tyrant, let me see her but once.]

Enter FRIAR ANDREW, his clothes torn and covered with dirt, and his face scratched.

CAMILLUS: Who have we here! Oh heavens! Friar Andrew!

COLONEL: What! My hector thus us'd?

HIDEWELL: What has befall'n thee, oh thou weak Brother?

FRIAR (*angrily*): What has befall'n me! You may behold what has befall'n me: dirt, wounds, and disgrace. The ladies may live in rat traps, or die o' the pips, for Father Andrew's assistance again.

HIDEWELL: Look, [forward undertaker and wretched performer,] there the lady stands, deliver'd by me!

ELENORA: My lord, is not this the Friar brought your first letter, after I was married, whom the Marquess caught and abus'd?

CAMILLUS: The same, madam.

[HIDEWELL: I said he had unfortunate lines, but he wou'd take no warning.]

ELENORA: Not to encourage anything that's ill, but because you have suffer'd in my cause, there's a cordial will revive the heart and wash out all stains. (*Gives him a purse of gold.*)

COLONEL: For me you have suffered too; and I beg would accept of this. (*Gives him more.*)

FRIAR: Spite of vows, in this necessity there's no refusing such a favour.

CAMILLUS: Come, Father, cheer up yourself; have recourse to your old friend Malaga. I'll provide for ye, that you shall go thro' no more dangers.

FRIAR: By St. Dominic [I had not need, for I have almost lost my life in this]!

Enter a SERVANT.

SERVANT: Sir, the Governor of Barcelona is come to wait on ye.

CAMILLUS: Godsme – in, Father! You wou'd not see him, I suppose.

FRIAR: See him! I'd sooner see the Devil. Well, I'll get a pretty wench to wash me without, and a good store of Malaga within, and try to forget past sorrows.

Exit {FRIAR}.
Enter GOVERNOR and his LADY, arm in arm.

GOVERNOR: My lord, your servant.

CAMILLUS: Yours in all obedience.

GOVERNOR (*aside*): Yonder he stands, the ogling rogue! I thought so. My Lord Camillus, before I talk to you, pray give me leave for some few words with that gentleman.

CAMILLUS: With all my heart.

GOVERNOR {*to COLONEL*}: Sir!

COLONEL: My lord.

GOVERNOR: Nay, o'th't'other side, if you please. Now, Tittup, speak what you promised.

LADY: Colonel Peregrine, my lord has been so good to forgive me what is past; and I desire for the future, as you are a gentleman, you wou'd, after this night, never see me more.

COLONEL: Madam, I obey.

GOVERNOR: And d'ye hear, if ye prove a man of honour, about threescore years hence I may leave ye Tittup for a legacy, and abundance of wealth, a world of wealth, by the honour of Spain. Nay, 'tis worth staying for.

COLONEL: Threescore years hence, quotha!

GOVERNOR: Now, my Lord Camillus, to you and the lady.

{GOVERNOR, CAMILLUS and ELENORA *go aside.*}

HIDEWELL: I wish we had some music. Since our success, I can't keep my heels on the ground.

COLONEL: If the company agree to it, I can procure my Lord Ambassador's {musicians} and send for my own.

HIDEWELL: I'll motion it presently.

{*Exit* HIDEWELL.}

[ELENORA: I freely submit, and will retire to what monastery you appoint. I hope my future conduct will satisfy the world of my innocency.

CAMILLUS: And mine, of my faith and constancy.]

COLONEL: What say ye now to music and dancing? Hidewell longs.

CAMILLUS: With all my soul; this is a jubilee which I'll keep whilst I've life.

ELENORA: But are we secure?

GOVERNOR: Fear not, madam; my guards surround the house – and am not I here?

Songs and dances; them over, the company comes forward.

[CAMILLUS:
Greatness was the attendant of my birth;
But love gives me Heaven upon earth.
These comforts my Elenora does impart:
Joy to my eyes, sweet raptures to my heart.

GOVERNOR:
Like you, here stands a happy man;
And I'll keep my Tittup, – that is, if I can.]

LOVE AT A LOSS
OR
MOST VOTES CARRY IT

Catharine Trotter

The curious life of Catharine Trotter Cockburn is so riddled with paradox that no one has yet constructed a coherent portrait. The most recent attempt is Constance Clark's meticulous collection of facts about Trotter's life and work; this is helpful, though hardly riveting.[1] There is ample evidence of Trotter's complexity, for she wrote about herself, and others in her time and since, have written about her. Depending upon whose description one reads, she was: a dainty coquette, a withered prude, a literary genius, a religious hypocrite, a woman of deep moral conscience, a child prodigy, a septuaginarian drone, a brilliant moral philosopher, a pretentious flirt, a lesbian, a dutiful minister's wife and devoted mother, a tormented intellectual, a tease. In her long life, from 1679 to 1749, she was quite possibly all of these, and more.

The Dictionary of National Biography concludes that her character was irreproachable, whatever that means. Her somewhat fictionalized autobiography, *Olinda's Adventures: or, the Amours of a Young Lady* (1693) must have invited reproach in some circles. It depicts her as a witty jilt, a manipulative coquette, a passionate young woman with strong sexual inclinations toward both men and women. A scurrilous portrait was later drawn in key novels by Trotter's one-time friend, Delariviere Manley. Yet the stories of 'Olinda,' as Trotter called herself, and 'Lais,' 'Daphne,' and 'Calista,' as Manley called her, cohere roughly with the story related of her early life in the authorized biography issued by Thomas Birch two years after her death.[2]

In sum, she was a well-born and intellectually gifted child whose father died at sea, leaving the family destitute and dependent upon the charity of relatives; she resorted to publishing and to coquetry to help provide for herself, her mother, and her elder sister; she adopted the Roman Catholic religion in adolescence; she was an ardent Tory and yet a devoted admirer of the Whig Churchills; she considered many proposals but took her time in choosing a husband. Birch adds to this tale the fact that despite considerable literary gifts, she failed to support herself by writing, re-converted to Anglicanism at the age of twenty-eight and then married a clergyman, and reared a houseful of children in the northern provinces. Once her children were grown, she returned to writing poems and philosophical essays. She was also a prolific letter-writer.

Manley, claiming she fell out with Trotter in competition for a man after several mutually supportive writing projects, depicts Trotter in three novels as an unwarranted snob, a lesbian, and a lascivious hussy 'fallen' to so many men Manley could not count them all. According to the identifying 'key' to Manley's novel, *Atalantis* (1709), after being jilted by the Duke of Marlborough, Trotter was taken in as the lover of Catherine Portmore.[3] Neither of these liaisons has been substantiated, though it appears likely that Trotter did have an early alliance with a notable military gentleman who *could* have been Churchill (she later dedicated a play to one of his daughters); and she certainly carried on an intense relationship with Lady Sarah Piers, to whom she dedicated *Love at a Loss*.

These aspects of Catharine Trotter's life are nowhere reflected in Birch's account, though hints of them remain in the papers he collected while compiling the *Works* (now available in the British Library Add. Mc. 4264 and 4265). Birch obscured Trotter's youthful peccadillos (he never mentioned *Olinda's Adventures*), whitewashed the coquette, and highlighted the moralist; but a note he wrote to himself during his dealings with her suggests that she took part in some of these decisions: 'Ask if not better to omit mentioning the Atalantis etc. Ask if not proper to give some reason for not publishing all plays mentioned.'[4] It is noteworthy that Birch did mention *Atalantis;* yet he gave no reason for not publishing all the plays, and he opted not to publish Sarah Piers' circuitously-worded, passionate letters to Trotter.

These letters require careful interpretation.[5] Some of the pages have been censored by razor and many are in disorder, yet they afford a glimpse at a social, sexual, and moral order which helps to explain the depiction of women's relations in some of Trotter's plays. While the letters are addressed to 'my dearest,' 'my darling,' 'my sweet,' and refer to kissing and lying together, not uncommon in romantic friendships of the time, they also touch on unnamed issues which Piers found troubling. In a letter dated 9 June 1697, Piers warns Trotter, 'the pleasing Wishess of the sighing fair, are not so easily suppress't,' while she denies that 'my inclinations move with that temperature you imagin.' By 19 September, 1698, the relationship seems to have escalated, for Piers writes, 'to send you my softest wishes, and remind you how much 'tis in your power to oblige me' before embarking on the following curious passage:

> . . . perhaps I have been guilty of some Errours that conveniently I can't justify, but if an unshaken faith in the future will atone for what is past, I distrust not of your pardon, I know you will forgive, I know your wonderous temper, and when I reflect what little reason I have to love where my heart is most inclin'd, I must acknowledge more is due to you, much more than nature well can give, who with tenderness the most engaging, receiv'd I fear not half so kind usage. Yet I ought rather to alay than aggravate what might conduce to my disadvantage, were not this sense of my indiscretion a sign of repentance . . . nothing can augment the present bliss, but such a dear companion as your Self; thus were I bless'd, my Elevated joys, I doubt would so transport my wandering Sense with some Romantick, wild extravigance to think my Self a Silvian Deity (Add. Ms. 4265, f. 287).

The syntax reveals the difficulty Piers had in finding words to express her concerns; she may also have feared being discovered or exposed. In a letter dated 24 June (no year), she writes, 'I covet little else but to Serve you, and to serve you so that I need not blush for it, for as much as I doat on your company I had rather be absent from you, than see you endure any perplexity I can't redress' (f. 320). It is certainly possible to deduce that Piers' inclinations in fact did move with that temperature Trotter had at first imagined, and that Piers found it impossible to suppress them; nor, apparently, did Trotter resist. Given the evidence of Trotter's earlier romantic friendships, mentioned lightly in *Olinda's Adventures* and portrayed in depth in *Agnes de Castro* (1696), Trotter may have been the instigator of the events Piers alludes to. Unfortunately, Trotter's letters to Piers are not on record.

Whatever Trotter's character and sexuality may have been, she certainly depicted women as capable of romantic, indeed erotic friendships with each other in her early work. But though as an old woman she wrote many letters to a niece whom she clearly loved, she left no hints of any passionate feeling, homoerotic or otherwise, after her marriage. Indeed she earned two distinct and separate reputations for writing in her lifetime. In her old age, as Mrs. Cockburn, she was widely respected for theological essays. A gentleman's letter to Thomas Birch avers,

> Mrs. Cockburn deserveth the first rank among the best moral writers. In strength and clearness of reasoning, in force and propriety of language, few have been her equals. Her manner and matter are greatly superior to all the performances of the whole sex in all ages and places of the whole world. . . .[6]

In her youth, as Catharine Trotter, she was admired as a poet and playwright. Lord Lansdowne and playwrights William Wycherley and William Congreve viewed her as the most accomplished female writer of the time, as their letters preserved with Birch's material attest. John Locke wrote to her, as did the Queen of Prussia, Leibnitz, Bishop Burnet and his nephew Thomas, and other social, political, and theological luminaries. George Farquhar, a novice playwright in Trotter's heyday, begged her for instruction and support.

It was a wise move for the young Farquhar to make. Trotter's tragedies had attracted considerable attention. One of them, *Fatal Friendship* (1698), had been a major success of its season, running at least six nights in a year when few new plays held the stage for three. Her poetry was often published and admired. And her one comedy, though unsuccessful onstage, was a stunning piece of work. *Love at a Loss: or Most Votes Carry It* premiered at Drury Lane on 23 December, 1700 but closed before a third performance (possibly after the first night), which meant that Trotter earned not a penny from its London production. Apparently it was never staged again, though it was published in 1701, with an affectionate dedication to Lady Sarah

Piers declaring, 'the censure [the play] met with, endear'd it to me, made me earnest
to have it clear itself of the injurious report it suffer'd under, by appearing in
print . . .' A letter from her son to Thomas Birch reveals that she revised it later in
life. That revision was in the hands of the son soon after her death but is not included
with Birch's manuscripts and has now been lost.[7] This is grievous, as an examination
of how the ageing theologian revised the play written when she was a sparkling
coquette might reveal much about the two aspects of her literary personality.

In any case, *Love at a Loss* is a dashing play of wit, featuring at centre a young
woman named Lesbia who has already been, before the play's point of attack, unable
to resist what she calls 'the yielding minute.' Lesbia is hopeful that she may yet secure
her future financially by marriage either to Beaumine, the fiancé to whom she
granted sexual favours, or to Grandfoy, with whom she had fallen in love before her
affair with Beaumine, and whom she loves still. The political astuteness and
originality of this storyline is completely unprecedented in its time. For in the first
place, while fallen women were stock characters of the drama, they were customarily
depicted as either guilt-ridden and destined for suicide, or slatternly and destined for
the streets. Secondly, the idea that a woman might be deeply in love with one man,
entertain a liaison with another, and return to the first with her love intact, and in
hopes of forgiveness, is still unusual in dramatic literature.

Lesbia is not the only radically 'new style' of woman in Trotter's play. Lesbia's
friend Lucilia is madly in love with her fiancé, Phillabell, but has written indiscreet
letters to a fop, Cleon, who threatens blackmail. A third coquette, Miranda, is flirting
manipulatively with Beaumine, though she is engaged to Constant, a dull fellow of
sterling virtue.

The play takes the very institution of marriage to task: its financial necessity for
women, its dubious value for men, its irrelevance to love, sexuality, or emotional
affinity. In scene after scene following a plot full of suspense in which at any moment
Lucinda's letters may be exposed or Lesbia may lose both her marriage prospects, the
young sophisticates, fops, and lovers revile marriage, praise flirtation, and pursue
their various passions. Central to the plot is the question, Which man *should* Lesbia
marry? Beaumine, the self-serving and cynical man she has had sex with and to
whom she is legally contracted? Or Grandfoy, the genuinely affectionate man she
loves? The playwright weighs the choice in favour of Grandfoy.

Unable to decide, just minutes before the final curtain, 'divided betwixt love and
honour,' Lesbia asks her friends to throw dice for her. Miranda suggests rather that
they put it to a vote. With comical intensity, each character casts a vote for first one
and then the other, until Miranda casts the deciding vote for Beaumine. He spits a
response, ''twas pure malice, Miranda,' yet in a moment of completely unbelievable
transformation, Beaumine pledges to marry Lesbia and be faithful to her. Lesbia,
disarmed by the sudden change, suggests that if she's to keep her side of the bargain,
Grandfoy had best 'be a stranger to us.' Grandfoy objects; Beaumine overrules
Lesbia's suggestion; and the play ends with a dance and a moral tag delivered by the
'reformed' Beaumine.

Surely Trotter didn't expect her audience to take the conclusion at face value. The
clever cynicism of the entire play; the obvious likelihood of a continuation of intrigues
between Grandfoy and Lesbia, Miranda and Beaumine; and the lifeless moralism of
Beaumine's concluding rhymed couplets, would have been more than sufficient to tip
the audience off to the real intentions of the principals. Those are underscored by
Lesbia's modest demand that Grandfoy absent himself and the resistance of
Beaumine and Grandfoy to that demand. The likelihood that the lovers would
continue their relationships despite judicious marriages might again have been
underscored by their behaviour during the final dance. This highly cynical response to
rakes' reformations had a precedent in Vanbrugh's popular *Relapse* (1696), which
made good fun of the fifth-act reformation in Colley Cibber's facile *Love's Last Shift*
(1696).[8]

Love at a Loss is a play about a society mired in materialism, stuffed with
hyperbole, blinded by its own verbal fireworks, and thoroughly charming withal. Love
is at a loss in a world which mandates marriage as a financial contract and precludes

sexual expression for women. Love is at a loss among people who value words for what they may obscure, who admire repartée above directness. Love is at loss when social forms and social lies prevail over honesty between lovers.

Yet Trotter suggests there is at least one arena in society in which one *may* place one's trust, and that is friendship. Lesbia relies on Lucilia, who confides in Miranda, who ultimately comes to Lesbia's support. Beaumine banters with Phillabell, but as drinking buddies the two men establish a good deal of mutual reliance. Friendship, between women or between men, is the one safe harbour in Trotter's tumultuous world, and through the characters' friendships the audience is invited to respect and admire them. This helps to explain how, for all its social comment, *Love at a Loss* remains fundamentally a laughing comedy with gusto. There are no villains here, and though love is legally and socially at a loss, these lovers pine, banter, tease, and arouse each other with lavish and often hilarious excess.

The success of a modern revival will depend in large measure upon skilful direction and fine acting, liberating the subtext. For most of the meaning as well as the comedy *is* subtextual. These lovers are too sophisticated, and too wary, to say what they mean. (Those who do, like Constant, are ridiculed by the cleverer ones.) Hot-house passions erect themselves beneath the mellifluous language designed to obscure them; and behind flirtacious fans, the women's entire lives are at stake in a dangerous mating game. Lesbia didn't become pregnant, so her indiscretion remained, like so much of her reality, hidden. Trotter's audience needed no reminding that if an orphan like Lesbia failed to snare a husband, she'd have to fling herself on the mercy of relatives, if she had any, or try to sustain herself as some gentleman's mistress (a short-lived career at best). Trotter's knowledge of the stakes reinforces her women's reliance on each other in this play, an aspect which might need to be emphasized subtextually in a modern production.

This is unquestionably an actor's play. All the women's roles are superb, with depth and range beyond even the very best men's plays of the era (one thinks of Congreve's brilliant Millamant, yet Millamant lacks the genuinely affecting qualities that Trotter's women exhibit in their exchanges with each other). The role of Beaumine offers similar range, and Grandfoy may be played with swashbuckling panache, while Philabell and Constant are comical caricatures, foils for the more verbally astute leads. Cleon is a flamboyant fop worthy of high Restoration comedy, while Bonsot is a lovable fool, the sort of stock clown who might, if well-played, steal the show.

The play is long. However with cutting the action can be made brisk; and there is ample opportunity for the inclusion of music, movement, and dance. The language is lush, graceful, glorious. Perhaps the original production was not well-staged. Whatever the cause of the failure of *Love at a Loss* on 23 November, 1700, it cannot have been the script, which vibrates with theatrical possibility.

---

[1] *Clark devotes sixty pages to her review of information about Trotter in a dissertation entitled* The Female Wits: Catherine Trotter, Delariviere Manley, and Mary Pix – Three Women Playwrights Who Made Their Debuts in the London Season of 1695–96 *(City University of New York, 1984, UMI No. 8409389), pp. 35–95.*
[2] *Birch's 'Account of the Life of the Author' serves as a preface to his edition of* The Works of Mrs. Catherine *[Trotter]* Cockburn, Theological, Moral, Dramatic, and Poetical, *a two-volume set published in London, 1751 (pp. i-xlviii).*
[3] *The edition of* The Novels of Mary Delariviere Manley *edited by Patricia Köster (Gainesville, FL: Scholars' Facsimiles and Reprints, 1971), includes a lengthy index annotated by Köster from 'keys' to the novels.*
[4] *Add. Ms. 4265, f.43, British Library, London.*
[5] *Lillian Faderman's* Surpassing the Love of Men: Romantic Friendship and Love between Women from the Renaissance to the Present *(William Morrow, 1981) is particularly useful here. Her chapter, 'The Fashion of Romantic Friendship in the Eighteenth Century' discusses relationships similar to that of Piers and Trotter. Faderman believes such relations should not be called 'lesbian,' in the narrow sense*

in which that term has been defined since the labelling systems of nineteenth-century sexologists became popular; nor were they merely sentimental. Faderman writes, 'We have learned to deny such a depth of feeling toward any one but a prospective or an actual mate. Other societies did not demand this kind of suppression' (p. 84).
[6] *Add. Ms. 4265, f.48, British Library, London.*
[7] *Add. Ms. 4265, f.198, 109, British Library, London; David Baker's* Biographia Dramatica *(London: Longmans, 1812) states in volume 1, p. 384, that the revised version was entitled* The Honourable Deceivers; or, All Right at the Last.
[8] *Jeremy Collier's* Short View of the Immorality and Profaneness of the English Stage *(1698), which certainly influenced Trotter, is credited with spawning a whole new approach to comedy, involving quick reformations, glib moral dictums, and increased sentimentality most notable in the works of Cibber and Farquhar. The rare quality of Trotter's play is that it does not ask the audience to believe in the reformation, but it offers a sop to theatre critics objecting to the immorality of the drama. Trotter presented herself as a theatre reformer even more clearly in the preface to* The Unhappy Penitent *(1701). It remains a mystery whether she was earnest in her desire to reform the stage, or whether she simply adopted this pose in an effort to reach a wider audience and to defend herself for writing plays.*

Characters:

Men
BEAUMINE, *a Gay Roving Spark*
PHILLABELL, *in Love with Lucilia.*
CONSTANT, *contracted to Miranda.*
GRANDFOY, *in Love with Lesbia.*
CLEON, *a Vain affected Fellow*
BONSOT, *a good-natur'd Officious Fool.*

Women
LESBIA, *contracted to Beaumine.*
MIRANDA, *a Gay Coquette*
LUCILIA, *in Love with Phillabell*
LYSETTA, *her Governess*

SERVANTS

ACT ONE

Scene One

{*Paris*}

Enter LUCILIA, *reading a letter, and* LYSETTA.

LUCILIA: Does the fool think to threaten me into love? Hearts must be won a softer way.

LYSETTA: Ay, madam, but our fear often does the men's business as well as our inclinations. [More women have sacrific'd their virtue to reputation than ever love has ruin'd; and if they can but make us kind, what need they care why we are so?]

LUCILIA: Cleon seems indeed to be of that opinion.

LYSETTA: Every man is, that would be master of his pleasure.

LUCILIA: Phillabell has told me a thousand times, he should not think me his, unless my inclination gave me to him.

LYSETTA: [Because he finds that his best friend, if he would refuse you from any other,] it does not much recommend his love.

LUCILIA: That's your notion, but ever since I have begun to know myself, your maxims are not oracles with me. You shall no more debauch my reason.

LYSETTA: Why, madam, what false maxims did I ever give you?

LUCILIA: Should you not have warned me of the deceit and treachery of men? Instead of that, what did you entertain me with, but tales of happy or unhappy lovers? All to insinuate the violence of Cleon's passion. How did you represent him to my vanity – adoring, dying for me? I thought it a fine thing to be courted in rhymes and ecstasies, tho' [even in that distinguishing age,] he never pleased me, which you knew. [And therefore, to move my pity, made my credulous ignorance believe, that if I wou'd not give him some hopes, he must infallibly die for me; the poor innocent thought she was oblig'd in conscience to save a man's life!]

LYSETTA: Lord! Madam, what ado is here about nothing! Where was the harm of writing a few kind letters to a man? Is there ever a lady in Paris that has not done more for half a dozen before she can resolve to marry one? [And a wise husband wou'd no more repine at that, than he wou'd that his clothes does not come directly to him from the weavers; all the little gallantries do but fashion her for his wearing.]

LUCILIA: [Phillabell loves too nicely, not to grudge the least kind thought for any other man,] and shou'd this Cleon expose *your* letters (for so I must call 'em, since I was but the scribe of what you dictated), I'm utterly undone, my reputation ruin'd; and what is worse, Phillabell lost for ever.

LYSETTA: That wou'd be a base baulk [to a young lady, just upon the point of yielding to her wishes]. Tomorrow is to be the happy day.

LUCILIA: Was to be, but Cleon's resolute to hinder it. Can you invent a way to countermine him? You have been cunning to undo me; employ your art for once to save me.

LYSETTA: Madam, whatever the event has been, my aim was never to undo, but to serve you. [If I had known that you cou'd never have lov'd Cleon, or foreseen your passion for Phillabell, I had not engag'd you so far; but since 'tis past recalling, we should only think of preventing future mischiefs.] But all my counsels will be suspected.

LUCILIA: Indeed I believe you wish me well; prithee advise me.

LYSETTA: You must by no means undeceive Cleon till you are married; persuade him that you love him still, and only marry Phillabell in obedience to your father. Give {Cleon} some hopes of making him happy afterwards.

LUCILIA: Well, and what will this do?

LYSETTA: Do? Is there any man that would not rather have another man's wife than make her his own? 'Twill do all that you would have it, make him as eager for the match as you are yourself; instead of preventing it, as his letter threatens.

LUCILIA: But can I endure he should imagine I would wrong Phillabell so basely?

LYSETTA: What are you the worse for his imaginations? Besides, you can easily dispossess him of 'em, when you have once secur'd your husband.

LUCILIA: Methinks 'tis so dishonourable a deceit I can't relish it.

LYSETTA: Nay if you scruple the cheat, you may keep your word with him.

LUCILIA: Prithee be serious.

LYSETTA: Well, madam, this is certain, unless you give him hopes false or true, he will expose all your letters to Phillabell; I need not make you apprehend the consequences.

LUCILIA: 'Tis such a fatal one, I would at any rate prevent it; but you know Cleon's not allow'd to visit me. 'Tis impossible for me to see him today in private, and to write a letter after the manner propos'd, you wou'd be putting it more in his power to ruin me, than I have ever done before.

LYSETTA: Ay, but at the same time you give him the power, you show him that 'tis against his own interest to use it. When you are once believ'd (which his vanity will help you in), and have gain'd a little time, twenty wiles may be thought of to get the letters out of his hands.

LUCILIA: My case is desperate, and therefore the remedy must be so; once more I will be govern'd by you. Cleon sends me word he shall be in the Walks this evening; you shall carry the letter thither to him.

Enter LESBIA.

LESBIA: 'Tis seasonable to wish you joy today, Lucilia; tomorrow Phillabell will give it you, and then my wishes would be needless.

LUCILIA: He is indeed a man to make a woman happy.

LESBIA: Ha, ha, ha, are you practising the decent gravities of a bride against tomorrow? Prithee, away with that sullen look, or I shall think you are

angry with this impertinent day for stepping between you and the wedding one.

LUCILIA: You are not so much in haste I find. [But, my dear, what if you shou'd marry Beaumine tomorrow, 'twould be friendly to keep me in countenance.

LESBIA: No, no, I won't lose the pleasure of making observations upon you.]

LUCILIA: But tell me seriously why you delay your marriage so long.

LESBIA: Phough, I came to divert my self with talking of your wedding, and you would make me dull with the thoughts of my own.

LUCILIA: Believe me, Lesbia, if I did not love you, I would not urge you farther. [But I am vex'd to hear some malicious reflections that are whisper'd of you, and must ask you why you give the occasion.]

LESBIA: Some fitter time I'll tell you.

LUCILIA: Lysetta, we wou'd be private –

Exit LYSETTA.

Now be free with me.

LESBIA: Well, if I must lay aside my mirth a while to tell you a sad tale – You have often heard me speak of one Grandfoy, whom I lov'd before I knew Beaumine.

LUCILIA: You have told me he was false.

LESBIA: I thought so, but he has since convinc'd me that I wrong'd him, tho' my suspicions were, you know, well grounded. He's still the man which he appear'd at first, all truth and goodness, and he loves me more than I can now deserve.

LUCILIA: I shall think you deserve a great deal of him, if you decline so considerable a match as Beaumine for his sake.

LESBIA: When you know my story, I fear you'll say Grandfoy ought to despise me.

LUCILIA: That's impossible, but pray, my dear, go on.

LESBIA: Just in the height of my

resentment against Grandfoy,
Beaumine first saw, and lov'd me. He
address'd to my mother, who easily
gave her consent, his fortune being
very considerable. To be short, her
commands were sacred to me, and I
believ'd it would be some revenge
upon Grandfoy, which was the chief
motive of my resolving to marry
Beaumine. He propos'd to have our
engagement secret whilst his mother
liv'd, because she design'd him for
another. No priest wou'd marry us
without her consent. He told me then
it was the tie of hearts that made a
marriage; but fearing mine should
change, to make me sure, he writ a
contract, which we both sign'd with our
blood; and to confirm it, he led me to
the Holy Altar, where he vow'd to
take me for his wife –. I don't know
how to tell you the rest.

LUCILIA: You e'en took him for a
husband, is it not so?

LESBIA: He often importun'd me to live
with him as such, and at my refusal,
lost all the natural gaiety of his
temper, and much avoided seeing me;
my mother dying, he came to condole
with me. I saw myself unguarded, and
willing to engage him in my interests. I
flatter'd him with all the artful
tenderness I could affect; this made
him press me more eagerly than ever.
Agreeable as he is, I never loved him
much, and yet, I don't know how he
found the yielding minute. Betwixt you
and I, Lucilia: is there not one
{minute} of which we are not master?

LUCILIA: I will believe so for your sake
[tho' I think it would be always in my
power to refuse a man any thing that
is not fit for him to ask]: but how did
Beaumine behave himself afterwards?

LESBIA: Very fond at first, but now
grows careless, and sometimes
insolent. Still he let me hope that he
would marry me after his mother's
death, which satisfied till Grandfoy
assur'd me she died just after mine,
tho' {Beaumine} conceals it from me.

LUCILIA: That does not look as if he
meant you fairly, but your contract will
oblige him to do you justice.

LESBIA: If it cou'd, I wou'd not marry

him against his inclination.

LUCILIA: What do you resolve on then?

LESBIA: I must first know certainly
what he intends.

LUCILIA: His intentions seem so
indifferent to you, that I must believe
yours are more for Grandfoy.

LESBIA: Indeed he shows so generous
an affection for me, it claims all my
gratitude, and since I find my
suspicions of him were unjust, did not
my honour oppose it, I confess I could
love him more than ever.

LUCILIA: Does he know of your affair
with Beaumine?

LESBIA: He does, and made me
promise that if upon the trial I found
Beaumine unfaithful, I would be
govern'd by him. To confirm my word
I gave him a ring, which was
Beaumine's first gift to me; you have
seen me wear it.

LUCILIA: Did not Beaumine miss it?

LESBIA: I told him I had lost it, which
he easily believ'd, not having ever
heard that I lov'd another, and I have
taken care as far as art would go, to
persuade him that I love him, for that
I thought both my interest and duty.

LUCILIA: I wish you may not find
yourself abus'd. The world is much
mistaken in {Beaumine}, if he has
any thoughts of marriage but to rail,
or make his jest of it.

LESBIA: A man of this age must no
more speak well of {marriage}, than
of religion, and yet perhaps there's as
few marriage haters as atheists.

[LUCILIA: What then can put the men
upon professing it? One wou'd think it
can be neither much for their honour
or interest.

LESBIA: At first to gain the reputation
of wit, by affecting a singularity in
their notions; and since that by
imitation, or humour, they are become
the common topics of raillery, many
take up with it for want of resolution
to bear with their being the ridicule of
their companions.

LUCILIA: And is this your opinion of
Beaumine?

LESBIA: I believe there's more humour and affectation, than any serious reflection in it; and] I have less reason to fear {Beaumine's} love of liberty, than some other chains.

LUCILIA: Why, are you jealous of him?

LESBIA: Only of his rambling temper; he takes care to give me no particular aim.

LUCILIA: He seems indeed to make love to every woman, and mean it to none.

LESBIA: Miranda and he were mightily pleas'd with one another t'other day. She happened to come in when he was with me; she gave him leave to visit her, and talks of him perpetually ever since. He does not seem to think much of her, or I should apprehend her a dangerous rival, she's so much of his own humour.

LUCILIA: But she's engag'd to another too.

LESBIA: Ay, and says she loves him.

LUCILIA: 'Tis strange she should; there can't be two more opposite tempers than Constant's and hers.

LESBIA: And what pleasure she takes in teasing and tormenting his gravity.

LUCILIA: And in pleasing every man else.

LESBIA: Well, coquette as she is, I should not be pleased to have Beaumine pursue the acquaintance.

LUCILIA: Then he has not made her a visit yet.

LESBIA: He does not own it to me.

LUCILIA: I shall see her today, and if I hear anything of him, you shall be sure to know it [for if he is not sincere, the sooner you are undeceiv'd, the better]. My dear, will you go to my closet with me? I have a letter to write in haste; 'twill be quickly done, you'll excuse me for a minute.

LESBIA: I expect to see Grandfoy immediately, and must take my leave of you.

LUCILIA: May all you undertake succeed to your own wishes.

LESBIA: I scarce know what I wish, only all happiness to you.

Exeunt severally.

Scene Two

PHILLABELL's *Lodgings.*

Enter BEAUMINE *and a* SERVANT.

BEAUMINE: Is your master busy?

SERVANT: He'll be at leisure to see you, sir, I am sure.

BEAUMINE: Tell him I'm here.

Exit SERVANT.

Egad, I pity this poor fellow. He might have been a fit companion for us men of spirit and pleasure, but for this damned, dull matrimony.

Enter PHILLABELL.

PHILLABELL: Beaumine! What sudden dearth of wine, or kind women, has reduc'd thee to thinking?

BEAUMINE: Only a sense of my friend's misfortune. I came to condole with you; faith, Phillabell, I am heartily sorry for thee.

PHILLABELL: For me! Why, what's the matter? I was never so satisfied, so easy, so full of joy, as in this minute.

BEAUMINE: Why, is your marriage broke off?

PHILLABELL: Broke! Heaven forbid! you wou'd have reason to condole with me then indeed.

BEAUMINE: And you are certainly to be married tomorrow?

PHILLABELL: I hope so.

BEAUMINE: Strange! but he's mad, poor man.

PHILLABELL: Why, did you hear anything to the contrary?

BEAUMINE: No, and therefore am amazed to hear such agreeable words, as 'satisfied,' 'easy,' 'full of joy,' out of the mouth of a condemned man, if thou art in thy senses.

PHILLABELL: Oh, a satire on marriage, is that your intent?

BEAUMINE: Faith, I would willingly reclaim thee, if thou art not too far gone to hear reason.

PHILLABELL: I cou'd never find any reason why a man shou'd be uneasy in the possession of a woman that he loves, only because he enjoys her without breaking human or divine laws.

BEAUMINE: What are laws but chains to our wills, our inclinations? [Destroyers of liberty, the dear prerogative of nature.

PHILLABELL: But Libertinism is not a privilege to be very fond of, and that's all we are denied.]

BEAUMINE: It's better to be lost with pleasure, than preserved in pain.

PHILLABELL: The pain of being always my Lucilia's – [won't much employ my philosophy to support it.

BEAUMINE: And are you sure you will be always of this mind?] Do you imagine she will be always young, always handsome, and that you shall always love her?

PHILLABELL: I am sure she will always have wit, good humour, and virtue, and by consequence, that I shall always love her.

BEAUMINE: But what if all that you call good humour should prove affectation, nothing else; and virtue, but the art of well dissembling?

PHILLABELL: To dissemble well is virtue, or what we can't distinguish from it.

BEAUMINE: Ay, ay, but the disguise is always laid aside when there's no further need of it. When you are entered into bonds, 'twon't be worth her pains. If you but saw the fond, endearing Lesbia, what arts she uses to engage me, how well she thinks 'em all return'd by one kind word or look. And then the tender niceness of her passion. She lost a ring the other day which I had given her; never was anything so moving as her complaints! I told her she shou'd have one twice the value, but she said 'twas the first present I had made her, and she fear'd the loss, a sad presage that she should

lose my heart. Nothing could comfort her but my repeated vows of never changing. Are there such tender sentiments in marriage? You'll find a cold civility the best part of a wife's entertainment, after a month's enjoyment.

PHILLABELL: I should expect no better, if I had chosen an unthinking coquette, or one whose broken fortune might make her snatch at the first hope of repairing it; but Lucilia's fortune equals mine. She has refused many considerable matches, and I have reason to think myself the only man that has found the way to her heart. I know she hates Cleon, and she treats with scorn or coldness the rest that languish for her. In fine, I have all the security for a lasting love and happiness, that reason can desire, or give.

BEAUMINE: Lasting! Why, thou hast nam'd the very bane of love and happiness. What that's old can charm to ecstasy? Or not be dull with being repeated?

PHILLABELL: And what that's new can be relied upon? Or how can you enjoy a happiness that you are always in danger of losing?

BEAUMINE: Relied on? O most firmly Phil, (Sings.)
'They still are constant whilst possest, and can do more for no man'

And faith, fickle as women are, they must be plaguy quick to make me complain of losing them; for if any of 'em should run out of my arms to another's (for then she is sure to have the start of me), I have always one in hand that supplies the vacancy.

PHILLABELL: [Nay that's the way indeed not to be much griev'd at their loss; for betwixt two, you can't be very fond of either.

BEAUMINE: You're mistaken, man, it makes me very fond of both; if they knew nature, a woman wou'd never fear losing a man. When the coyness or jealousy of one has vex'd him, he flies to another that with kindness restores his good humour; and when her over-fondness has cloy'd him, he returns to the first for fresh appetite; for by one of these extremes, the women always lose us: they are either so capricious, they grow troublesome, or so tender, they grow dull; but temper'd thus, they give the relish to each other.

PHILLABELL: If you cou'd convince the women of this doctrine, you might both have your ends by it; but whilst they are of another opinion, whatever advantage it may be to them, you'll hardly find your account in it.] He that pursues two hares will catch neither.

BEAUMINE: Still he has the greater pleasure in the chase, to observe their different crossings, windings, and little arts; sometimes their very fear, you know, makes 'em run full into the hound's mouth. But if you do not give over too soon, there's none of 'em but may be wearied out; then seize the panting quarry, and she's yours.

PHILLABELL: Well, give me the woman that resigns herself upon deliberation and solid reason, that as it makes the gift more valuable, so more secure.

BEAUMINE: That is, more insipid.

[PHILLABELL: There's no disputing tastes. The very trouble of continual fresh pursuits wou'd make variety disgustful to me.

BEAUMINE: Which gives me the highest relish. But I need not endeavour to convince thee; thy wife will do it effectually, since thou art resolv'd to purchase wisdom at the dearest rate, experience. What a lamentable figure thou'lt make, preaching it to others, as a fellow at the gallows does honesty, when 'tis too late to make use of it himself.] – But I'll leave you to prepare for your solid blessing. Will you meet me in the walk this evening?

PHILLABELL: If I have nothing else to do, perhaps I may.

BEAUMINE: Egad, I beg your pardon, I forget thou'rt a man of business. Honest matrimony. Adieu.

PHILLABELL: Well, well, laugh on, I am contented you shou'd have your jest, so I secure my happiness,

With a chaste wife, like my Lucilia, true.

BEAUMINE: I, with a mistress, ever gay and new.

Exeunt severally.

ACT TWO

Scene One

LESBIA's *Lodgings.*

Enter LESBIA *and* GRANDFOY.

GRANDFOY: I wou'd not appear in your defence, till you have try'd Beaumine to the utmost, that he may have no pretence against you.

[LESBIA: I never gave him any yet, nor can he find an excuse now for deferring our marriage, since the only obstacle he pretended, is remov'd by his mother's death.

GRANDFOY: But I advise you not to take notice of your knowing it, nor shew any distrust of him. If he has the least honour, the confidence you seem to have in him will be a stranger engagement.]

LESBIA: But shou'd he still refuse me?

GRANDFOY: You promise then to be dispos'd by me; I wear the pledge of your fidelity.

[LESBIA: Won't it be a bold venture to put myself in the power of a man I have injur'd?

GRANDFOY: Unless in your unjust suspicions of me, you only have been injur'd, your misfortune with Beaumine has a thousand excuses on your part, as unhappy as it makes me.] Oh, Lesbia, that I should ever think it reasonable to wish you another's! [To force a man to deprive me of all I value!]

LESBIA: 'Tis scarce reasonable indeed to value me now so much, as to care whose I am.

[GRANDFOY: I have such an opinion of your sincerity and virtue, that even now, would you consent to be mine, I should receive you as the greatest earthly blessing, but that you have refus'd me unless Beaumine, by a declar'd infidelity, entirely release you.]

LESBIA: Imagine with what difficulty I do it, whilst I receive such proofs of love from you, whom I have had too much kindness for, ever to be indifferent to, or equally to value any other.

GRANDFOY: Curse on that fate that forc'd me from you so abruptly, to make me lose that kindness, by seeming false then, when I lov'd you most, and ever must, tho' now your heart's another's.

LESBIA: I fear, Grandfoy, you are still but too dear to it.]

GRANDFOY: Yet you refuse the offer I have made to marry you.

LESBIA: 'Tis the only return I can make to so generous an offer. If my honour did not oblige me to it, I owe it to your love and good opinion, for 'tis the only way I can deserve 'em.

GRANDFOY: How little does Beaumine deserve this treasure that values it so lightly! [I must approve the virtue that undoes me; and to preserve it as free from suspicion as it is of guilt,] I'll leave you, since you expect Beaumine. For your sake I would not have him know me, unless he force me to revenge your wrongs.

LESBIA: You are in all things noble.

GRANDFOY: If you are for the Walks this evening, I shall see you again. Cleon sent this morning to desire I wou'd meet him there. He has something to ask my advice in, I suppose some love adventure, for that's his only business.

LESBIA: His only discourse indeed, but the great talkers of intrigues, as of religion, have usually the least of either [and indeed whatever a man studiously affects to seem, 'tis a shrewd sign he's conscious of not being it in reality.

GRANDFOY: But the reality of intrigues are generally private, and only to be known by talking of 'em, which, believe me, is the chief part of the pleasure to many of our sex.

LESBIA: I fancy only to those that are allow'd no other part, but they who are truly well receiv'd among us, if not in gratitude to those who have oblig'd 'em, will be cautious to secure their designs upon others; love is not to be rais'd like valour, by emulation.

GRANDFOY: I don't know what it may do towards kindling a flame, but I am sure 'twill increase it; many a woman from a little liking to a man, has become passionately in love, only upon finding another was pleas'd with him.

LESBIA: Then she must know it by her rival's indiscretion, and not his vanity, for that only shows his weakness, but the other, the force of his merit; but indeed, if Cleon should rely upon that, his Mistress would scarce find any occasion of jealousy; {Cleon's} vanity appears too grossly. The good-natured fool, his brother {Bonsot}, is the more supportable.

GRANDFOY: Poor Bonsot, he always means well; but unluckily {he} makes more mischief by officiously endeavouring to prevent it, and pretending to know everybody's business.

LESBIA: Then his bulls are diverting enough, they fall so naturally from him.

GRANDFOY: As near relations, I must bear with {both of them}, and would hide their follies.] But we shall forget ourselves, till we give Beaumine occasion of jealousy [which, tho' sometimes our sex find their ends in, 'tis always a dangerous expedient for yours, for what you gain in inclination, you lose in our esteem].

Fear of a rival will enflame desire;
But the distrust of her soon quench the fire.

LESBIA: That way leads to the back door. You'll be secure from meeting him.

Exit GRANDFOY.

Few men would use as Grandfoy does such a confidence as I have had in him [but sure never any woman made the experiment before me; if the lover can but be kept ignorant, no matter what he discover, when secur'd a husband; I must own those women have more courage than I. Cheating in all other cases, may be only playing the knave; but any deceit in marriage must be egregiously playing the fool, when the very injury we do, gives the power of revenging it].

Enter BEAUMINE.

BEAUMINE (*aside*): Ay, at home, you're as sure of finding an old mistress, as a creditor that expects you to pay him an old debt, in good humor too, I warrant. (*To her.*) I was afraid, madam, you had not been come home yet.

LESBIA: How could you imagine that, when I had hopes of seeing you?

BEAUMINE: Ay, I thought so. Well, this is the Devil. Faith, Lesbia, I do what I can to be very fond of you, but if you will take pains to hinder it, I cannot help it.

LESBIA: I don't know that I have done anything to displease you.

BEAUMINE: Why, there it is, you should do something to displease me.

Love is an active, restless fire,
That without agitation, must expire.

LESBIA: I thought a constant fuel of lasting worth and kindness would preserve it.

BEAUMINE: It may keep it in, but 'twill burn very dimly without blowing, Lesbia.

LESBIA: I wish I knew the art of doing it.

BEAUMINE: Why you should go abroad, when you're sure I shall come to see you; look angry or cold upon me, without telling me why, when I would caress you; and when I expect you should be fond of me, make me suspect you are thinking of another. In short, vex, perplex, and disquiet me, that supplying me always with something to employ my thoughts on, they may have no leisure to wander.

LESBIA: [I rather take care by the regularity of my conduct, to show you what you may always expect from me; for] tho' these arts may be agreeable in a mistress, you would scarce be pleas'd with 'em in a wife.

BEAUMINE: Nay, thou hast thought of a way now to put a man out of his humour with a vengeance [but the worst contrivance to raise an appetite you could have found out]. You have all of a wife but the name, and you must bring it in, to spoil a man's fancy.

LESBIA: I like your raillery, Beaumine, since I don't doubt but your serious thoughts are to make me that in earnest, which the name of, serves you for a jest.

BEAUMINE: Ay, ay, there will be a time for serious thoughts, respect and reverence, which wives should have [and that you know, is paid to antiquity, Lesbia]; but love and raptures for the young and free.

LESBIA (*aside*): Thus I can never be satisfied, or angry with this man! (*To him.*) Is it impossible for you ever to answer seriously and directly, Beaumine?

BEAUMINE: If you would have my thoughts, I wou'd counsel you against the most unaccountable extravagance you are designing.

LESBIA: What's that?

BEAUMINE: You have now a great deal of my love; it's certain marriage won't add one jot to it, and very possible it may extremely lessen it. [Now would anyone in their senses, that were in possession of a good estate, without any prospect of bettering it, put it to the chance of a die, whether they should keep it or lose it?] I am thy own, and keep me as thou hast me. (*Sings.*)
'Thus ever frolic, ever gay.'

LESBIA: Thou art the most agreeable, tormenting devil. But pri'thee, tell me, what am I to expect?

BEAUMINE: Expect? Why, that the old woman will die, and that –

LESBIA: But will the old woman ever die, Beaumine?

BEAUMINE: Humph! pugh, what's age and death to us, my love? They are melancholy thoughts. We've life, and youth, and liberty, my Lesbia, (*Sings.*)
'And life a thousand years a day.'

LESBIA (*aside*): Thus may this gay humour fool me on for ever. I must try him farther. (*To him.*) Well, you are the maddest fellow! Sure there is not your peer in France, unless Miranda. 'Tis pity fate has not joined you. What did you think of her?

BEAUMINE: I thought very well of her while I saw her, but have not thought at all of her since. [She's a very coquette, pleas'd with every man, and pleases all whilst with 'em; but no sooner out of sight, than she forgets, and is as easily forgot.]

LESBIA: She has not forgot you so soon, I assure you; but have you not refresh'd her memory?

BEAUMINE: Not I, upon honour.

LESBIA: I'm glad of it.

BEAUMINE: Why? You would not have been jealous.

LESBIA: No, but I think 'twill be better you should not visit her at all, for I know she likes you.

BEAUMINE: Not visit her because she likes me! Now hang me, if I can find that out to be a good reason.

LESBIA: It might be dangerous to fan a fire that's yet but kindl'd.

BEAUMINE: Nay, I have no design to see her. But what whim of yours is this? She likes anything for her diversion.

LESBIA: But talks of you in heroics.

BEAUMINE: A new humour.

LESBIA: And is very importunate to know, if there's any *amour* betwixt you and me.

BEAUMINE: Curiosity, I hope, did not satisfy her.

LESBIA: She seemed so much concern'd, I cou'd not deny her positively; but betwixt raillery and earnest, left her in doubt, which made her so uneasy, she said, she would soon see me again, and hoped I wou'd be more sincere with her.

BEAUMINE: By no means, I charge you. Women of her humour are always prying into the intrigues of their companions, to make 'em the jest of the next company. Never trust any of your own sex, especially such a giddy thing as Miranda.

LESBIA: Since you desire it, you may be sure I'll be cautious, tho' I know she was serious.

BEAUMINE: I suppose you can't think

you have any reason to fear her.

LESBIA: If I had distrusted you, I wou'd not have told you of such an agreeable rival; and I expect in return of the confidence I have in you, you should avoid a woman that I believe loves you.

BEAUMINE: Egad, a very nice piece of honour, I must have no mind to a handsome woman, because you have let me know she has a mind to me! [Well, as far as flesh and blood can reach it, I'll act this romantic lover.]

LESBIA: Then you won't visit Miranda?

BEAUMINE: No, since you would not have me, not that I think there's any danger in it, but I'm very indifferent in the matter. If she happen to fall in my way, and mischief should ensue – remember you were my tempter.

LESBIA: I dare trust you.

BEAUMINE: Well then, to put my virtue to the proof.

Going.

LESBIA: Where are you going?

BEAUMINE: To Miranda.

LESBIA: Pshaw, you're always fooling, but I have business.

BEAUMINE: So have I, but what's yours about?

LESBIA: Our marriage.

BEAUMINE: And mine is love. I cannot think of two things at once, so directly opposite, [so first for that of greatest moment].

Going.

LESBIA: But will you tell me –

BEAUMINE: How Miranda receives me? What favours she refuses, what she grants? All, all.

LESBIA: But *Beaumine*.

BEAUMINE: But *Miranda*.

LESBIA: Pugh, that's a jest.

BEAUMINE: Then you don't believe I'm going to her?

LESBIA: No, I'm sure you won't.

BEAUMINE (*aside*): Now the devil take her for not being jealous, [that I might

have a right to deceive her, for I'm afraid I cannot forbear; but 'tis no matter, there's no truth in these cases;] and since

We are all false alike in love, 'tis
    clear,
He that dissembles best, is most
    sincere.

Exit BEAUMINE.

LESBIA: You magotty, barbarous, good-humoured, ill-natured toad; he is gone as fleet as winds, but I as fast shall fly,

Since, while a stale, tried lover I
    pursue,
If he escapes me, I secure a new.

Exit LESBIA.

Scene Two

MIRANDA's *Lodgings.*

Enter LUCILIA *and* MIRANDA.

[LUCILIA: Nay I protest you're to blame, Miranda, to use a man thus, that dotes upon you.

MIRANDA: If he does not like the humour, what makes him dote on me? We're both pleas'd with one another, only have different ways of showing it; he's fond of my gaiety, I laugh at his gravity; he whines, I sing; he takes care to show his fidelity, I to make him jealous; that's his way, this is mine, we take several roads, but I fear both lead to the same dreadful end, we shall e'en meet at last in matrimony, tho' I am for going the farthest way about.

LUCILIA: Since you are resolv'd to go through the journey, 'tis the wisest way to make it as short as possible, for fear you should spend too much of your stock of love, or be robb'd of it by another upon the road, and not have enough to subsist on when your travels are over.

MIRANDA: I'm not so extravagant in my expenses of it, and for robbers, there's more danger of them in our place of rest; for tho' matrimony is too strong an edifice to be demolish'd, its guards and enclosures are weak and

easily broke thro', and love is a
treasure not to be confin'd, it slips like
water from the hand that would
restrain it; if you would secure it, leave
it loose and free.]

LUCILIA: But 'tis impossible you can
love Constant, and not have a mind to
marry him.

MIRANDA: Indeed I don't love him so
well, but that I had rather torment
him, than he should torment me;
rather have variety of diversions lie
heavy upon my hands, than the affairs
of my family. I like the squeaking of a
fiddle better than the squalling of
brats; and an obsequious, humble
servant, better than a surly lord and
master.

LUCILIA: I fancy 'tis some other
humble servant you like better. This
Beaumine you were talking of, runs
mightily in your head.

MIRANDA: In my head! in my heart, in
my sleep. I dream of him, sigh for him,
die for him. O, 'tis the easiest, gayest,
wildest, most engaging, everything that
suits my humour. I long for him again;
if he likes me well enough to visit me,
I shall grow so fond of him.

LUCILIA: Why, you can't love 'em
both.

MIRANDA: I'll swear, I do extremely. I
love Constant best at a distance;
Beaumine when he's with me. To think
of one; laugh with t'other. He diverts
me; t'other improves me. One will
make the better husband, t'other the
more agreeable gallant.

LUCILIA: Well, wildly as you talk, I
don't doubt but you'll make a very
good wife!

MIRANDA: I don't doubt but he'll
make me so: take a full revenge of my
tyranny when he has got the power in
his hands. Therefore I resolve to reign
as long as I can. But here comes my
sovereign-elect.

Enter CONSTANT.

I thought, sir, you had business with
my uncle, and therefore left you
without hopes of this happiness so soon.

CONSTANT: I thought, madam, you
had business, that you ran from me so

abruptly [when I was talking to you of
what concerns me nearest; but it seems
'twas only to be rid of me; I'm sorry
my company is so displeasing].

MIRANDA: 'Tis a strange lover that
won't give his mistress leave to think of
him; I came but to sigh for you in
secret.

CONSTANT: Sigh in secret, when we
may smile together? O Miranda, sure
you abuse my doting heart, and make
my love your sport.

MIRANDA: Why, what's love, or
anything else good for, unless to divert
us?

[CONSTANT: I might have thought
indeed, your sprightly temper could not
long brook my heavy, sullen nature,
but tell me freely I am troublesome;
and as I never ask'd your uncle his
consent, till you permitted me, so will I
not now use his authority, but leave
you free, to choose a humour that may
suit you better.

MIRANDA: Don't disturb yourself
about that, I shall quickly be as sullen
as you, when we're marry'd, no doubt.

CONSTANT: That wou'd but hinder our
resemblance then, for sure that happy
day that calls you mine will quite
dissolve the earthly part of me, refine
this mass, and make me spirit all.

MIRANDA: Leave you the ghost of your
departed Love,
And me to mourn in tears my
    wretched fate,
That yours expir'd too soon, mine liv'd
    too late.

There's rapture for your rapture,
Canstant {sic}.

CONSTANT: Well dear tormentor, don't
weary out my love then, ere you use it,
but cherish it whilst young and
vigorous, and it will be immortal.

MIRANDA: Then I must keep it in its
native air, for they say marriage is a
very cold climate.

LUCILIA: I believe indeed it kills the
hottest hasty plants, but preserves and
often produces such solid fruits as are
most fit for constant nourishment, and
bears sweets of its own growth too,
Miranda.]

MIRANDA: Well, seriously, Lucilia, I have been trying this month to compose my face for the wedding day; for I fancy if one has not a most reverend countenance, one will never be thought in earnest at so unreasonable a thing as taking for better or for worse. It looks so like a jest or stark madness.

CONSTANT: Keep your mad countenance then, and do it in jest.

MIRANDA: Ay, but that surly {countenance} of yours, Constant, has such a husbandly air, 'twill spoil the jest; I never look upon it but I'm afraid I'm married already.

CONSTANT: I'll endeavour to put on a more agreeable one; turn Merry Andrew, anything to please you.

[MIRANDA: Then 'tis resolv'd we will be kings no more.

CONSTANT: O when my life? My joy, now I am gay as thou art.]

MIRANDA: Nay, that has undone all again. Those laughing eyes bring to my thoughts that charming fellow that danced and sung himself into my heart. I must have some time to drive him out again, and then, Constant –

CONSTANT: Who? What is't you talk of?

MIRANDA: O such a grace, such an air, such a humour; if you knew him you must be fond of him for love of me, he's just my counterpart.

CONSTANT (aside); I know she rails, yet it tortures me.

MIRANDA: What, in the dumps? Nay, don't be jealous.

CONSTANT: No, no, but 'tis intolerable cruelty to make your sport of what my life depends on.

MIRANDA: It's in concern for your life I would delay this marriage. For, if in the height of my passion, the tempter shou'd come my way – he makes an attack; duty opposes; inclination assists him; prohibition strengthens it. Nature prevails, runs away with me. You pursue and cut his throat; I break my heart; you can do no less than stab yourself to complete the tragedy, and

prevent all this mischief –

CONSTANT: We'll take care to avoid the tempter.

MIRANDA: That can't be done without having him always in my thoughts. No, no, Constant. You have a better way of curing a woman's love, being perpetually with her. And since you have found it so effectual an experiment, I'm resolved to try it upon my new inclination, till he has said all the fine things he can, show'd all his humours, played over all his tricks, left nothing farther for imagination to work on; but grown as dull to me as a book I have just read.

CONSTANT: Or as I am to you now.

MIRANDA: Then you'll be new again, like one that has been long out of print! And I am always fond of the second edition, revised, corrected, and amended. [But be sure you take care never to let me peruse it thro'; reserve something for my curiosity, Constant. For you know the best books, when we have studied 'em perfectly, are thrown aside, or only kept for show, and any trifling novel that we never met with before, entertains us better.]

CONSTANT: Thou art never to be thoroughly known. The more I study thee, the more I am perplex'd; [find something clear enough to engage my search, but still too doubtful to determine on. Wou'd you provoke me first to break a contract you repent? Or] is't to try my constancy, you thus torment me? Are you not satisfied? What fool but I could have endur'd so much? But, madam, I'm not made to bear forever.

MIRANDA: What, is it 'nangry now? And what would it do? Can it break its cage? Flutter about, tire itself, and hurt its wings; and to what purpose?

CONSTANT: I am your slave, Miranda, but 'tis the more ungenerous to use a creature in thy power so inhumanly. I dote upon thee, dote on that very humour that distracts me. Be serious once to free me from the fear of losing thee, and ever after I wou'd have thee gay, as nature form'd thee.

MIRANDA: For ever after I am sure, be

dull enough, and therefore now indulge my natural gaiety; but let me see what time of the moon is it? About the full, I may be dispos'd.

CONSTANT: Still in raillery, I beg thee, I conjure thee –

MIRANDA: Well, I am good-natured, and since you are so impatient –

CONSTANT: O speak.

MIRANDA: I am resolved –

CONSTANT: When, when, my charmer?

MIRANDA: As soon as possible – to engage my charmer, grow weary of him as fast as I can, return to you with new pleasure, then here's my hand on it.

CONSTANT: [O torture, torture.] 'Tis too much, Miranda. You may find, fond of my prison as I am, I'm not so strongly chain'd as you imagine.

MIRANDA: Alas, and will you leave me?

CONSTANT: Well, madam, you shall no more insult.

*Exit.*CONSTANT.

MIRANDA: Not these two hours, I'll engage.

LUCILIA: Nay he can never return after this.

MIRANDA: Only half a dozen times a day, he makes and breaks these noble resolutions.

[LUCILIA: I'm sure you deserve to lose his love, and for my part, I'm amaz'd it has subsisted so long with such ill usage.

MIRANDA: O! The men's love is not so easily starved as surfeited. 'Twill live upon the lightest airy hope, tho' soon destroy'd with fondness. We lose lovers by over care, than neglect, Lucilia.

LUCILIA: You wou'd make 'em very ungenerous creatures, but I believe gratitude is as strong a tie to them, as to us.

MIRANDA: Just as strong indeed, and if you wou'd speak your heart as freely as I do, you wou'd own we take most pains to appear agreeable to a new acquaintance; put on our best looks, show all our wit, all our good humour, everything that may engage, whilst a lover we have well enough secur'd not to fear losing, is receiv'd and entertain'd as negligently as a cousin German.

LUCILIA: On the contrary, if I would use any arts, it shou'd be to please a man, who by proofs of a lasting affection had engag'd mine, and I cou'd never think it return'd with sufficient tenderness.

MIRANDA: Think, but I speak of what we do without thinking, the natural effect of such a composition as mankind are of.] Vanity is inconstancy.

Enter BEAUMINE.

LUCILIA (*aside*): Of which behold the very abstract! Lesbia must know this.

MIRANDA (*aside*): This wild creature here! And who the deuce expected him?

[LUCILIA: There was no need of expectation to make the blessing dear.

MIRANDA: Psha, because I jested.] (*To* LUCILIA.) Would he were hanged for coming.

LUCILIA: Nay, now I shall believe you love him in earnest.

MIRANDA: I'll swear, so shall I too, I was never so confounded in my life. (*Aside.*) Love him – Ay, I love him well
enough, anywhere else – but methinks here – I don't know – I wish he had not come.

LUCILIA: Well, I'll leave you, for I believe he wishes so too, finding me here.

Exit LUCILIA.

BEAUMINE (*aside*): A very odd reception. Maybe she doesn't know me again; but I'm sure Lucilia does, and this goes to Lesbia immediately. But no matter; I know how to make peace with her, when I have settled my new conquest.

MIRANDA (*aside*): Wish she had not seen him here. What can that mean? Is she my rival too?

BEAUMINE (*to* MIRANDA): I fear I am unwelcome, madam, tho' I had not ventur'd without your permission.

MIRANDA: Pardon me, sir, I was persuading the lady to stay, [the more to oblige you in return of this favour].

BEAUMINE: The lady knew better how to oblige me.

MIRANDA: I don't doubt but she knows much better how to please you.

BEAUMINE: She has only put me in the way of being pleas'd, but that depends upon the fair Miranda; which if she design, she need only be herself again; indeed that gravity is no more becoming, than natural to you.

MIRANDA: Why, d'ee think I affect it?]

BEAUMINE: I can't tell whether you are displeas'd with seeing me, or mightily pleas'd, and have no mind to show it. Those eyes must better inform me.

MIRANDA: Whatever they say, I find you can make a favourable interpretation of it.

BEAUMINE: I confess, madam, I love to be easy [and to give everything the most advantageous sense it will bear, if it ben't the way to truth, I am sure it is to happiness].

MIRANDA: Giving yourself false hopes is the sure way to meet with disappointments.

BEAUMINE: Not at all. Vanity gives a man confidence, and that's successful with the fair as well as the great.

MIRANDA: Why, do you believe any woman ever loved a man because he had the vanity to fancy she did?

BEAUMINE: [At least it gives him a chance for being belov'd, which he can never have without the courage to attempt. For example,] Madam, had I modestly said to myself, 'Beaumine, thou'rt a very disagreeable fellow. Miranda can never like thee; 'tis in vain to hope it,' I had certainly not come near you, you had thought of me no more, or I had lost the advantage of your thoughts, however favourable.

MIRANDA: And you have the impudence to tell me you believe I shall like you?

BEAUMINE: And does not every man that tells you he likes you, mean the same thing? But I beg your pardon, madam, I confess 'twas very indecent, so unmodish a thing as speaking truth to a lady.

MIRANDA: [Which is so far from offending me, you could not have oblig'd me more, than by telling me your thoughts, to give me the pleasure of disappointing you; and to show you how vain, how mistaken you are, how little an opinion I have of you,] I must tell you, when you came in, I was thinking you the most fickle, inconstant, falsest thing in nature.

[BEAUMINE: Now cannot I help thinking, you wou'd not have troubled your head whether I was false or not, if you had not been concern'd in it.

MIRANDA: And do you imagine I can like a man I have such an opinion of?]

BEAUMINE: We are naturally fond of our own resemblance [and by that rule to gain Miranda's good graces I can't be too false, or too *volage*].

When present we'll love, when absent agree;
I think not of Iris, nor Iris of me.

MIRANDA: Nay, now you have vanquish'd, there's no resisting that, the very image of my own heart. [I can make the exchange without missing it.] But not a word of sighing, dying, fidelity, constancy, or any of that dull form. [For 'twill immediately be sensible of being out of its element, and return upon the wing.]

BEAUMINE: [And upon peril of losing mine,] let me never hear you have the least remembrance of me when I am away from you; not a word of me in heroics to Lesbia.

MIRANDA: For fear of spoiling your *amour* with her?

BEAUMINE: [What, jealous? That's against the very end of our agreement. But I don't care if we do clear accounts to this day, and begin upon a new score of roving.

MIRANDA: In which we'll strive to out-do one another in extravagance; but first, how far are you engag'd with Lesbia?

BEAUMINE: That you may judge yourself, whether she can have any concern in me.] She told me you had a penchant to my person.

[MIRANDA: By which I conclude she was jealous.

BEAUMINE: And do you think then she would have ventur'd to let me know of so dangerous a rival?]

MIRANDA: 'Twas a raillery no doubt.

BEAUMINE: Indeed she did rail enough upon it, that the gay, the free Miranda, should be caught at last; therefore not only for fear I should suspect you of constancy, but if you would not be the subject of her mirth, speak of me for the future with more caution.

MIRANDA: [And Lesbia's jest, I suppose, has occasion'd me this favour.

BEAUMINE: Why really, madam, I might protest, and lie, and swear; I could neither eat, nor rest since I saw you. But if you'd have the truth, I have always found among all other attractions, kindness only has resistless charms, and by the means you've gain'd, secure your conquest.

MIRANDA: A way by which most of your sex are lost; but why may not you be as particular as I am?] This plain dealing of yours has charmed me beyond all things, and sure 'tis as much out of the road for a woman's affection to be engag'd by sincerity, as man's to be secured by kindness.

BEAUMINE: [Ay indeed, you are seldom to be satisfy'd, unless we engage for as much more love than we have, as we are willing to release you from paying; but] I am no dissembler, madam, and must confess my love for you is none of those violent passions that will of course abate; it's in so moderate a degree, that even your fondness could not lessen it.

MIRANDA: And mine so indifferent, your sincerity can't disturb me [so without scruple, confess what interest Lesbia has in you].

BEAUMINE: [Really, madam, she's at present very indifferent to me, but I believe I shall shortly have a violent passion for her; she's going to ruin an honest friend of mine, and I shall hate her heartily for it.

MIRANDA: How will she ruin him?

BEAUMINE: Marry him. How can a woman ruin a man else?

MIRANDA: O mischievous! But to show you that I know she is not indifferent to you, she said herself, you would wish she had not been here at your coming.

BEAUMINE (apart): And thereby hangs a tale. (To her.) Faith, madam, she was in the right on't, I had much rather have had you alone. She knew my thoughts, and comply'd with 'em, I thank her, the first favour she ever did me, or I ever wish'd from her.] So now, I hope all past accounts are cleared.

MIRANDA: And for the future.

[BEAUMINE (sings):
    'We'll neither believe what either can say,
    So neither believing, can neither betray.'

And at this rate our loves must be eternal; there's no danger of quarrels or satiety.

MIRANDA: Ay, if all lovers had follow'd our example, we had not heard so many complaints of faithless nymphs and perjured swains.

BEAUMINE: But they must be perpetually dangling at one another's elbows; and the little time they are parted, enquiring after every action or step they take, for fear they should go astray.

MIRANDA: So tire one another when together, and torment themselves assunder; and no wonder they soon break a knot, that with drawing too straight fits uneasy upon them, and is the weaker itself, bursts upon the least irregular motion.

BEAUMINE: Well, madam, that we may

profit by others' follies, I believe it's time to part before we are weary of one another.

MIRANDA: For now we have told all our thoughts, we are in great danger of growing dull next time we meet, ten to one, we shall be quite of another mind, and so new again. In order to it, I'll give you a song made by a heroic lover of mine, perhaps it may infect you with sighing, whining, dying love. – Who's there? Desire the gentlewoman in the next room to walk in.

{*Enter* SINGER.}

You'll oblige us, madam, with the song I gave you last to learn. (*After a song.*) Well, Beaumine, how does it affect you?

BEAUMINE: I melt, I languish, am all transport, now (*Sings a line of the song.*)

'What shall I say to work upon thy Soul!'

MIRANDA: O most apish! How ridiculous a man appears when he would cross nature! He may as well expect to be finely shaped by putting on another man's clothes, because they fit well upon him they were made for, as to please, by affecting the most agreeable humour in another. It hangs as awkwardly upon him, and is as easily perceiv'd not to be his own.]

BEAUMINE: Then I must e'en stay from you till I am so much forgot, I will be new again.

MIRANDA: Which need not be long, I assure you. Out of sight, out of mind.

BEAUMINE: A pleasant way of inviting me to return soon,

Thus while the artful sex in words deny
The secret sense, their kind looks comply.

Exit BEAUMINE.

MIRANDA: Thus we gain lovers, and secure our fame,
We promise nothing, and they nought can claim.
They fancy pleasures when we speak of pain,
And hope's enough, their passion to maintain.

Exit MIRANDA.

ACT THREE

Scene One

The Public Walks.

Enter LESBIA *and* LUCILIA.

[LESBIA: By his manner of speaking I cou'd not imagine he wou'd visit her; this is a new way to deceive by speaking truth.

LUCILIA: A sure one, 'tis so little expected from a lover.

LESBIA: I'll never forgive it him. What pretence can he have to excuse this?

LUCILIA: If he get off now, 'twill be a masterpiece of his art indeed.

LESBIA: Impossible.] I wish we may see Grandfoy here tonight; he said he was to meet Cleon in the Walks, and I wou'd have his advice how to behave myself now, before I see Beaumine.

LUCILIA: I'm mistaken if that is not Beaumine, coming this way with Phillabell.

LESBIA: The very same, and gay as innocence itself.

LUCILIA: There's no avoiding 'em now, they're so near, they see us.

LESBIA: Well, I won't disappoint you, for I know you wou'd be so peevish all this evening; if you should not speak to {Phillabell} now, there would be no enduring you, tho' he was with you so lately.

LUCILIA: You're mistaken; though I never think I see him too often, I could have spar'd it now, since Cleon is to be here. Their meeting might prove of ill consequence [considering the coxcomb's design I told you of; 'tis not yet the time he appointed me to send my answer, but we'll go off soon, and oblige them to go with us, if we can].

Enter BEAUMINE *and* PHILLABELL.

BEAUMINE: So the friends are together, and all's out. [Well, I must take the old way of complaining first, when we know ourselves in fault.]

PHILLABELL: I'm pleased at this unexpected good fortune. Madam, the sight of you gives me soft pleasures

that compose my soul transported.
[Now my happiness approaches, with
my impatience of one day's delay, and
joy to think it is but one.]

{PHILLABELL *and* LUCILIA *go off
to the side.*}

BEAUMINE: Indeed, Lesbia, I did not
imagine you had so much indiscretion,
but women can no more forbear
talking of their *amours*, than an ill
poet of his verses; [tho' they equally
expose their folly, by what they design
to gratify their vanity with, and usually
prove as tiresome to their hearers,
unless such as have ill nature enough
to divert themselves with every thing
that's ridiculous in another.]

LESBIA: I don't know what you aim at,
but I think women deserve to be
laughed at, that boast of any kind
thoughts for such faithless things as
men are.

BEAUMINE: You'll guess what I mean,
when I tell you I have seen Miranda,
and know all you said to her.

LESBIA: You'll know what I mean,
when I tell you I heard that before,
and guess what you said to her.

BEAUMINE: [Really, madam, so you
may,] you gave me cause enough to
suspect you had let her know of our
engagement, and I resolv'd to see her,
to find out how far you had discover'd.
I was never so out of countenance in
my life.

LESBIA: 'Twould have been a wonder
to have seen that indeed, for I'll swear
you have an extraordinary assurance.

BEAUMINE: To be so laughed at, to
hear you so ridiculed, [for being over-
reach'd by a creature that professes
abusing everybody; you wou'd have
been asham'd to have seen yourself so
describ'd, so mimic'd so] – I did not
know what to say for myself or you.

LESBIA: She abused you, if she told you
I said anything positive.

BEAUMINE: Positive, but such signs,
such things – O Lesbia, Lesbia, that
you cou'd be caught by such a shallow
artifice.

LESBIA: I'm sorry, sir –

BEAUMINE: Well, you know I love
you, and can forgive you anything; but
I hope you'll be more cautious
hereafter.

LESBIA: I think, Beaumine, 'tis time
our engagement were made known to
everybody.

BEAUMINE: Ay, ay,
We'll write each other's names on
every bark,
The winds shall bear our vows to
distant climes,
And Echo every tender word rebound.

LESBIA: Good romantic sir, will you
condescend for once to answer directly
a little intelligible sense?

[BEAUMINE: O! that were to wrong my
love. A lover, and speak sense? To
answer in cross purposes, in broken
murmurs, and disjointed words,
expresses passion.

LESBIA: Do you think I'll be always put
off with this trifling, Beaumine?

BEAUMINE: O! mighty things have
been produc'd from trifles. The
cackling of geese once sav'd the
capitol; men's promises have gain'd
many a fair one, and women's favours
lost 'em many lovers. Trifles, trifles all,
but great effects.

LESBIA: Is not that to tell me I have
lost you, by what you think a trifle?

BEAUMINE: No, to show you I don't
think your favours a trifle, and have
no mind you shou'd lose me, I wou'd
have 'em still favours, the more to
engage me, and not turn all to duty.

LESBIA: Had you talk'd thus to me at
first, Beaumine –

BEAUMINE: You had lost a great deal
of pleasure, Lesbia, and laugh'd at me
for a fool.

LESBIA: Which is something better than
a knave.

BEAUMINE: Good words, good words,
madam. Knaves are precise,
protesting, plotting, thinking creatures;
but you'll find this mad, maggoty
fellow, a very honest fellow at last.

LESBIA: At last.]

BEAUMINE: Well, if you'll have me

marry you just now, I'll run and fetch a Priest immediately.

Going.

LESBIA: I think you're mad. Why, Beaumine?

BEAUMINE: O Gad, I forgot, the canonical hour is over. (*Sings.*)
'But if I ever play the fool, dear
  Cloris, I am thine' –

Well, (*turning to* PHILLABELL.) What can you have to say to one another all this while? [You are agreed upon the premises, are convinc'd of that mutual affection; and to answer for the future, can only serve to call the sincerity of the present in question.

LUCILIA: Why so, sir? I think 'tis rather a proof of the present, a sign we find it so great, we believe it will always last.

BEAUMINE: Ay, madam, but if I hear a man swear to a thing done out of his sight, tho' it may happen to be true, I shall think he has a large conscience, and scarce believe him in what he might know; and indeed, we may as well swear to any thing done in Japan, as {to} our future inclinations, they are no less out of our knowledge or power.

PHILLABELL: I think a man [that knows himself not to be of a wavering temper, if he has well consider'd the merit of his choice,] may venture to promise for his constancy, without prejudice to his honour.

BEAUMINE: But to what end should he promise? Will it secure his inclination one minute the longer? [O but it secures the woman he would engage. Madam, my friend's a very honest fellow. I believe he thinks what he says; but 'tis your fault, if you take his word for what he cannot know. We had rather you should rely upon the power of your charms; and] if the ladies will force us to add perjury to our natural levity, the sin must lie at their door.

[LESBIA: 'Tis a folly indeed to rely upon their word for future inclinations, since few of 'em can answer for their future actions.

BEAUMINE: Really, madam, our actions are generally guided by our inclinations; this is not an age of much mortification. But are not you for walking, ladies?]

LUCILIA: I'm a little tired. What think you of going off, Lesbia?

LESBIA: I'll wait upon you, madam.

PHILLABELL: We'll attend to your coach, ladies.

LUCILIA: Maybe you would not leave the Walks so soon.

PHILLABELL: Well, come back and take another turn or two. Tomorrow early as the day, I'll visit you [and hope your wishes]. My fair bride will meet me.

LUCILIA: You never yet could come too early [for 'em].

BEAUMINE: What a deal of tenderness they are going tomorrow to destroy! (*Sings.*)
Would you, would you love the Nymph
  for ever,
Never, never, never, never let her be
  your wife.

Exeunt.

Enter GRANDFOY, CLEON, *and* BONSOT.

CLEON: Let me expire! My false nymph, going off with her lover! Before my face! In the very place where I sent her word I would be tonight! The inexpressible confidence of a faithless woman!

BONSOT: Nay, brother, don't be angry, I dare say she meant no affront to you, only to make him believe she don't care for you.

CLEON: Then she's the greater jilt, brother.

BONSOT: Humph, pugh, Lord, you will think the worst of everything! Do but look how loath she is to leave you. She stands still all the while she goes.

GRANDFOY: That's an extraordinary art indeed.

CLEON: I don't doubt her affection. But the fellow's rich, if she consulted her honour or happiness. Is such a *grossiere* as Phillabell to be preferred to me? I protest, I almost pity her.

GRANDFOY: Ay, ay, e'en let the weakness of her choice be her punishment; 'tis below your resentment.

CLEON: Nay, 'tis not that I value the creature, but then to disappoint my rival will be a good revenge for his presuming to hope, where I had once made my pretensions. Therefore he shall see all her letters. I can't but think how silly the fellow will look, ha, ha, ha.

GRANDFOY: But you don't consider what a kindness you'll do your rival, in preventing his marriage with such an undistinguishing coquette. I fancy they'll better revenge you upon one another.

CLEON: Egad, thou art right in that, Cuz.

BONSOT: Ay faith, that's well said, [I hate mischief; and then you know, brother, 'twould vex you more, if she should refuse you, after you had shown so much concern for her].

[CLEON: Impertinent suppositions! To show you the impossibility of it, I'm now positively resolv'd to pursue my design.

BONSOT: Hay, why, I meant, in case, d'e see –. Pugh, brother, you are so hasty. – I would have said, psha, do not be so ill-natur'd. – But I mean, that if, suppose, he should be very fond of the honour of being your rival. – Ay, d'ye mind that now? And so force her willingly to marry him.]

CLEON: Then wou'd I, after they are married, expose her letters to the whole tawn {sic}; that will be an immoderate pleasure, rat me.

BONSOT: That might breed quarrels now between a man and his wife.

CLEON: She'll be the more sensible of the ill judgment of her choice.

BONSOT: Phough.

GRANDFOY: O but that is not en cavalier. ['Twill be look'd upon as vanity.]

BONSOT: [Ay this will do – but now I think on't better, I don't believe he'll

be angry.] Being a very humble sort of man, he's likely to be proud that you shou'd be vain of his wife's letters.

CLEON: Vain! No, no, the town know well enough, if I wou'd boast, there are ladies of more wit and better judgment than Lucilia, that have afforded me de quoy.

BONSOT: Ay brother, the lady, you know, that never work'd in her life, and made you a cravat all with her own hands.

[GRANDFOY: What, she drew the picture of his cravat?]

CLEON: [O no,] she really made the very lace I have on, [now you know women of a great deal of wit never work; but as love once rais'd a blacksmith to a painter, so it made her descend from her nicer speculations to this mechanic employment,] that I might wear the product of her fingers.

GRANDFOY: O wonderful effect of passion! I confess.

CLEON: Ay, if you consider the elegancy of the work.

BEAUMINE and PHILLABELL enter here unseen.

GRANDFOY: O extremely elegant (examining the lace).

CLEON: That's a very fine ring. I never saw thee wear it before; some lady's favour undeniably, come confess, confess.

GRANDFOY: Why, yes faith, 'twas a lady's favour.

CLEON: She must be of quality, by the value of the present.

GRANDFOY: It was given her by another lover, his first present too.

CLEON: O most obliging! But how did he bear it? (Here {BEAUMINE} sees the ring.)

BONSOT: Ay, if he should hear of it now what a deal of mischief might come on't.

GRANDFOY: I laughed heartily at the pains he took, and the presents he made, that she might be the less afflicted at the loss.

CLEON: Kind cully – so she pretended she had lost it.

GRANDFOY: Ay, the jest is – (*Seeing* BEAUMINE) pr'thee, Cleon, turn this way.

CLEON: This is the place I appointed to send the answer of my letter.

GRANDFOY: Damn your letter, pr'thee come.

Exit GRANDFOY *and* CLEON *in confusion.*

BONSOT: Hey day, what vagary's this? He's afraid of somebody, I think.

BEAUMINE: Ha! This confirms me – damn'd jilt.

BONSOT (*aside*): And this gentleman seems angry. I have a good mind to stay and hear what he says [that I may prevent their quarrelling together whilst they're asunder].

PHILLABELL: How now, Beaumine! What's the matter?

BEAUMINE: Did you know him that turn'd off just now?

PHILLABELL: Very well, 'tis my coxcombly rival, Cleon, don't you know him?

BEAUMINE: Pox of your rival, t'other, he with the ring I'd know.

BONSOT: Ay, it's so.

PHILLABELL: But why so fretful?

BEAUMINE: Plague! do you know him? Can't you answer?

PHILLABELL: Why, I do not know him, but what if I did?

BEAUMINE: O dissembling witch!

PHILLABELL: What's this passion for? Who has offended you?

BONSOT: I hope, sir, you are not angry with the gentleman you inquire after; he's a relation of mine, sir, and a very honest gentleman, I dare say. If he offends anybody wilfully, it must be without his knowledge.

BEAUMINE: Then you may give him the knowledge, sir, that he wilfully wears a ring I may make bold to take from him, sir.

BONSOT: O Lord, sir, as for that, if you have a mind for the ring, I'll engage 'twill be at your service; my cousin's a generous person, that does not value such a trifle, nor the person he had it from, in comparison of your friendship, I dare say, sir.

BEAUMINE: Why, do you know the person he had it from, sir?

BONSOT: Ay, sir, anybody may know her; a mere common creature, she's kept indeed by a coxcomb, a soft-headed cully.

BEAUMINE: You know him too, sir, I suppose.

BONSOT: A fellow not worth knowing – but the wench is very fond of my cousin, and a man does not know how to deny a woman.

BEAUMINE: Very well, sir –

BONSOT: I tell you the plain truth, to show you that you need not quarrel with my cousin about the ring; for he does not care this for it, nor the lady neither. You may have them both, if you please, sir.

BEAUMINE: You are very impertinently civil, sir.

BONSOT: O Lord, sir – nay I must say that for myself, I am a very civil, good-natured fellow. I can't abide to see people when they are at quiet and in good humour, quarrelling with one another.

PHILLABELL: That's a strange sight indeed, sir.

BONSOT: Ay, sir, I hope you'll persuade your friend not to be in a passion for nothing; about something of a ring and a lady, a jilt not worth his concern, sir.

BEAUMINE: That I am very well convinc'd of, sir. Your cousin and the lady, and the ring, may go to the Devil for me, as they please, sir.

BONSOT: Oh sir, your very humble servant, that's all I desire; that they may have leave to go to the Devil in quiet, sir, I have no more to say, [Sir. I'll be sure to tell him how civil a person you are, and I don't doubt he'll have the same complaisance for you; begin your journey when you will. He's none of the hottest choleric fellows; whenever he's in a heat against any 'tis in cold blood. Your very humble servant, sir,] I'm extremely obliged to you indeed, sir.

Exit {BONSOT}

PHILLABELL: What a soft officious fool this is! but pr'thee what concern have you in the ring you talked of?

BEAUMINE: By heaven, the very same I gave to Lesbia.

PHILLABELL: Ha, ha, ha, ha, ha, why, thou can'st not be jealous, what of Lesbia! The fear of losing thee, you know, will keep her faithful.

BEAUMINE: Who cou'd have suspected?

PHILLABELL: O never think it, she valued not the loss; but as a sad presage thy dearer heart would follow. Ha, ha, ha.

BEAUMINE: Prithee leave thy fooling.

PHILLABELL: Were she a wife indeed; but Lesbia, she whom nothing cou'd console, but thy repeated vows of never changing. Ha, ha, ha.

BEAUMINE: Lesbia false! where shall we look for truth?

PHILLABELL: Not in a woman that has sacrific'd her honour, but such a one as my Lucilia. O what a treasure! This makes me more impatient to be master of it; 'tis an age till tomorrow. Wou'd she this night were mine.

BEAUMINE: Why, truly when a man is to be hang'd, a night's reprieve gives him but so much time to torment himself with the apprehension. O I cou'd curse the whole jilting, hypocritical sex.

PHILLABELL: They all are Lesbias, but thou may'st rail, thy malice cannot reach Lucilia: the abstract of all goodness, so true, so innocent. [I had much ado to persuade her t'other day, that any woman cou'd be false to her husband, or even pretend to love where she did not.

BEAUMINE: And you believe her? Is there any of 'em that cannot talk of sincerity?

PHILLABELL: O! 'tis stamp'd on all her actions. Then she's so reserv'd, she hated Cleon for his impudence. He has made her blush a thousand times with the liberty of his discourse and actions.]

(Enter LYSETTA with a letter, which going to hide as she sees PHILLABELL, she lets fall accidentally.)

Is not that her governess?

BEAUMINE: She's in mighty haste. What have we here? A *billet doux*?

PHILLABELL: I believe 'tis Lysetta's. You had best call after her.

BEAUMINE: The direction gives me a curiosity to open it. (*Reads it to himself.*) Nay now, Phil, I'm made a convert to marriage.

PHILLABELL: What can have wrought such a miracle!

BEAUMINE: Why a proof of thy Lucilia's virtue and sincerity. Do you know her hand?

PHILLABELL: Perfectly.

BEAUMINE: Is this like it?

PHILLABELL: The same to Cleon, some severe repulse I suppose.

BEAUMINE: Ay, really, 'tis a pity to use the poor man so severely.

PHILLABELL: She never thinks she can use him ill, or me well enough. (*Reads.*)

'You are ignorant of what force the first engagements have; and you as little know my heart, when you imagine it capable of loving any thing – but you.'

Am I awake!

'If I marry Phil, 'tis to obey a cruel father, who will sacrifice me to his interest –'

the rest is more baseness. It can't be Lucilia's.

BEAUMINE: No, no, Lucilia's! you know she hates the impudent fellow, for making her blush so often.

PHILLABELL: I can scarce credit my own eyes.

BEAUMINE: O! why should you,

against so much sincerity? 'tis stamped on all her actions. [I dare swear 'tis in this – she can't think it possible for a woman to be false to her husband, or pretend to love where she does not, there's a treasure!] 'Tis an age till tomorrow; shan't we have a wedding tonight, Phil?

PHILLABELL: I'll not believe it.

BEAUMINE: Never, never, were she a woman that had sacrific'd her honour indeed, but one so reserv'd as thy Lucilia. Ha, ha, ha, prithee let's have the wedding tonight, Phil. Come, hang delays.

PHILLABELL: Torment me, am I thus paid for all my doting love and generous trust?

[BEAUMINE: The sure reward of trusting. What should hinder people from being false, when they are certain not be suspected?

PHILLABELL: 'Tis a base principle.

BEAUMINE: A woman's principle.]

PHILLABELL: Nay, I can join with thee now in railing.

BEAUMINE: Let's bid defiance together, to the whole ensnaring, damn'd, lying sex.

[PHILLABELL: Agreed, and yet there was such pleasure in believing, I could almost wish I had not been undeceived. Had she but truth, she were an angel.

BEAUMINE: Maybe so, for I am sure she could not be a woman.] Betwixt you I, what a couple of coxcombs we are to dote upon what we despise! I see you love this Lucilia still, and to confess the truth (now neither of us can laugh at t'other) I find Lesbia's infidelity strikes deeper at my heart than I thought any of her sex could reach. [She has in gaining and losing, spoilt more of my good humour than the whole kind could be worth in exchange. O! a mere liking only, she is young and airy.

PHILLABELL: And new.

BEAUMINE: Ay, if you could add kind, I do not know but those two monosyllables might have more force

to make me bear Lesbia's inconstancy than all Seneca's morals.] But there is an old mistress of mine that still rivals them all: the faithful bottle. Shall we try it?

PHILLABELL: I care not if I do, for I fear I shall never forget Lucilia, but when I forget myself.

BEAUMINE: Come along then, this is a mistress we can both enjoy without being jealous of one another.

Love's niggard spirit must the bliss engross,
Companions would the happiness destroy,
But wine does all its charming pleasure lose,
Unless we generously share the joy.

Exeunt.

Enter LUCILIA *and* LYSETTA.

LYSETTA: Ay, this is the unlucky place.

LUCILIA: There's no hopes of finding it. I am undone; I shall be exposed to the whole town. Nay, for ought I know, Phil himself may have found it.

LYSETTA: This comes of a woman's taking pains to do good, labouring out of her own vocation. O! Madam, there's Cleon coming this way, now you may e'en carry your message yourself, that it may be sure not to fail.

LUCILIA: 'Twill be the likelier to fail. I cannot speak such things as you made me write [or if I should, 'twould be with so much constraint, he must perceive it false]. You know I can't dissemble.

LYSETTA: I know you have practis'd it as little as any woman, but trust nature, madam, trust nature – [and consider a young husband will do you a great deal of good. Your sincerity, – e'en have none at all, 'tis not a virtue for this designing world. nay, on my conscience, I don't know why it should not be thought as much a vice to prostitute our minds to every fool, as our bodies. Truth is the chastity of the soul, and should not be expos'd to any man that would put it to the proof. Here he is, have a care of your metaphorical chastity, or you may be forc'd to keep the real one, for Phillabell. And if that does not frighten you –]

LUCILIA: Peace, fool.

Enter CLEON.

CLEON: [I hope I have not miss'd the letter, for I cannot positively determine whether I shall condescend to hinder her marriage or not, till I know how she expresses herself.] Here in person! This is excess of civility indeed; I always thought her well-bred. This is an unexpected favour, madam –

LUCILIA: And undesigned, sir, I assure you.

LUCILIA: O! Sir, the most unfortunate accident: my lady sent me with a letter to you, but meeting with one here, I was afraid should see me, I dropt it in my surprise. My lady, in a fright, came here to look for it, but in vain. 'Twas gone, and nobody knows what mischief may be done with it.

CLEON: Was the subject of it dangerous?

LUCILIA: Indeed it was.

LYSETTA: It complain'd of your injustice in suspecting my lady's love, because she was forced to marry another; and said such kind things of hereafter.

[CLEON: Was there a superscription?

LYSETTA: Ay, ay, your name was upon it.

CLEON: O very well, that will be an excuse for what it contains to those that know me.

LUCILIA (*aside*): Ridiculous vanity! There need not much pains, I find, to persuade this thing he is belov'd.

CLEON: So, madam, you marry Phil to express your aversion very emphatically! But how do you show your affection for me?

LUCILIA: By not marrying you.

CLEON: That is a favour, I confess, but not very particular; I've a world of rivals in it.

LUCILIA: That can't be avoided, but you are the only person I particularly

resolve never to marry.

CLEON: As proof of your fondness.

LYSETTA: Ay, sir, my lady fears she should have such a world of rivals, she cou'd never be easy with you.

CLEON: O Lard {sic}, madam, there's no danger, but really I think when a man is singularly eminent, he shou'd never marry; for he injures the person he bestows himself upon, by exposing her to the envy of your sex, and {he injures} the rest by giving 'em despair. It was worth the care of the government in this scarcity of persons of merit, to forbid monopolizing 'em.

LUCILIA: Indeed I wou'd not injure my sex so much as to monopolize such an extraordinary person as Cleon. (*Apart.*) This fool can't be flatter'd too grossly.

[CLEON: Well, madam, since you are pleas'd to prefer me to Phil in your esteem, I won't disturb his imaginary felicity; but I was thinking it might not be amiss to show some of your obliging letters to my friends, that might justify to the world (who might judge you by your choice in a husband) the niceness of your wit and judgment.

LUCILIA: O by no means, sir, they'll conclude you would not have done it by my consent, and take it as an effect of my vanity.

CLEON: You are in the right, madam, there may be cause to suspect it, and vanity is of all follies the most odious.

LUCILIA (*aside*): And yet he thinks himself agreeable! (*To him.*) Nay really I think vanity a very harmless thing. It does nobody any hurt; those it deceives are the better for it, having no other quality to make 'em satisfy'd with 'emselves. The rest of the world know that like all other artificial lights, 'tis only to supply the defect of the natural, and as they burn the brighter in the darkest nights; so it appears most, where there's least merit.

CLEON: Justly observ'd, madam. Vanity is a very charitable flatterer. I have known it encourage an unbred, ill-drest fellow to make love to a lady that everybody knew I was well with.

LUCILIA: That might make him despair of pleasing her indeed, but I hope the lady judg'd better of your merits.

CLEON: Yes faith, madam, she judg'd him blockhead enough, for that dull animal a husband. Avoided me, to secure her virtue; and carry'd him out of town, to show she was asham'd of him. And if that did not mortify his vanity –

LUCILIA: And secure him from jealousy, it show'd her discretion, as great as her judgment.

CLEON: No, strike me dead, it had been wiser to have stay'd, and giv'n him a cause of jealousy. The only excuse a woman can have for marrying a man she does not love, is to secure her pleasure with the man she does. 'Tis a way among the women of condition to contrive for their interest before they marry, and their inclination after. But the rustic had infected her with his stupid society; 'twas only want of modish conversation, a finish'd good breeding.

LUCILIA: Well, to show you I am better bred, and not to be spoil'd by the stupid conversation of a husband, I'll always have it with the ceremony of a new; and the coldness of an old acquaintance, never have the same diversions, and seldom the same bed.

CLEON: Very courtly upon honour. Then for your lover, madam, he must make one in all your avow'd pleasures for a blind to the secret stol'n ones: be always with you at cards; hand you to your coach from the play; be very free together in public, to appear the more innocent. Then he must be very intimate with your husband, to make him the more secure of you, – and the town the more suspicious.

LUCILIA: I don't doubt but with your instructions to prove as modish a mistress as a wife. I promise never to avoid you, to secure my virtue.

CLEON: Then I have no obstacle to fear, for all the women I have address'd to, wou'd never see me again, knowing the only way to conquer was to fly. I shall certainly attack, madam, and then you will not find your virtue in danger – but no virtue at all, I am positive.

LUCILIA: Indeed, I positively believe there will be no virtue at all in the case. I shall not once struggle with my inclinations to resist you.

CLEON: A, a, it wou'd be in vain, but a little for decorum – the poor thing is strangely fond.] Well, madam, that I may be happy hereafter, I will be secret now, and if you please, appear at your wedding more gay than the bridegroom.

LUCILIA: You'll be a welcome guest. But I dare stay no longer – live upon hopes, substantial food enough for thee –
Vain, empty things, more solid cou'd not bear.
Who're nothing else themselves, must live on air.

Exit {LUCILIA}.

CLEON: Well, I profess this is a very generous age. [These married men are at the expense of what we don't care to do, and we in return do for them, what they never cou'd do.]

In mutual charities we pass our lives,
They keep our mistresses, we please their wives!

Exit.

ACT FOUR

Scene One

MIRANDA's *Lodgings.*
Enter MIRANDA *and her* WOMAN.

MIRANDA: Oh, ay, I'm within to her. Desire her to walk up.

Exit WOMAN.

This is a very quick return of my visit, how fond Lesbia and I grow of late. There are not such dear friends and constant companions in the world, as women that are jealous of one another.

Enter LESBIA.

LESBIA: I could not deny myself the satisfaction any longer, and I hope you'll take it kindly. For there's nobody I desire more to be believ'd a friend to, than Miranda.

MIRANDA: And nobody, I assure you, desires more to be yours. But how can I think you mine, when you are not free with me? You always speak with so much reserve.

LESBIA: Indeed, if I had any secret to impart, I should do it freely; but since Beaumine has been to visit you, no doubt he has convinc'd you, you had no reason to think there was anything between us; you may engage with him as you think fit, without any injury to me.

MIRANDA: I engage with him! Lord, I but jested – sure you did not think me serious – I had a curiosity indeed to know your *amour*; but did you imagine I cou'd have any design upon such a vain, pert, unaccountable creature?

LESBIA (*apart*): This is certainly affected. I'll be hanged if the traitor has not cautioned her, too, against trusting me. (*To her.*) You gave him much better epithets once, Miranda; [but instead of thinking him that charming fellow, I find now you extremely dislike him].

MIRANDA: [No extremes indeed;] he's perfectly indifferent to me.

LESBIA: It's true, that's all he deserves to be. I see nothing extraordinary in him.

MIRANDA: You thought much better of him once too, Lesbia. (*Apart.*) Now have I a shrewd suspicion, this faithless swain has made us distrust one another, that he might the better deceive us both. Well, if it is so, I'm resolv'd to torment her, and be reveng'd of him. (*To her.*) Well, my dear, since you assure me you have no concern in him, I'll confess my weakness; that 'twas with all the difficulty imaginable I constrain'd myself for your sake, not to make a return to such tender, engaging things, as I thought him uncapable of saying.

LESBIA: O villain – no doubt he can say what he pleases, madam.

MIRANDA: O! but in a manner so persuading – and yet, till you confirmed it, I wou'd not believe him, tho' he vow'd he had no love for you, and told me all you said to him of me.

LESBIA: Traitor! – as a friend, Miranda, I advise you not to rely too much upon what he tells you; for to my knowledge, you are not the only person he makes addresses to.

MIRANDA: Nor is he the only I'll receive addresses from (*Sings.*) 'He's fickle and false, and there we agree –'

We shall have the more adventures to entertain one another with. So {you} be diverting always, always new, and I'll engage to secure him the more, by not endeavouring to confine him.

LESBIA: Secure him! Sure you forget you're engag'd to Constant.

MIRANDA: No, but I'm in hopes very soon to torment him out of his love or his senses, that I may have my liberty.

[LESBIA: Phough, now I find you jest indeed.

MIRANDA: The Devil's in me, I think, I'm so posses't with this giddy humour; it gives a tincture to my most weighty affairs. But if I cou'd look languishing, and sigh – O the dear charming man! there is no joys {sic}, no life without him! 'twould not half express my heart. Now I have found he's not insensible, and then you know his fortune's very considerable, I can't see how I can do better.]

LESBIA: Whether you are in earnest or no, Miranda, I must tell you seriously, it won't be for your reputation to receive from a man of {Beaumine's} wild character.

MIRANDA: Really! I'll swear I shou'd not have thought so, having met him at your lodgings.

LESBIA: I intend to get rid of him as soon as I can.

MIRANDA: O! If everybody throws him off, I'm resolv'd to receive him, [for by being so scandalously general, he'll be forc'd to be particular; and 'tis many a pious man's case, who wou'd never have been honest if he had not lost his credit, never virtuous if his appetites had not decay'd. 'Tis the best thing you can do for his reformation, and my happiness].

LESBIA: Well, madam, however you flatter yourself, I don't doubt but you'll find yourself as unhappy with him as he has made others. So your servant, madam, I shan't trouble you more with my counsel, but you'll repent –

(*Going.*)

MIRANDA: What? Nay, Lesbia, I can't let you go now, 'tis so obliging to be mov'd at this rate for your friend's good – come, come, had not you better confess what this concern enough discovers? If you would be sincere with me, I could tell you a secret worth two of yours [and wou'd give you more satisfaction than all your own art or resentment ever can].

LESBIA: Perhaps I cou'd tell you something too, that wou'd undeceive you, but I have no great encouragement from the use you made of what I hinted before for your advantage – repeating it to Beaumine, and ridiculing me for it.

MIRANDA: The lying toad! may I never have a secret of my own worth keeping, or another's worth telling, if I said one word of it. [But 'twas a wonder I did not; for if I discover anything of myself that can make a jest, out it comes at all adventures. But] when I am thoroughly trusted, tho' with a jest, I can keep it without bursting, and faithfully will, I promise you.

LESBIA: Then I will own to you, Beaumine and I are so solemnly engag'd, that if he has made you any proposal, he's the most perfidious man on earth.

MIRANDA: Nay, then 'tis past jesting, and I must tell you, what I said was only to try you. All his discourse to me was mere gallantry, and with his usual gaiety of humour; yet by the care I find he has taken to hinder us from confiding in one another, I apprehend he may have some farther design.

LESBIA: Then if you've none upon him, you may assist me [in one I have of consequence].

MIRANDA: With all my heart, for whatever little inclinations I may have, they only amuse me for the present, and endear Constant to my serious thoughts, whose plain dealing and true affection I find no where equal'd, and {he} will get the better of my fickleness at last.

LESBIA: But that I desire you to disguise from Beaumine, and to pretend you are dissatisfied with Constant, which will encourage {Beaumine} to declare himself, if he has any serious designs, and you carry it on handsomely.

MIRANDA: Let me alone for that; I have acted an indifference for Constant long enough to be perfect in it.

Enter MIRANDA's WOMAN.

WOMAN: A gentleman, madam, that calls himself Bonsot, inquires if you are here.

MIRANDA: O! By all means let him come.

(*Exit* WOMAN.)

That creature can never be unentertaining. [If we furnish no occasion for his good nature to do mischief in, the elegancy of his bulls must divert us.]

Enter BONSOT.

BONSOT: Since you command me to do myself this honour, {I} hope, madam, you'll forgive my intruding without your leave, where I have no business, being 'tis a concern of consequence brings me here.

MIRANDA: Then it seems, sir, you have business here.

BONSOT: Ay, with this lady, madam. I went to wait on you at your lodgings, and was told you were at Miranda's. So having something to say to you, I came to let you know it, because I can't inform you of it here.

MIRANDA: Pray use your liberty, sir.

BONSOT: Your very humble servant – Why, look you, madam, my brother sending me, I came of my own accord, to desire you will tell your friend Lucilia that he don't know, but he's very certain, Phil found the last letter she writ to him. For I saw {Phil} just in the place where it was lost, mightily concerned at a paper he had in his hand. I knew by his voice he was in a passion, but he was not within hearing.

LESBIA: I thought you heard his voice.

BONSOT: Ay, madam, but I could not tell what he said, for tho' I was pretty near, 'twas at a good distance.

LESBIA: Well, sir, I'll be sure to tell her what you don't know, but are very certain of.

BONSOT: That would be very kind, madam, but if I could meet with him I warrant I'd appease him.

Enter MIRANDA's WOMAN.

WOMAN: A gentleman below, madam, desires to wait on you.

MIRANDA: Who is it?

SERVANT: The young brisk gentleman that I told your ladyship would make a rare gallant for you when you are married; but he looks sullen enough now for a husband.

MIRANDA: Beaumine, on my life, let him come up –

(*Exit* WOMAN)

Now {Lesbia,} if you'll step into that closet, you may be witness of the whole scene.

LESBIA: With all my heart, this is lucky. But should not Bonsot retire too?

MIRANDA: No, he may stay if he'll be sure not to discover your being here.

BONSOT: You need not fear me, madam, I never discover a secret.

MIRANDA: In, in, he's coming.

Enter BEAUMINE.

BEAUMINE: I was told, madam, Lesbia was here.

MIRANDA: She's just gone.

BEAUMINE: Do you know whither, madam?

BONSOT: No, sir, I can assure you she does not know.

MIRANDA: Now, do you think to make me jealous, or is it to make yourself new? It is indeed extremely new; but no very taking way of addressing to a woman by showing a concern for another.

BEAUMINE: Faith, madam, the concern I have for her at present, need disturb nobody but myself, for I do hate her heartily.

MIRANDA: Which would not disturb you, if you had not rather love her heartily.

BONSOT: Nay, why so, madam? I don't believe the gentleman had rather love her; but a man may love a woman that he hates, and then 'tis not his fault.

MIRANDA: So you have mended the matter.

BEAUMINE: A man can't bear to be impos'd upon.

MIRANDA: And how can a woman impose upon a man, when they have no interest in one another? As you would have me believe.

BEAUMINE (*aside*): Damn her, I shall be an extravagant lover indeed, to lose a new mistress, for grief that I have lost an old one.

BONSOT: There you are too hard again, madam. Mayn't a woman impose upon a man, merely out of a jilting nature, tho' she have no interest at all in it? Especially if she find him fond and credulous.

BEAUMINE: I have a rare advocate. Well, madam, in anger as well as in wine there is truth. I confess, Lesbia once had such an interest in me, as would have cost the best part of my possessions to satisfy; but thanks to the virtue of her sex, she has forfeited.

MIRANDA: What, a debt upon your estate?

BEAUMINE: Upon my liberty, the most unreasonable of debts; but I'm released and – seiz'd again by another, but there's no more bonds and judgments against me: I shall only be your prisoner at large, you may call me in when you please, Miranda.

MIRANDA: How can I trust you, when Lesbia that had so fast confin'd cou'd not secure you? – Come Beaumine, honestly own, you broke loose from her to give yourself to me. It'll be the better compliment, and more generous to her than to wrong her every way.

BONSOT: Really, the gentleman seems to me a very honest gentleman, that wou'd not wrong any lady unless it were in a just cause. I warrant if he 'had not been in love with you or somebody else, he would never have forsaken her [but when a greater merit claims his heart, d'e see, a man has right of his side to do wrong to the less worthy].

MIRANDA: Most solidly and eloquently argued.

BEAUMINE: 'Tis such a well-meaning blunderer – I'm extremely obliged to you, sir.

BONSOT: Not at all, sir, I always endeavour to make a right understanding between any persons that I am acquainted with, tho' they are absolute strangers to me.

BEAUMINE: Ha, ha, ha, very charitably done indeed, sir. But madam, on my honour I have not injured Lesbia – Ha, I feel my liberty [(*Repeats.*) lighter by what I've lost, I tread on air]. Have a care of yourself, Miranda; she has left a plaguy deal of love upon my hands, and if you should be forced to bear it all –

[MIRANDA: I dare undertake it, like Aesop's choice of the bread, tho' the heaviest burden at first, being our constant subsistance, 'twill waste every

day, and soon be light enough.

BEAUMINE: Then you must resolve to have no other subsistence.

MIRANDA: Oh such a dry diet – a little variety to make it relish the better, but if you are for devouring us so fast, let's e'en make but one meal on't: marry, and there's an end. What think you of that, Beaumine?

BEAUMINE: Think, ay – Faith, we must e'en do't without thinking, or we shall never have the courage.

MIRANDA: Nay, but I'm serious.

BEAUMINE: What, before we're married? time enough after; this is a time for gaiety and joy.] Ha, my fair bride, here let me plight my vows on this soft hand.

CONSTANT *enters, unseen.*

CONSTANT: So close!

BEAUMINE: But now I think on't, there's a matrimonial rival in the case, he'll certainly forbid the bans.

MIRANDA: Ah, name him not, I am so sick of his fulsome, whining stuff.

BEAUMINE: I'm afraid there's more love than you'll confess, by what I have heard of the matter.

MIRANDA: They talk of putting us together indeed, but sure you're more a man of this age, than to think love a consequence of marriage.

[BONSOT: Ay, pox, love is never any part of the concern in marriage. Some indeed marry only for love, but then –

BEAUMINE: Ay, madam, 'tis sometimes the cause of it.] Love has many extravagant effects.

MIRANDA: [His love makes him so indefatigable a tormentor, that] if you cannot free me, I must marry him at last, for that's a sure way to be rid of him.

CONSTANT: Fortune has found you a quicker way. My passion now no longer shall torment you, nor I be more the subject of your mirth.

MIRANDA (*aside*): What must I say now? If I undeceive him, it will discover Lesbia's secret. Besides, I lose the dear pleasure of teasing him.

BONSOT (*aside*): What can I contrive now?

CONSTANT: Is there excuse for this ungenerous usage? [Had I by violent means or indirect pursued you – but how oft, Miranda, with bleeding heart, and gushing eyes, have I sworn rather to place you in another's arms, than fetter you in mine against your will? Why then, if I were so uneasy to you, could you not rid yourself with honour of me?] Why this unfair proceeding?

BONSOT: Nay, sir, I must needs say, the whole fault was partly mine, of their being so good friends. For when they first met, this lady was jealous of another, and he was in an anger; they seem'd to have very little kind thoughts for one another. But you must know, I, sir –

CONSTANT: Have very well reconciled 'em since, I see, sir. [So far engag'd anger and jealousy between 'em! O faithless woman – What pretence.

MIRANDA: Well, who can tell when to believe these lovers? 'Twas but yesterday he swore, I was too great a good to be engross'd. Nature design'd me an universal blessing. And now I must make nobody happy but himself.

CONSTANT: Miranda, you're a woman – Sir, this is no proper place for our dispute.

Going.

BEAUMINE: Now must I fight with him for having taken his mistress from him, and with her relations for not taking her.]

BONSOT: Oh, madam – Pray, sir, hear me, for you must know, I was with them all the time they were alone, tho' somebody, that shall be nameless, would have had me go, but I assured her, I could keep a secret.

CONSTANT: You would have obliged her more, in giving her a privater opportunity, no doubt. [(*Apart.*) O torture!

BONSOT: Pugh, that was as I told you, a person that must be nameless.

CONSTANT: Sir, I am not in a humour to be fool'd with –

Going.

BONSOT: Fool'd, sir!]

MIRANDA: This is carrying the jest a little too far, tho'. Constant –

CONSTANT: Madam.

MIRANDA: I would know upon what terms we part, before you go.

CONSTANT: Terms of never meeting. I know no other can be made between us.

Going.

MIRANDA: But one thing more – [I am considering which of us must wear the willow. Can you resolve me?]

CONSTANT: Am I your jest?

MIRANDA: Well, but in earnest now, stay but a minute.

CONSTANT: What, to be more abused? I have been fool'd enough.

(*As he is going,* LESBIA *comes out of the closet and stops him.*)

LESBIA: Stay to be disabused.

CONSTANT: I know enough.

BEAUMINE: Lesbia here! then I'm afraid, 'tis I have been fool'd.

BONSOT: Lord, that she should discover herself! But do what she will, I'm resolved not to betray my trust.

LESBIA: Nay, you shall stay and hear the truth.

BEAUMINE: I know, madam, that you are a very virtuous, generous person.

LESBIA: Thou the basest of men, but I have not leisure to upbraid thee, till I have justified my friend.

[BONSOT: So, more mischief forwards; I must not betray my trust.]

LESBIA: Miranda had not now a thought of wronging you, for 'twas at my request, to try Beaumine's truth, she gave him this obliging reception. Bonsot can witness.

BONSOT: I scorn to betray my trust, madam – As for me, sir, I can't say Lesbia was here before but I can affirm this to my knowledge, that Miranda had no design of quarrelling with you, but you not being here, d'e see, and this gentleman a very engaging person, she could not be so hard-hearted, you must think, as to put him quite in despair.

CONSTANT: Do you insult me, sir?

BONSOT: Sir –

MIRANDA: He does not know his humour.

BONSOT: Why should you be so peevish, sir? What if she had sent him away in despair, and he had gone and hang'd himself?

CONSTANT: Then you might have hang'd with him for company, sir.

BONSOT: Oh, oh, oh, to do you service, sir.

LESBIA: An officious coxcomb not worth your anger. But what I have asserted –

CONSTANT: [You'll pardon me if I believe herself;] she has not offered to deny, but justifies her infidelity.

LESBIA: That was, I suppose, her too-scrupulous care to conceal what I entrusted her with; but I saw there could be no other proof of her innocence but my appearing, which must convince you 'twas a plot between us. What else could I be hid for? You need not conceal it now, Bonsot.

BONSOT: Nay, nay, don't think to draw me in so. I know better things. This is all to make a difference betwixt you and Miranda; now I see the drift on't, but (To BEAUMINE.) don't mind her.

CONSTANT: Your witness is not well enough instructed.

BONSOT: Oh, as to that I know all, and if you will have it, Lesbia did hide her self indeed, not that there was any plot against Beaumine; but Miranda having a desire to be alone with him. (To CONSTANT.) Not that she designed to injure you, sir, intending you should know all. (To BEAUMINE.) Not that she would have betrayed you, sir, but for fear he should discover it. (To CONSTANT.) Tho' there was no harm, but you might have been jealous, and made a fighting business on't. (To BEAUMINE.) So you might

have been kill'd, sir. (To .) And your life in danger, sir. (To BEAUMINE.) But the lady having a great value for you, sir. (To CONSTANT.) And fearing to lose you, Sir. And as I was saying – ay pox, I'd fain have you both satisfied.

CONSTANT: What impertinence is this?

BEAUMINE: Is it not my turn to complain now, madam? Well, there is no confiding in you women. your vanity or jealousy is sure to betray us; but if ever I trust two that know one another, with the same secret again – You are the strangest incontinent creatures.

MIRANDA: And have you the impudence to complain of us, that you were endeavouring to deceive!

BEAUMINE: Why, have not you both deceiv'd me?

MIRANDA: Hang me, if I could not be fond of him again for this humour. But you, I hope, Constant – are now convinc'd.

CONSTANT: Yes, madam, [tho' before I took pains to cheat myself,] now every act of your disdain and coldness upbraids the folly of my blinded passion, that would believe they rise from any cause but strong aversion.

MIRANDA: One would think a woman of my fortune need not be so desperate at these years, to bestow herself upon one that is her aversion.

CONSTANT: You knew my nature fit to work on, and now I should deserve to be so used, be made the tool you meant me for, if I again believed. [But no, Miranda, I've broke my chain, and here I throw it from me. Thus from my injured heart, I'll throw you too, for ever.]

Going.

MIRANDA: O come back, I beg you.

CONSTANT: Never.

MIRANDA: Then he is lost indeed, and I am wretched.

BONSOT: But, sir, pray consider, as the lady was saying, she's a young lady, and a rich lady, and might have anybody she pleases. I would marry her with all my heart, myself, tho' I'm resolved never to marry, so what need can she have –

CONSTANT: None of me, sir, so pray give me leave.

BONSOT: Nor of any man for a *tool*, sir, for this I can say, she had no design to have a gallant, for as soon as the gentleman talk'd of love to her, she proposed marriage.

CONSTANT: She was very forward it seems. I must be gone, sir.

BONSOT: Forward, sir? Oh I suppose that. Nay, hear me, sir.

As CONSTANT *offers to go,* BONSOT *still stops him.*

CONSTANT: Provoking coxcomb.

LESBIA: This is barbarous. For shame, Constant! You won't leave her thus, in tears.

CONSTANT: Tears? Come, madam, you need not hide your mirth. I can laugh with you now. (*Taking her handkerchief from her face.*) Ha! She weeps indeed! O – let those precious drops fall on this bosom, soften this stubborn heart, that would contend against your virtue and its own persuasion.

BONSOT: Ay, I knew I should reconcile 'em at last.

MIRANDA: Why will you believe? These tears may be dissembled.

CONSTANT: No, thou art itself, and my proud heart wanted but this excuse for its submission. Can you forgive me?

MIRANDA: Indeed you were unkind, tho' you had reason, for I confess, I have not used you well.

CONSTANT: Do you confess it? ['Tis too large atonement. O that in this soft minute I could hear my charmer speak me happy.] Tell me, Miranda, when will you be mine?

[MIRANDA: Indeed the apprehension of losing you was so dreadful to me, that now, methinks, I can't be secure of you too soon.

CONSTANT: Shall it be tomorrow then?]

MIRANDA: You dispose of me.

CONSTANT: Tomorrow then, Miranda, makes us one. O my transported soul leaps at the thought! [as if it would break forth, to speak its joy! It will not stay, but flies to meet with thine through this lov'd bosom, and take an earnest of our coming bliss. Tomorrow, my Miranda, O my love!]

LESBIA: I wish you would take an earnest large enough to subsist on a day or two longer. I shall be at a loss else, how to divide myself between you, {Miranda} and Lucilia.

BEAUMINE: You may engage yourself here, if you please, madam. For I believe Lucilia will have no great occasion for you tomorrow, unless it be to condole with her.

LESBIA: Condole with her! for what?

BEAUMINE: For being disappointed of a good-natured cuckold, madam, that's all.

BONSOT: That is pity!

LESBIA: Scandalous! [You are such an enemy to virtue, none that profess it can 'scape your censure.] What is't you mean by these accusations?

BEAUMINE: Why, I mean that a very civil letter which she design'd for her gallant fell by chance into Phillabell's hands, at the very same time that the ring you had given yours, happened into the sight of your humble servant.

LESBIA: I suppose you both wanted an excuse [for your constancy, and so fell upon this invention] –

BONSOT: No indeed, madam, 'tis not his invention. The thing is true, only 'tis a mistake. A ring there was, but you know, sir, I told you 'twas given by a wench, a very jilt.

BEAUMINE: I believe you, sir, indeed.

[CONSTANT: As you have been an instrument in this division, I hope, Miranda, it will be your care to reconcile these lovers. I must leave you to give some orders for tomorrow's happy business.]

Exit CONSTANT.

MIRANDA: Come, what say you to it? Will you accept me for arbitrator? I'll be a very impartial judge.

BEAUMINE: Lesbia, I have still some regard for your honour, and would be loath to publish your baseness.

MIRANDA: Will you, Beaumine, do her justice, if she is innocent, and can clear herself?

BEAUMINE: Ay, ay, if the sky fall, madam.

[LESBIA: I don't doubt my justification; but that must be deferr'd.

BEAUMINE: Venus forbid! Upon the assurance that was impossible, I was just going to make her the promise.

LESBIA: Methinks, Beaumine, it wou'd become you, at this time, to answer Miranda's question in a more serious manner.

MIRANDA: Seriously then, be it known, Lesbia, there is a law that excludes anyone from witnessing in their own cause.

BONSOT: That's a very silly law tho', for does not one know their own cause best, and are most concern'd to clear themselves, right or wrong?

BEAUMINE: Therefore, sir –

LESBIA: But if I shou'd bring proofs?

BEAUMINE: Ay, ay, there are proofs that the earth moves, and that it does not move, everything can be proved. [But where we are concern'd the strongest argument is always on the side our inclinations are for; so first make me sensible you were innocent.]

LESBIA: Are you resolved then?

BEAUMINE: Never resolve anything. I did resolve to believe you faithful; you resolved to deceive me. Both have been disappointed. [Little said's soon amended. Words are but wind. All promises are either broke, or kept. Proverbs flow against you.]

LESBIA: Intolerable trifler, Beaumine, I shall find a way to force a juster answer from you.

BEAUMINE (sings):
'Women's rage like shallow waters.'

BONSOT: Egad I love to see people merry. Come, madam, [never spoil company, you see this gentleman's pleas'd.] Here's nobody out of humour now, but you.

LESBIA: Here nobody has cause, but I.

[BONSOT: Pugh, not a whit, I'll engage Beaumine will never give you any farther trouble.

LESBIA: Prithee, Bonsot, I'm not in a humour now to be pleas'd with your good natur'd impertinence.

BONSOT: Ay, ay, this is always my reward for taking pains to do good. When people are in a peevish mood, presently I'm impertinent.]

MIRANDA: Come, come, a truce with your anger till a better opportunity of clearing the debate.

LESBIA (apart): I had almost forgot Lucilia. She must know of the letter he talks of. (To him.) Adieu, my dear, 'tis late, and time to leave you.

Exit LESBIA.

BONSOT: I must follow her [for I never leave people till I have argu'd, or teas'd, 'em out of their anger]; and, sir, if you don't find her as fond of you as ever she was in her life, next time you meet, say I'm an officious, impertinent, insignificant fellow.

Exit BONSOT.

BEAUMINE: That will be an extraordinary obligation indeed, sir.

MIRANDA: Well, Beaumine, you must consider too it grows late, and that I must begin to think of the virtues of a wife's discretion and obedience.

BEAUMINE: [Ah! that's a virtue I must have too, but mightily against my will when you command me to leave you; this has been a very tragical day to lovers. Phillabell his mistress false; Lesbia lost a believing coxcomb; I my hopes of the most agreeable woman in France; and she I'm afraid will find herself in a greater distress than any of us, for, in faith Miranda, what ever the unexperienc'd may fancy of marriage –

As those who furrow'd fields at distance view,
May think 'em smooth and flowry as they show;
But he that enters, curses what they praise,
Finds 'em deceitful, toilsome, rugged ways.

Exeunt severally.

ACT FIVE

Scene One

The Walks.

Enter BONSOT with GRANDFOY.

BONSOT: Cousin, I say, trouble yourself no more about this matter. Beaumine is thoroughly satisfied, for you must know, I told him the person you had the ring from was a common jilt, a wench you had no value for, and he presently believed me.

GRANDFOY: Your folly's so ridiculous, it mocks my anger. [Wou'd thou cou'dst once be sensible how unluckily thou ever toil'st against thy own designs, thy good nature then wou'd surely silence thee –] To be always meddling where you have nothing to do, in things you know nothing of!

[BONSOT: Ay, ay, I know nothing. I don't know that he was in such a passion with you – If I had not hindered him, he'd have cut your throat before now, without giving you time to say your prayers.

GRANDFOY: Better he had, than she had been abused, the woman in the world whose honour I am most concern'd to vindicate, and most to him.

BONSOT: Why, her honour's none the worse for what I said of her. But to please you now, I'll go to him and tell him I was mistaken; the lady never had a kindness for any man but you –

GRANDFOY: That will mend the matter, indeed.

BONSOT: Well, then you shall see how I'll manage it –

Going.

GRANDFOY: Prithee, Bonsot, be quiet. All the kindness I ask of thee, is never to intend me any.

BONSOT: But wou'd not you have me do justice to a lady you say I have wrong'd?

GRANDFOY: No, no, I am just going to Beaumine, where I have appointed him to meet me, and shall find a way to do her justice myself.

BONSOT: O ho, then I'll go with you.

GRANDFOY: Indeed you shan't, sir.

BONSOT: Try me but once –

GRANDFOY: Pray hold your tongue, sir.

BONSOT: Well, I will hold my tongue then, if you'll let me go, for I know you'll begin a quarrel now, and put Beaumine out of his good humour, and then he'll never let you go to the devil in quiet, Cousin –] O, there's my brother's rival. I must talk with him. Wait for me but a little while now.

Enter PHILLABELL.

GRANDFOY: Little enough, I promise you – a lucky deliverance.

Exit GRANDFOY.

BONSOT: Sir, your humble servant – Happening to see you take up a letter in the Walks, I imagine it might be one my brother expected there, because he did not receive it.

PHILLABELL: If he would know what it contained, no doubt the lady that sent it will inform him.

BONSOT: Ay, sir, but that is not the thing now. [I can tell you more, because you have reason to take it ill, to show you have no reason, sir.

PHILLABELL: No reason, sir?

BONSOT: Not a dram, sir, upon my word, for you must know –] All the kind things in it, were only to pacify my brother, for fear he shou'd show you the rest of her fond letters, not but she really design'd to marry you.

PHILLABELL: I don't question it, upon my word, sir.

BONSOT: Ay, sir, to be sure she was in earnest with you, she admitted you to the house, when he cou'd only see her by stealth.

PHILLABELL: Confound 'em.

BONSOT: And then, you have a much better estate than he, sir.

PHILLABELL: I believe she was sincere with that, sir.

BONSOT: So I hope I have satisfied you, [and since you know she design'd you her sober choice, and only to play the fool a little with him; you won't be angry if he shows you her letters,] and I may leave you with joy, sir.

PHILLABELL: Joy, sir? you busy trifler – hence, and don't provoke my rage. What devil sent thee, when I am going to Lucilia, whom I wou'd meet as calmly as if I were not injur'd.

BONSOT: Injured? why don't I tell you, sir, I'm certain she designs to marry you.

PHILLABELL: Thy folly gives thee a privilege to abuse men safely. There's no way to resent it, but by flying from impertinence.

Exit PHILLABELL.

BONSOT: Psha, psha, as I was saying, sir – Phough, why so fast, sir – [That men shou'd be such enemies to truth, they don't care to hear it, tho' for their good!] Everybody runs away from me, [when I wou'd tell it 'em,] as if I were a monster – O yonder's Beaumine; I'll go satisfy him [and then to see what humour Lesbia's in, and then to my cousin, and my brother's. I'll go to 'em all round; I do take a deal of pains, and do a world of good – to no purpose].

Exit BONSOT.

{Scene Two}

{LUCILIA's *Lodgings*}

Enter LUCILIA *and* LYSETTA.

LUCILIA: This comes of taking your pernicious counsels; they have always been fatal to me.

LYSETTA: I'm sure I meant well, tho' it falls out so unluckily. Who cou'd dream of such an accident?

LUCILIA: Dream! for ought I know the fool hir'd you to betray the letter to Phillabell.

LYSETTA: Nay, madam, I know you can't suspect my fidelity to you.

LUCILIA: How dare you talk to me? Get you out of my sight.

LYSETTA: Dear Madam, have patience; if you'll be advis'd all may be well yet.

LUCILIA: You're very free of your wise counsels indeed, but I'll hear no more of 'em.

LYSETTA: Nay, good Madam, be pacified; I know I have been the cause of this misfortune, and therefore I would fain do you some service that may recompense it.

LUCILIA: What recompense, what service can you pretend to do me? Has he not seen the letter under my own hand?

LYSETTA: If you can but deny it confidently enough, I don't doubt your coming off, for all that.

LUCILIA: Deny it! What, when he has the proof in his possession? What could that signify, unless to show him I had joined impudence to infidelity?

LYSETTA: Nay, it must be managed artfully; you must seem angry with him as if you suspected a forgery. you know I can counterfeit that hand; insinuate that to him cunningly. Do you observe me, madam?

LUCILIA: Well, what does all this tend to?

LYSETTA: It's a nice business, and will require no little artifice, but let all your care be, very slyly to give him a suspicion of me.

LUCILIA: Do you think he'll be imposed upon so? It can but make him doubt at most.

LYSETTA: Ay, but I have a further plot. We may be thankful for this time to be prepared for him before he comes, instead of repining at the accident. How lucky it was that Lesbia should hear of it [and that you were not at home when Phillabell came last night, before she had given you notice of it].

LUCILIA: I shall be little the better for it, I'm afraid.

LYSETTA: Look you, madam, take my advice. He's a lover, and by consequence credulous. That will make him believe you enough to have a mind to examine me; and being jealous, he'll probably doubt you enough, to do it immediately, that we mayn't have time to lay our heads together. 'Tis very likely he'll come directly from you, to look for me. Then let me alone for the rest of the project. I engage to return him to you, the most satisfied, humble thing, begging pardon, calling himself a jealous pated coxcomb, and you the most innocent injur'd –

Enter a young WOMAN, *servant of* LUCILIA's, *niece to* LYSETTA.

WOMAN: Madam, here's Phillabell coming up.

LYSETTA: Dear madam, will you follow my directions?

LUCILIA: Well, well – Be gone, I hear him.

LYSETTA: Niece, come with me hussy, I have business with you, quick quick.

Exit LYSETTA *and* NIECE.

LUCILIA: I hate deceit, but sure 'tis of all others the most innocent to cheat a man to a belief of truth. How my heart trembles.

Enter PHILLABELL.

You seem disturbed. Can there be any cause of sadness of this day?

PHILLABELL: Why, madam, not on this?

LUCILIA: Does Phillabell ask why! He who so often swore this day wou'd pay the sum of all his wishes.

PHILLABELL: [Alas, there's nothing man so much deceives himself in, as the means to his own happiness;] I thought to make you mine the certain way, but unless your heart cou'd be secur'd, all other ties is {sic} wretched slavery.

LUCILIA: That you need not doubt [for whom I've laid aside my virgin-modesty, to confess I lov'd you].

PHILLABELL: You have told me so indeed, but are you sure th'obedience of a daughter has not sway'd you against your inclination?

LUCILIA: Heav'n can witness, that you are much less my father's choice than mine.

PHILLABELL: Have a care, madam, what you call Heaven to attest, and deal with me sincerely, for I am come as one that truly loves you, to offer you my service [in whatever way can best conduce to make you happy].

LUCILIA: Your service! Can anything in nature make me happy but your love?

PHILLABELL: I wou'd not have you make a sacrifice, and if you fear t'offend your father in refusing me, confess it generously. [I'll take it upon me, seem to fall off, and whatever his resentment may proceed to, I promise you to bear it all, rather than expose you to it.]

LUCILIA: I don't know what you mean. This is strange language to me.

PHILLABELL: Does this speak plain enough? (*Gives her a letter, and whilst she reads, says.*) So unmoved! She must be practised sure in falsehood.

LUCILIA: What's the design of all this?

PHILLABELL: You best know that, madam.

LUCILIA: I know it! What to disguise your own inconstancy, must you tax me with such baseness?

PHILLABELL: Why, you won't pretend to deny your own handwriting, I hope.

LUCILIA: My writing! Who dares say I writ it?

PHILLABELL: O woman! Woman!

LUCILIA: This is a masterpiece of villainy indeed!

PHILLABELL: I was not prepar'd for this turn, I confess. But who can reach the depths of woman's artifice?

LUCILIA: 'Twill be enough to wrong my love by your infidelity, without this forgery to injure my reputation. This from a man whom I despised all others for!

PHILLABELL: I forge it! I have not the art of counterfeiting so well as you, madam, but I may learn in time of so perfect a mistress.

LUCILIA: You have found a much better for your purpose, I assure you.

PHILLABELL: That wou'd be a prodigy, indeed.

LUCILIA: There's few can exceed my

sweet governess, who I don't doubt was employ'd in this contrivance.

PHILLABELL: Employ'd by whom? for what?

LUCILIA: To sacrifice my honour, for your base ends.

PHILLABELL: O madam, you need not distrust her; 'twas not she betrayed you. Fortune was my only friend in this matter.

LUCILIA: Indeed, I shall hardly take your word for it. Perhaps you imagine I don't know her skill in counterfeiting my hand, tho' she might have told you I did.

PHILLABELL (aside): Is't possible there can be a deceit in this? If my reason wou'd be as soon convinc'd as my fond heart, I could not think her false one minute. [Lysetta counterfeit her hand, to what end? And yet I can see nothing of that confusion, or disorder in her looks, which guilt wou'd naturally have, upon so unexpected a discovery.] What can resolve me in this hell of doubts?

LUCILIA (apart): So there's some hope; it begins to work. (To him.) I see you are surprised to find your accomplice so soon suspected.

PHILLABELL: Madam, I thought you had known me too well to believe me capable of such villainy. If you are innocent, we are both abus'd.

LUCILIA: I thought too my virtue had been better known, and I will clear it, if my false governess dare deny it. There may be ways to force the truth from you, and her.

PHILLABELL: There may be ways too, madam, to make her own whatever you please.

[LUCILIA: You may prevent that if you please, but I suppose you'll be loath to lose so good a pretense for denying my innocence, if I should make it appear.

PHILLABELL: O cou'd you look into my heart, Lucilia, it wou'd tell you, that with the forfeiture of half my reason, I wou'd believe you're wrong'd, so much I wish it; but tho' I shou'd be easily convinc'd, yet for your sake, that there may be no room left

for malice,] I'll tax your governess with this forgery, as if I knew it hers, that perhaps may induce her to confess it.

LUCILIA: You may do as you think fit.

PHILLABELL: Till then believe I suffer more than you. What different effects does passionate love produce!

Fearful to lose, we quickly jealous grow.
And wishing to be loved, soon think we're so.

Exit PHILLABELL.

LUCILIA: Now, if Lysetta play her part as well, who can condemn this harmless artifice? [The main points, that I love Phillabell, and despise Cleon, are truths. Where then wou'd be the virtue or wisdom, to let him know some disagreeable circumstances which wou'd make us both really uneasy, tho' there were only an imaginary reason for it. But happy are those who have rul'd their lives with so much prudence, that every action may appear barefac'd; for to be forc'd to the least disguise is some violence to an honest nature, and tho' 'tis not disus'd to injure others, 'tis a corruption, at least a blemish, to do injury to itself. Yet wou'd the men dissemble no otherwise with us, we cou'd easily forgive 'em, but they with baser arts,

All their past faults, with impudence reveal,
And only those which they intend, conceal.]

Exit LUCILIA.

Scene Three

The Walks.

Enter BEAUMINE *and* GRANDFOY.

GRANDFOY: [Thus, sir, least my sword shou'd fail to do her justice, I have endeavour'd to convince you how little Lesbia has deserv'd such unhandsome usage from you, and am ready to confirm the truth of what I have said with the hazard of my life.] We need go no further; this place is private and convenient.

BEAUMINE: To give me satisfaction, sir, for you have done me such an injury.

GRANDFOY: I thought, sir, what I have told you with so much frankness, and Lesbia's letters, which you saw, refusing the offer I had made to marry her, and mentioning on what account the ring was given me, were proofs that we never injured you.

BEAUMINE: Why, that's the mischief on't. You have convinced me she has been so honourable that I must be married, the greatest misfortune you could have drawn me into, that I know of, indeed, sir.

GRANDFOY: Then it seems you don't love her, sir.

BEAUMINE: Because I have no mind to marry her? Then no man ever did love, for no man ever had, or can have a mind absolutely to marry any woman.

GRANDFOY: [Why, sir, has not many a man married merely for love?

BEAUMINE: Ay, sir, and many a man has taken a house he liked, with a considerable fine upon it, because he knew it would not be let otherwise, but I'll be hang'd if any man had not rather have it without.

GRANDFOY: And be the more unwilling to pay it, after he has been long in possession.

BEAUMINE: But rather than forfeit his word, or his house, for I find there's love as well as honour in the case.]

GRANDFOY: Well, sir, [if you resolve to do her justice upon any motive, 'tis all that Lesbia can require of you; but] since we both have a claim to her, nothing but our swords can decide it.

BEAUMINE: O, yes, sir, she can do it much better, for [tho' it's true, women are seldom favourable to merit, we must own they are better judges than the most judicious sword in Europe. The advantage is,] the person she rejects will be in a better condition than may be his chance if we fall to cutting of throats. For him she chooses, I can't promise it, indeed.

GRANDFOY: You talk very little like a lover; I wish her choice were placed where 'twou'd be welcomer. But I prefer Lesbia's satisfaction to my own and therefore am content to submit to her sentence.

BEAUMINE: Wisely resolv'd, sir. [A man of honour should not decline fighting upon any reasonable occasion but where it can answer the end – If it be for revenge, stabbing a man is a very substantial one; but for a mistress, how the devil does my sword know her inclinations? If it happen to dispatch the man she likes, I am sure to be hated the more for it; if a man she dislikes, there was no danger in him. So it can never be to any purpose.] Come, sir, let us try other means, capitulate with the lady – (*Sings.*)

Women by force of arms can ne'er be won,
Unless the guards within, betray the town.
Sound a parley, ye fair, and surrender.

Exit, singing with GRANDFOY.

Scene Four

LESBIA's *Lodgings.*

Enter LESBIA, {Bonsot}[1] *and* LUCILIA.

LUCILIA: You see how dear this foolish gallantry had like to have cost me, if your timely notice had not put me on my guard.

LESBIA: This comes of being so hasty to run into an *amour*. Before the heart engages, we must retreat, and know not how to do it with honour. But when love leads us on, however dangerous the consequences are, it makes 'em easy to us.

LUCILIA: But 'tis indeed a strange folly to hazard our reputation, only for the vanity of securing a conquest. The

---

[1] The name of Bonsot was inadvertently omitted here, in the original. However, with suggested cuts, Bonsot need not appear until the next scene.

prize is so little worth, in respect of the venture.

LESBIA: What think you of the contrary fault, affecting an indifference for those we really love?

LUCILIA: That's as much a greater folly, as our own happiness is of more consequence to us, than other people's opinion.

LESBIA: How blind we are to our own faults! Now don't you see that what you have been condemning, you are at this instant guilty of, flying Phillabell, when you most wish to meet him; and seeming angry with him, when you know he's in the right.

LUCILIA: But 'twou'd not be wise to know it, as our affairs stand, and I have ordered Lysetta to tell Phillabell I am at your lodgings. If he comes here I can't avoid him, and so give him an opportunity of reconciling himself, without seeming to desire it.

BONSOT: I'll engage, madam, he'll come, I'm sure I said enough in your defence to satisfy any reasonable man.

LESBIA: No doubt. A little harmless artifice is sometimes necessary, and for a young beginner, you have performed pretty well, but] Lysetta's part was managed with wonderful dexterity.

LUCILIA: The design indeed was cunningly laid, and happily effected.

LESBIA: Hold; is not that Phillabell's voice below?

Enter PHILLABELL *and* LYSETTA.

LUCILIA: I think it is. (*Pretending to be going.*) Now for my last deceit, madam, I'll take my leave of you.

LESBIA (*holds her, pretending difficulty*): Nay, now indeed you shan't.

PHILLABELL: Be so just to hear what I have to say, before you condemn me, madam.

LUCILIA: I have heard you say too much.

PHILLABELL: But hear Lysetta, madam. (*To* LYSETTA.) Come, you must speak the truth.

LYSETTA: I beg your pardon, madam.

I did not think any harm wou'd come on't, but truly I did write some letters in your name to Cleon; indeed I did not intend to do you any injury by it.

LUCILIA: No injury! What else could induce you to it? Who set you on?

LYSETTA: Nobody set me on, but Cleon took care to pay me so well for deceiving him, that I thought it worth my pains.

[LUCILIA: It seems, Phillabell, you have great power with her, to make her confess all this.

BONSOT: What, is she jealous of her? – Oh, madam, there's nothing in that but money too; he has only given her money enough, take my word for it.

LUCILIA: So I imagine, sir.

BONSOT: Psha, you think 'twas upon some slippery account now, but 'twas only to make her own this cheat, I can answer for him.

PHILLABELL: Prithee give me leave to vindicate myself, Bonsot.

BONSOT: With all my heart, sir, now I have satisfied her as to the main point.

LESBIA: Ay, like all other universal friends, commanding every one alike, their praises always injure.]

PHILLABELL: I took her in the very fact, madam. My good genius led me thither just as she was writing, and so intent upon her treachery, I came into the chamber unperceiv'd, heard her admiring with her niece her skill in counterfeiting your hand so perfectly. When I had heard enough, I snatch'd the paper, which was to the same effect of that I show'd you. It having miscarried, she was writing it again, which left her no room to deny her guilt, nor me to doubt your innocence.

LUCILIA: 'Twas happy, since it proves a means of putting an end to this cheat, and gives us power to punish the author of it, which she shall find severely.

PHILLABELL: But first, Lucilia, let us think of our own happiness, that no new chance may cross it.

LUCILIA: 'Tis not enough that you believe me innocent, since Cleon, and perhaps by his vanity, many others, suspect me of infidelity. I must not let you share in my dishonour.

[BONSOT: Why, madam, 'twill make your part the less.]

LYSETTA: If I might hope for pardon of my fault, by making some kind of reparation, I wou'd tell Cleon how I have all this while abus'd him.

[BONSOT: And let me alone to appease him, I'll tell him 'tis all but a sham, to a certain purpose.

LUCILIA: I hope he knows his brother well enough to esteem what he says as it deserves.

LESBIA: Upon those terms I must become her intercessor.

PHILLABELL: And I have reason to join with you.

LUCILIA: You have too much power with me to be refused anything you desire.

PHILLABELL: Then you are mine again. At your feet receive my thanks, and let this hand give me possession.

As he kneels, {BONSOT,} BEAUMINE, GRANDFOY, *and* CLEON *enter.*

BONSOT: See now how good friends I have made you, and here come my Cousin and Beaumine together. I thought I had made up matters between them too.

BEAUMINE: So this is the way on't! When the women have played us false, we must submit, and beg pardon, for having the impudence to see it.

PHILLABELL: O Beaumine, my Lucilia's innocent.

BEAUMINE: Ay, ay; so they are all, if they have but cunning enough.

PHILLABELL: Thou'rt a mere infidel.

BEAUMINE: No, faith, Phillabell, no offence to thee. I'm as credulous a coxcomb as yourself. [Prithee don't laugh at me; there are two evils you know, that go by destiny.

PHILLABELL: Of which I shou'd least expect marriage to be thine, indeed.]

GRANDFOY: My cousin Cleon,

madam, met us as we were coming hither, and wou'd needs have me bring him to wait on you.

LESBIA: Being your relation, he must be welcome to me, but I'm sorry it happens at a time when things are in such a posture that I cannot be so easy, much at liberty as I shou'd, to be entertained by so extraordinary a person.

CLEON (*apart*): That is, she would be alone with me. (*To* LESBIA.) O, madam, I shall find a happier opportunity, but since I cannot enjoy it now, I'm extremely pleased to meet such good company here. I have a great respect for these lovers, and wish you joy with all my heart, upon my word, sir.

PHILLABELL: O, I thank you, sir, but must desire another favour of you. You received some letters in this lady's name, which I expect you shou'd return.

CLEON: In that lady's name, sir? Then it seems she is not asham'd of her name, that she has told you where to find it. – I protest, I resolv'd to conceal 'em, but if you have a mind to have 'em published, madam, I can put 'em in the Press. They will be a very extraordinary *Epithalamium*.

LUCILIA: Sir, you have been deceiv'd. Those letters never express'd my thoughts.

CLEON: Very probable. Women's words seldom express their thoughts. I did not doubt but you had more kindness for me than they expresst.

LYSETTA: Ah, sir, my lady never thought one word of what was writ. 'Twas all of my contrivance. I confess, sir, I was loath to let you despair –

[BONSOT: Hark you, brother, this is only a plot to make you part with your mistress the more easily. But don't you seem to know it, and ye don't be angry neither.

CLEON: But seem as good natur'd a fool as you? Brother, you had the best contrivance last night in the Walks to keep me from despair – but not one word of your ladies' thoughts.

LUCILIA: I'll be sworn I spoke truth, but abusing a man is complimenting him, when vanity's the interpreter.]

LYSETTA: – Well, sir, since the deceit is discovered, I suppose you won't think my letters worth keeping.

CLEON: Her letters – *Madam la Gouvernante*, [when you grant me the favour, I desire it may be in the same shape you made me the promise in last night.

LYSETTA: Ay, ay, sir, this shape is only put on, that we may keep it with the more security.]

CLEON: O, I apprehend.

PHILLABELL: I hope, sir, you believe Lucilia had no hand in deceiving you?

CLEON: Pasitively, {sic} I assure you, sir.

PHILLABELL: And be so ungenerous to refuse the letters.

CLEON: Sir, I happen to have 'em all about me. I had some thoughts you might have a curiosity to know how well she cou'd write before you married her. They're at your service, sir, if you please to peruse 'em. (*Gives PHILLABELL the letters.*)

PHILLABELL: I have not the curiosity indeed, sir. Here, Lysetta. (*Gives them to LYSETTA.*)

CLEON: The best bred husband in the world, rat me.

[BONSOT: I told you I shou'd satisfy him, sir. Now you must know he thinks the letters were Lucilia's for all this.

PHILLABELL: Does he so, sir? I shall find a way then, to convince him they are not.

BONSOT: Hay, why are you angry at that? Nay, rather than you shou'd quarrel, I'll tell him myself, that she only order'd Lysetta to write 'em.

PHILLABELL: What you say is of so little consequence, I care not what you tell him.

BONSOT: Ay, ay, this is always my reward. But for all that, I shall never give over –

PHILLABELL: Being impertinent, I dare engage for thee. 'Tis the happiest,

tho' the most incurable distemper a man can have, and both for the same reason: he can never be made sensible of it.

BEAUMINE: Among the many interposers in affairs they have nothing to do with, who, when they laugh at this officious meddler, will consider him as their own picture?

LUCILIA (*aside*): Well, I am happily come off, but through such dangers, such anxieties, as might warn all our sex against those little gallantries with which they only think to amuse themselves. But tho' innocent, too often gain 'em such a character of lightness, as their future conduct never can efface. Nay, tho' I have succeeded better, I find within, all is not as it shou'd be. A secret check, that so entire a confidence as Phillabell has in me, is not return'd with that plain, open, artless dealing it deserves: that will be the lasting punishment of my childish fault.]

LESBIA: Grandfoy tells me, Beaumine, you will both submit to my choice between you.

BEAUMINE: So we agreed, madam. I'm impatient to know which blessing I must lose – you, or my liberty.

Enter CONSTANT and MIRANDA.

LESBIA: Miranda! and married, I'll engage, by that affected gravity.

LUCILIA: Miranda, married at last!

LESBIA: I hope, sir, I may give you joy?

MIRANDA: Ay, you may give him joy. For it's the first day of his reign.

CONSTANT: Of my happiness indeed, but 'twou'd be ungrateful to use it to the prejudice of your power, from whom I have receiv'd it.

MIRANDA: I begin to be terribly afraid I shall certainly love you, and you have loved me so fast, you must be near the end of the race before I am set out.

CONSTANT: O! 'tis an endless race; endeavour but to overtake me.

BEAUMINE: This is a dreadful omen to me, madam; there was so much sympathy between us, I'm afraid it reaches to our destinies, too.

MIRANDA: Do the planets incline to conjunction then? I cou'd not forbear coming to inquire how your affairs went.

BEAUMINE: Very ill indeed, madam. [There is but a woman's inclinations betwixt me and ruin, which wou'd certainly give her to that gentleman, if I were as fond of marrying her, as he is. But your sex's darling, contradiction, I fear will carry it].

MIRANDA: What, Lesbia in profound meditation?

LESBIA: Advise me, Miranda. I'm a little puzzled in this affair.

MIRANDA: Divided betwixt love and honour?

BONSOT: Now, I advise you, madam, in this case.

LESBIA: What, without knowing it?

BONSOT: Let it be what it will, I am never of honour's side. It's good for nothing but to make people uneasy, and I would have everybody please themselves, whether they can or no.

LESBIA: You must teach 'em the art then – But prithee shou'd I, out of a foolish scruple, tie myself to Beaumine, when we are weary of one another?

MIRANDA: Or lay the yoke upon a fresh lover, that will hold out longer.

LESBIA: And bear it easier. How shall I resolve? I think they had best throw dice for me.

MIRANDA: E'en put it to the vote.

LESBIA: With all my heart.

MIRANDA: What say you, gentlemen? Lesbia is so unwilling to disoblige either of you, she's resolved to be his, that has most voices for him.

BEAUMINE: What she pleases.

GRANDFOY: I shall never dispute her will.

CLEON: This is extremely new; but I don't know why it should not be brought into custom to marry, as well as to divorce by vote. [Unless indeed, that getting rid of our wives will be more for the general good.]

MIRANDA: Well, sir, which are you for?

CLEON: Since there is so good a relief, for him that will soonest be weary of her.

GRANDFOY: That I grant, is on Beaumine's side.

MIRANDA: What say you, Constant?

CONSTANT: I am for him that loves her best.

GRANDFOY: That favours me.

BONSOT: I am for him that won't quarrel with her.

BEAUMINE: That's likely to be me, for I shall be least with her.

LUCILIA: I am for him that can plead most right in her.

BEAUMINE: Ah the devil! That's me again.

PHILLABELL: I am for him that she loves best.

MIRANDA: And I for him that she loves least.

BEAUMINE: That has undone me! 'Twas pure malice, Miranda.

LESBIA: The odds are on Beaumine's side, whether I declare I love him least, or best, there's a vote for him. His right is indisputable. He says he shan't quarrel with me, and he's weary of me already, so there can be but two against him.

[BEAUMINE: You'll find hereafter there were more. My late suspicion of you gave me such disquiets, as show'd me how dear you are to me; and the proofs of your innocence confirm my love, with my esteem.

LESBIA: Which to preserve, and for all our quiets, I propose for the future, Grandfoy be a stranger to us.

BONSOT: Oh! That's cruel – Sir, my cousin has a great kindness for you, and your lady, I'll engage he'll do her no harm.

BEAUMINE: Oh no, sir.]

GRANDFOY: I must submit, but may

have still, I hope, some pretence to
your friendship.

BEAUMINE: You have deserv'd it, sir,
and are welcome to share with us this
day's diversions.

CONSTANT: I have ordered some
music. With your leave, madam, we'll
employ 'em.

[After a Dance.]

PHILLABELL: 'Tis time now to think
upon the ceremony that yet remains to
make us master of our wishes.

BEAUMINE: Which performed, I
resolve to show those married men
[whom I have laugh'd out of the
fondness, or civility, for their wives;
that I have learn'd by their weakness,
how to avoid giving 'em a revenge,
and will so shamelessly boast of loving
mine, that 'twill put raillery out of
countenance. And by preserving my
complaisance for her, show] {that} I
know how to value myself.

For treating them with rudeness or
    neglect,
Does most dishonour on ourselves
    reflect;
If that respect which their own merit
    drew,
We think, by their becoming ours, less
    due.
And as in choosing, we their worth
    approve,
We tax our judgment, when we cease
    to love.

ANTIOCHUS THE GREAT
or
THE FATAL RELAPSE

JANE WISEMAN

Jane Wiseman was a round, brown woman, writing tragic soliloquies by candle-light in her tiny room under the front stairs of the Wright's house in Oxon. She met Susanna Centlivre at market one day in front of the yellow onions; they swapped recipes for French onion soup, which led to an invitation to Susanna's house for coffee on Jane's next free afternoon. There Jane, in a blue muslin borrowed from her mistress, met George Farquhar, who introduced her to Catharine Trotter, who led her to Mary Pix, who gave *Antiochus* to Elizabeth Barry, who decided she absolutely had to stage it and play the part of Leodice.

No. Jane Wiseman was a lanky, red-faced blonde, brazenly coining blank verse while polishing banisters, the Wright children hanging off her skirts. She was the John Clare of women's history, a rough-cut genius who heard voices in her sleep and wrote them down in stolen moments between boiling the pudding and slicing the quince. One night she bribed Joseph, the groom, to take her to the theatre, where she watched Dryden's *Absalom and Achitophel* from the second gallery. Inspired, she went home and wrote the first scene of *Antiochus*.

I created these and a hundred more scenarios in my obsession to put the dressing of reality on the handful of surreal facts that are all we know of Jane Wiseman's life, which are as follows: a 'Servant in the Family of Mr. Recorder Wright of Oxon,' Jane Wiseman wrote one play, *Antiochus the Great; or, The Fatal Relapse* (staged in 1701 and printed in 1702), after which 'She married a young Vintner, whose Name was Holt; and with the Profits arising from her Play, they set up a Tavern in Westminster.'[1] She belonged to a literary clique composed of Captain William Ayliffe, the historian Abel Boyer, and playwrights Susanna Centlivre, George Farquhar, Ned Ward, and Tom Brown.[2] And according to Susanna Centlivre's biographer, 'Susanna and Jane Wiseman were clearly good friends, who planned their diversions together and who may have helped one another in writing their plays.'[3]

Where did Jane Wiseman come from? What were the circumstances that led her to work for Mr. Wright, to become associated with an artsy crowd, to meet Susanna Centlivre, to write a tragedy about aristocratic Babylonians? Did she teach herself to write verse drama by reading samples in Mr. Wright's library? How did she even learn to read? Was Mary Pix the force behind Centlivre as well as Wiseman? Did Wiseman write other plays which were never performed, never published? Who was this man Holt? Do manuscripts, letters, or details of Wiseman's life still exist, perhaps in an attic in London or a box of uncatalogued manuscripts in some library basement? I never found a clue.[4]

Whoever encouraged her, Jane Wiseman certainly attracted prodigious support for her play. Elizabeth Barry, a friend of playwright Mary Pix and one of the three managers of Lincoln's Inn Fields theatre, was the greatest tragedienne in the English-speaking world in 1701. She played Wiseman's female lead. Charles Gildon, at that time highly respected both as critic and playwright, wrote the words to a song for her third act. The part of Antiochus was played by George Powell, Drury Lane's lead male actor, on special loan to Lincoln's Inn Fields for this production.

Moreover, the costuming was expensive. While middle-eastern plays were common, and some form of oriental garb must have been staple costume stock, Wiseman called for the Babylonian attendants of Antiochus to be dressed differently from the Egyptian attendants of his reluctant wife, Berenice; she also stipulated that Act Three should begin with a 'masque,' and that for this scene, eight principals and 'several lords and ladies' be dressed 'in Masquerade.' In order for a serving-woman's first play to be staged at large cost to a company teetering on the brink of bankruptcy, someone of influence must have been behind it. Was it Elizabeth Barry herself, eager for the thunderous role of Leodice? Was it Wiseman's literary crowd?

Someone's faith in Jane Wiseman's play paid off. It ran at least three nights in a difficult season when few new plays were that successful, and it may have run longer and been revived (records for the season are not specific, and confusion arises later with another play of the same name). Since we know that Wiseman earned enough from its proceeds to purchase a tavern, she must have had a very full third night indeed, if not a sixth. The only other information about Wiseman, or about the play's reception, is what she herself published with the play – in her dedication to 'John, Lord Jefferies, Baron of Wem.'

Here she wrote that the play was 'the first Fruits' of her muse, and that 'The Reception it met in the World, was not kind enough to make me Vain, nor yet so ill, to discourage my Proceeding.' She said the play was criticised for 'want of Business,' for which she apologised, promising to do better with her next play; she defended the character of her hero; and finally she answered the cruellest criticism of all: that of not actually being the author. She stated with good humour that the critics 'have chose one of our best Poets for my Assistant, one I had not the happiness to know, 'till after the Play was finish'd.'

Oddly enough, the man to whom Wiseman dedicated her play was the son of George Jeffreys, an arch-Tory who served as Lord Chancellor to James II until the Glorious Revolution of 1688. George Jeffreys was called 'the Butcher of Monmouth' for having been instrumental in the execution of ninety-seven Whigs involved in the Duke of Monmouth's rebellion, and for doing nothing to avert the deaths of about two hundred more. Little is known of his son John, other than that he was married at the age of fifteen to a daughter of the seventh Earl of Pembroke, and he died the year *Antiochus* was published, at the age of twenty-eight.[5] Jane Wiseman's tribute to him is the only one I was able to find.

Did she offer it as he lay on his deathbed, or did he die unexpectedly, soon after the play was published? Did she actually know him? Was he, like his father, a Tory? And if so, what does that say about Wiseman, whose one friend of record was Susanna Centlivre, a passionate, pamphleteering Whig? Did Jeffreys respond to Wiseman's dedication at all? Did he support her or the production in any way? Like the other clues to the mystery that is the life and work of Jane Wiseman, this one only leads to more questions.

Wiseman's play has thus far attracted almost no critical attention. Nancy Cotton gives it a quick plot summary and then dismisses it as 'mediocre.'[6] Fidelis Morgan mis-reads the play, stating that in the conclusion 'Leodice's brother accidentally kills Berenice;' Morgan's only critical assessment is that the play 'is that of a writer learning the craft.'[7] Out of the mass of moulding playscripts that Cotton and Morgan must have read in the course of their research, it was no doubt inevitable that they should overlook, misjudge, or misread one or two, though it seems odd that they should both have missed the forceful, ranting poetry and outspoken sexual politics of this unlikely author.

For *Antiochus* is an astonishing achievement. If it were *not* the first play written by a self-educated serving woman to be professionally produced in London, it would still merit a good deal more press than it has received. The plot, though interesting, is the least of its virtues. Set in Babylonia, the tragedy explores the psychological destruction of two heroic women by the self-serving Prince Antiochus. Although the women never confront each other in the play, the action proves they were never actually rivals, as Berenice actually found the Prince repulsive.

This does not appear to be where the play is going when the curtain rises on the scorned former mistress of Antiochus. Leodice declaims to Cypre, her devoted companion, 'She comes, she comes; the hated Berenice comes, And I must fall to make my Rival way'. Wiseman knew the convention of female rivalry popular in men's plays of her time, and she must have enjoyed duping the audience into believing it was about to see another pair of tempestuous females tear each other's eyes out in competition for the man of their desires.

Leodice reveals that Antiochus has broken his promise to marry her and legitimize their child; he has married the Egyptian, Berenice, instead. However the audience soon learns that Berenice was engaged to marry a fellow Egyptian, Ormades, whom she loves; her father gave her to Antiochus as part of a military treaty, and she arrives in Babylon in a state of isolation, distress, and mourning, relieved only by the tenderness of her devoted companion, Irene. What complicates the plot is the virtue of Berenice, who believes that since she is now married to Antiochus (though she cannot bring herself to bed with him) she must reject Ormades, who has followed her to Babylon in disguise, hoping somehow to free her.

The fourth act climaxes as Antiochus has promised to rendezvous with Leodice, but on the way to Leodice he hears that Berenice is meeting secretly with Ormades. In a towering double-standard fury, he rushes in on the couple and reviles Berenice, not knowing she has just virtuously told Ormades to leave her forever. Ormades stabs himself, and in the final act Leodice poisons herself and Antiochus; and Leodice's brother, attempting to murder Berenice, is executed by guards. The plot is at first glance fairly typical of heroic tragedy, offering the standard conflict of love and honour, a love triangle, and a littering of the stage with dead bodies at the end.

However its focus on a complex female protagonist, Leodice, who is not entirely heroic but certainly not villainous, is most irregular. Wiseman invites her audience to sympathize with the ravings of Leodice, to understand that she was violated by Antiochus' breach of contract, and to be awed by her decision to destroy both herself and Antiochus. One almost feels like cheering when Antiochus consents to drink the 'wondrous cordial' Leodice offers him. Yet by comparison with Berenice, Leodice is unreasonable, immoral, out of control.

There may have been a racial issue in the play. Berenice, after all, is Egyptian. It is difficult to know exactly how the English perceived the Egyptians in 1701, but early in the play Leodice asks, 'Must her curst Race possess the daz'ling Crown?'. If Wiseman was suggesting that Berenice was of an oppressed race, as this line implies, then the characterization of Berenice as the central model of virtue in the play and the sole survivor of its tragedy takes on added interest. So does her revulsion at Antiochus. This hypothesis requires more evidence but gains weight from the popularity of Aphra Behn's portrait of the noble and virtuous Oroonoko, who kept his word no matter how many white men he saw break theirs, and from the history of many women writers' concerns for other oppressed people.

While Wiseman's position on the politics of race is not yet fully substantiated, her position on the politics of gender is patent in this play. She depicts a universe in which the exercise of male prerogative brings destruction; the sexual double standard leads to man's abuse of power and his exploitation of woman.

All politics aside, Wiseman's play is also a poem. Berenice has a gift for well-worded prophecy and a bond with other women that gives her understanding beyond her husband's imagination. When in Act One, scene two, Antiochus promises, 'Each day shall bless us with some new delight,' Berenice answers, 'That were to make us wretched./Pleasures like luscious Banquests cloy the most./And constant Blessings dull and tasteless prove'. She knows Antiochus as he doesn't know himself, for she echoes the experience of Leodice, whose availability, like that of a wife, has caused her to grow dull and tasteless to Antiochus. Much later, when Berenice is faced with a choice of poison or a dagger with which to kill herself, she cannot choose. She asks, 'I wou'd not Live; Then why this strange Confusion?/To die is but to sleep, and yet I fear:/Poor Coward, Nature, how art thou perplext?'.

The rhythm of Leodice's ranting is sometimes hypnotising: 'Tell me of Poyson, Daggers, Death, Confusion./These be the Subjects I wou'd treat on now;/These be our Theme, but mention Hope no more', or 'His soft, resistless, dear, deluding Arts/Deceiv'd her to his Arms, as they did me'. In her confrontation with Antiochus he spurns her cruelly, declaring, 'I am in love with Vertue, yours is lost,' and she answers with a warning to all women:

> Oh! Let all fond believing Maids by me be warn'd,
> And hate as I do, base ungenerous Man;
> Whom if you trust, you're sure to be betray'd;
> Fly from their power, laugh at their Complaint;
> Disdain their Love, and baffle their Designs;
>
> So you may scape my Sufferings, and my Faults.

Wiseman doesn't reserve poetic utterance for her heroines alone. Ormades, who has some of the most exquisite speeches in the play, realizing at his moment of death that Berenice still loves him, speaks lines worthy of Shakespeare: 'Why did I live to hear these tender words?/I shou'd have dy'd in Peace, and thought it gain'.

Wiseman's play stands alone among all the tragedies of its time in one final respect. Her curtain falls on a virtuous female couple, Irene and Berenice, heading off for a life in the wilderness together. Berenice vows to 'seek some lonely unfrequented Shade,' and asks Irene to go with her 'And prove the kind Companion of my Life,' to which Irene answers, 'To the Worlds utmost Limits I would wander,/ To follow you in Power or Distress'. Where was the precedent for that, in English drama?

[1] *Giles Jacob's* Poetical Register *(London, 1719), Vol. I, p. 301.*

[2] *This information appears in an odd anonymous volume entitled* Letters of Wit, Politicks and Morality *(London, 1701), p. 21.*

[3] *John Bowyer,* The Celebrated Mrs. Centlivre *(1952, reprinted NY: Greenwood, 1968), p. 28.*

[4] *My search yielded nothing more than the printed version of* Antiochus *filed with books, and nothing whatsoever filed with manuscripts under the name of Jane Wiseman or Jane Wiseman Holt in any of the following places: the British Library, the Bodleian, Trinity College Library in Dublin, Marsh's Library in Dublin, the Humanities Research Center in Austin, the Newberry Library in Chicago, the London Public Record Office, the National Portrait Gallery in London, the York Public Library, the Fawcett Library in London, Harvard University Library, the Sophia Smith Archives at Smith College, nor any of the Five College Libraries in Massachusetts.*

[5] *Information taken from* The Complete Peerage *(London: St. Catherine Press, 1929), Vol. 3, pp. 83–85.*

[6] *In* Women Playwrights in England c. 1363–1750 *(Lewisburg: Bucknell University Press, 1980), p. 156.*

[7] *In* The Female Wits: Women Playwrights on the London Stage 1660–1720 *(London: Virago, 1981), p. 64.*

Characters

Men
ANTIOCHUS THE GREAT, *King of Asia and Syria*
ARTENOR, *brother to Leodice*
SELEUCHUS, *his friend*
ORMADES, *an Egyptian Prince, in love with Berenice*
PHILOTAS, *an Egyptian, his friend*
ARCHUS, *the Queen's Eunuch*

Women
BERENICE, *Queen, secretly in love with Ormades*
LEODICE, *sister to Artenor, seduced by the King and now forsaken*
IRENE, *favourite, lady to the Queen*
CYPRE, *favourite to Leodice*
CHILD, *to Leodice*
GUARDS *and* ATTENDANTS

SCENE, *Babylon*

ACT ONE

A Room of State

LEODICE, CYPRE, *and* WOMEN

LEODICE: She comes, she comes; the hated Berenice comes,
 And I must fall to make my Rival way:
 Curse on all Cowards, those slow dregs of Phlegm!
 For Treason was not what the Rout dislik'd,
 Mischief was ever welcome to their Wills:
 But Courage fail'd, and the Slaves durst not Fight;
 Else I had still been sole Commandress here;
 Still Reign'd, in spight of an Usurping Queen,
 Who by the Priviledge of an empty Title
 Possesses all my Right.

CYPRE: The Change indeed is sad, yet do not grieve;
 Great Hearts shou'd know to brave malicious Stars.

LEODICE: Canst thou believe so poorly of Leodice,
 To think my Soul can lose by Fortune's Frowns?
 By the Immortal Powers, I scorn her Rage;
 And still am great, and still will so continue,
 'Till I think fit to end the busie Scuffle.
 Nor shall the sprightly Boy I've born to Empire
 Tamely resign to a lawful younger Brother.
 Whilst I survive, I'll teach him to Contend;
 And when I die, by Fates severe Decree
 My watchful Genius shall attend his Steps;
 Inspire and lead him to revenge my Wrongs,
 My ravish'd Power and my injur'd Love.

CYPRE: Hark! By these shouts they must be near at hand.

LEODICE: Away then, let's retire and plot Revenge,
 For with them comes my Artenor, my Brother;
 Who shares my Injuries, and will my Vengeance.

Exeunt

Enter ANTIOCHUS, BERENICE, ARTENOR, SELEUCHUS, PHILOTAS, IRENE, *and* LADIES. ANTIOCHUS *attended by Babylonians,* BERENICE *by Egyptians.*

ANTIOCHUS: This day be sacred to my Queen and Heaven,
 That thus have doubly blest Antiochus
 With matchless Beauty, and with glorious Peace.
 Let my free Subjects taste unbounded Joy;
 And let each Slave today, forget his Task.
 Let the loud Peals of Gratitude be heard,
 That distant Egypt may receive the sound,
 And learn from thence how Berenice is ador'd,
 Who condescended thus to wed a Foe,
 And Crown his Arms with soft transporting Love,
 Who sought her Father's Empire and his Life.

BERENICE: Alas, Great Sir! To me there's nothing due;
 My Royal Father laid his strict Command,
 And I the humble Creature of his Will,
 Without dispute obey'd. 'Twas much indeed,
 A Stranger and in Arms against himself!

He lov'd you, took you to his aged heart,
And gave you thence the dearest Pledge he had;
Which worthless as it is, if you are pleas'd,
Be all your generous Thanks apply'd to him.

ANTIOCHUS: Much to his Goodness I shall ever pay;
Much to the Gods that so inspir'd his Mind.
But oh! to thee, the source of all my Joys,
To thee my grateful Soul for ever bends;
For thou wast Mistress of thy Lover's Fate,
And hadst alone the Power to make me blest.
Thy Father gave thy hand, but cou'd no more;
And that without thy heart had made me wretched.

BERENICE: Nay, now you over-rate that Trifle;
For with my hand the sure Descent was given
Of Egypt's Ancient Crown.

ANTIOCHUS: Oh, be not thus unkind, to wrong my Love,
And think that sullied with ambitious Falsehood:
No! though thirst of Greatness drew me to the War;
Though Fame and Empire then were all I sought;
Yet when I heard of thy Angelick Form,
Thy wondrous Vertue and eternal Charms,
My hopes and wishes took another bent.
All that were by, can witness to my Love;
For when we met to treat of Peace and thee,
Ambition was no part of my concern:
I thought not of a Crown, but of thy Beauty.
And having urg'd thy Father to an Oath,
Thou shoud'st be mine, I had no more to say;
The rest was by my faithful Lords debated:
For Love and Expectation rais'd my Soul
Above regarding Articles of State!

BERENICE: Forgive me, Sir, if I have spoke amiss;
And let the just Obedience of my Life
Preserve your Love, and shew me grateful.

SELEUCHUS (aside): Both Soul and Body of Imperial make.

ANTIOCHUS: Come to my arms, far dearer than my Soul;
To doubt my Passion, shews how well thou lovest.
Such kind Suspicion gives me new delight,
And I am blest beyond a Mortals share.

BERENICE: What shall I say to this excess of Love?

ANTIOCHUS: Say any thing, that I may hear thee talk:
For charms are in thy Words, and Transport springs
From the bewitching Accents.

BERENICE: Oh, you are good, and will o're-look my faults:
Nor frown to meet a Sadness in my Eyes
Not suiting with this Extasie.
The Cause will claim your Pardon and your Pity.
'Tis owing to a Daughter's Tenderness,
Who, just parted from the best of Fathers,
Cannot forbear some Tears to his dear memory,
Who sheds the same for me.

ANTIOCHUS: Forbear, thou best and kindest of the Sex;
Cease to lament what thou shalt never miss:

For thou in thy Antiochus shalt find
A thousand Blessings more than thou hast lost.
The watchful pious Care of Philadelphus;
The eager fondness of unpractis'd hearts;
The extasie of Passion at full growth;
And all that constant Faith which Heaven commands.

BERENICE: Sure none can boast a happier State than I,
(*Aside.*) Nor less regard it.

ANTIOCHUS: Then bannish Sorrow from thy lovely Breast,
It has no warrant to inhabit there:
The ugly and the old, the crawling Slave
Opprest with want and scorn, let them lament,
'Till anxious grief gnaw through their meagre forms,
Leaving them in the silent Arms of Death.

BERENICE: That certain cure of all our mortal ills,
And safe retreat for Monarch and for Slave.

ANTIOCHUS: But long may we be Strangers to its Shade:
We have no griefs to heal, no ills to shun;
Possest of all that's valuable here:
Plac'd high in Power, and smiling Love our Friend.
Each day shall bless us with some new delight;
And thronging Joys prevent our very Wishes,
'Till Heaven, to compleat and crown our Joy,
Forgives us Natures Debt, and makes us
Both immortal.

BERENICE: That were to make us wretched.
Pleasures like luscious Banquets cloy the most;
And constant Blessings dull and tasteless prove:
In vain you'd look for new Delights to charm.
At best we are but cheated with a shew,
An empty Vision of Variety!
Which when our restless Appetite receives,
We own the Disappointment.

ANTIOCHUS: Whence Learn'd thy Youth these grave unequal Thoughts?
Thy Charms deny the Morals thou woud'st teach.
Every succeeding hour augments my Joy,
And shews new Beauties to my wondering Mind:
But lead we now where Mirth and Pleasure wait,
There let thy Smiles crown my Exalted State;
And all thy Monarchs Happiness compleat.

Exeunt.

Manet ARTENOR *and* SELEUCHUS.

SELEUCHUS: She's gone.

ARTENOR: Curses attend her!

SELEUCHUS: I know thy Grief; but do not curse the Queen,
She must be Good; or were she not, that form
Wou'd force a Blessing from the rudest breath.

ARTENOR: She may be beautiful, and good as Angels,
In gross the whole perfection of her Sex;
But she is rais'd upon my Sister's Ruins,
And I am sworn her everlasting Foe.

SELEUCHUS: She is indeed the Master-piece of Nature.

ARTENOR: But she must fall
From the exalted top of tottering Power,
To low Contempt and Scorn.

SELEUCHUS: What canst thou mean?

ARTENOR: I mean, Leodice must rise again,
My banish'd injur'd Sister.
Come, thou'rt my Friend, and may'st assist me nobly:
What! lost in Thought? Thou canst not fear for me;
I have it in my Brain, to set all right again.

SELEUCHUS: Ah, poor Seleuchus!

ARTENOR: Ha! Why that Sigh, and these dejected Looks?
Now, by my Life, thou shalt not hide from me;
I've us'd thee like a Friend.

SELEUCHUS: And I'll return it, nay, o're-pay the Tract:
I love the Queen.
My Eyes this hour have suck'd the Poyson in:
Nor can Despair expel the frantick Passion.
Though Birth and Marriage, Love, and every Barr
Which Fate can set 'twixt happiness and me,
Oppose my Folly; yet I cannot turn,
But must adore, though sure to be undone.

ARTENOR: Now, as thy Friend, I pity thee;
But have no power to condemn the Chance.
By this, thou'rt doubly bound to my Designs;
Both Interest and Friendship make thee mine;
For know, the Plot I've laid may serve thy ends.

SELEUCHUS: You talk'd of Ruin to the Queen.

ARTENOR: I'll tell thee,
Antiochus was not the Man she chose;
But marry'd in obedience to her Father.
The brave Ormades, a young Native Prince,
Had Lov'd her long, and was agen belov'd,
But they conceal'd their Passions; why I know not.
And while the Prince was busied in the War,
Her Father forc'd her to Antiochus's Bed,
In spight of all my subtile Opposition.

SELEUCHUS: Is this thy Cordial to a fainting Friend?

ARTENOR: Alas! Thy Brains are stupify'd by Love;
Or woud'st soon discern the health I offer.
This Tale improv'd, will give the King suspicion,
Which her unlucky Coldness will augment.
Those Tears consider'd, I can hardly think
The Tribute cou'd be paid to an old Father.
I know the King is apt for Jealousie:
But shou'd I urge it, he'll suspect my Interest.

SELEUCHUS: Say this were done.

ARTENOR: Then anxious days and restless gloomy mights
Wou'd breed indifference, and wrangling discord,
'Till all conclude in endless Separation.
Then he'll remember his young smiling Image,
That hopeful Centre of my vast Ambition;
And joyfully restore him to his favour.

My Sister then, that fallen Star shall rise,
And shine with glorious Lustre, bright as ever:
Her smiling hours will then dance round agen,
To the same pleasing measures as before.

SELEUCHUS: But what have I to hope?

ARTENOR: Thou lov'st the Queen, and she's above thy reach;
When she's disgrac'd, she's nearer to a level,
And thou perhaps may'st joyn in her Revenge.
Ormades is far off, and a new Lover
Will blot his memory with ease:
Come, Lovers are short-sighted; What say'st thou now?
Have I not lifted thee to a fair Prospect?

SELEUCHUS: Thou hast, but with such dangerous ways between;
Such craggy Mountains, and such steep Descents,
That much I fear: But tell me, Artenor,
What must I do to work the fatal Mischief?

ARTENOR: Hint what thou hast heard
With subtilty and caution, to Antiochus,
Thou shalt not want wherewith to amuse his Head.
All this I learn'd from the Queen's Eunuch,
Whom I brib'd, and molded for my own.
I'll to Leodice, and comfort her,
Without whose Aid we shall but Plot in vain.
She's yet at Court, though banish'd by the King;
And cou'd she meet him in a lucky hour,
And for a while forget her haughty temper,
We need not doubt Success.
I must prepare her for the great Design.
Now to thy Task; away, lose not a minute:
If possible, let us prevent a mischief yet unborn:
At night there is a Mask; there we shall meet.

Exit ARTENOR.

SELEUCHUS: Yes, I am going.
But oh! a moment, let me think; on what?
To ruin what I love!
To blast the Glories of a Bridal Queen,
In hopes she'll love me for the grateful Service!
Madness beyond example. Yet Artenor,
Who never Plots in vain, he leads me on:
Down all my fears; each timerous thought be gone.
I wou'd by nobler means obtain my Bliss,
But scanty Fate affords me only this.
Then, Oh! ye Gods, if I a Traytor prove,
Acquit your Slave, and lay the Fault on Love.

Exit.

ACT TWO

Shouts at a distance, 'Long live Antiochus and Berenice'.

Enter LEODICE, *followed by* ARTENOR *and* CYPRE.

LEODICE: Oh! Whither shall I flie,
  To 'scape the noise of these accursed Clamours?
  Now I cou'd stoop to Banishment, or Death,
  And give up all my Title to Revenge;
  Oblige the ungenerous, faithless, cruel king,
  And free my Rival from her evil Genius. (*Shouts agen.*)
  Hark! they shout agen! Now Plagues and Tortures,
  Great as those I feel, seize on them all,
  And teach their bellowing, hoarse Plebeian Tongues
  To rave and curse as I do.

ARTENOR: Forbear these wild Complaints, thy Brother's here;
  And came to bring thy labouring Spirit ease.

LEODICE: Ease! name it not; there's no such thing for me:
  Ungrateful perjur'd Tyrant!
  Thus to reward my everlasting Love.
  How often have I sate in awful State,
  And view'd with scorn the trembling wishing Crowd,
  Where all that lifted their presumptious Eyes,
  Bow'd to my Charms, and offered up their hearts;
  Where sighing Princes have confess'd my Power,
  And gaz'd to adoration!
  These, these will point at my Prodigious Fall;
  Laugh at my Wrongs, and glory in my Fate.
  Oh that distraction wou'd relieve my Brain,
  And free me from the sense of what I am!
  Disgrac'd and Banish'd! Oh, my swelling heart!
  Give me revenge, ye Gods, or I shall burst.

ARTENOR: For Heaven's sake have Patience for a while;
  Think how to appease the King,
  Who will be furious when he finds you here.

LEODICE: Ease! name it not; there's no such thing for me:
  Ungrateful perjur'd Tyrant!
  Thus to reward my everlasting Love.
  How often have I sate in awful State,
  And view'd with scorn the trembling wishing Crowd,
  Where all that lifted their presumptious Eyes,
  Bow'd to my Charms, and offered up their hearts;
  Where sighing Princes have confess'd my Power,
  And gaz'd to adoration!
  These, these will point at my Prodigious Fall;
  Laugh at my Wrongs, and glory in my Fate.
  Oh that distraction wou'd relieve my Brain,
  And free me from the sense of what I am!
  Disgrac'd and Banish'd! Oh, my swelling heart!
  Give me revenge, ye Gods, or I shall burst.

ARTENOR: By all that's good, I bring you Hopes in earnest.

LEODICE: Away, away;
  Or talk of something nearer to my Soul:
  Tell me of Poyson, Daggers, Death, Confusion,
  These be the Subjects I wou'd treat on now;
  These be our Theme, but mention Hope no more.

ARTENOR: Yet wou'd you hear me, all might be retriev'd.

LEODICE: Oh never, never; he's marry'd!
  And Berenice must live and die a Queen.
  Had his bewitching Charms betray'd her Vertue,
  His soft, resistless, dear, deluding Arts
  Deceiv'd her to his Arms, as they did me,
  I then might hope.
  I know my Youth and Beauty great as hers,
  And cou'd not fear, upon the square of Fate;
  But she, with curst Egyptian subtilty
  Has wrought my Ruin, sure, and bound him fast.
  Gods! Must I see this envy'd, hated Rival
  Shine on a Throne which I shou'd have adorn'd?
  Must her curst Race possess the daz'ling Crown?
  And will no Power prevent her lavish Fortune?
  Was every Blessing Cast and Stampt for her?
  That thus he doats upon the worthless Bauble,
  Crowning her Pleasures with excessive Love.
  Confusion, that he basely robs me of:
  From me he catch'd the first uniting Sparks;
  I kindled in his Breast the generous Flame;
  And from my Store he has inrich'd the Queen.
  Oh! Torture, Treachery, and Wrongs unparallel'd!

ARTENOR: Still will you let your Passion blind your Eyes;
  And deaf to Interest, ruin all for ever?

LEODICE: I will be Calm; but yet 'tis very hard
  To enjoy the chiefest Blessings Heaven cou'd give,
  And lose them all on one unlucky hour!
  To fall from Love and Empire in one day!
  Who but my self wou'd have out-liv'd the Loss?

ARTENOR: Yet hear Me:
  If you'd stand this almighty shock of Fortune,
  And combat with the Powers that will your Ruin;
  Conceal this high wrought Fever of your Soul,
  And keep your Rage for more important use.
  First, undermine the Queen: It may be done,
  She's not so fixt as your Despair suggests:
  The Marriage was precipitate and rash:
  The King has once been false, and may agen.
  You have a Son may tempt him to relapse.

LEODICE: Say on, a glimpse of Comfort seems to bless me.
  So the poor wretch in some sad Dungeon chain'd,
  After a long despair in painful darkness,
  Spying through a small Cleft the cheerful Light,
  Rises with Joy, and shakes his lighter Chains,
  Fancies he shall be free without delay,
  Believes the Gods were mindful of his Prayers,
  When the next hour perhaps is doom'd his last.

ARTENOR: Throw off this melancholly from thy Soul:
  Persue thy Fortune, she'll agen be kind.
  Cast off those Robes, and put on Sable Weeds;
  Such sad solemnity will move the King.
  But see! we're interupted, let's retire;
  In private we'll consult what's to be done.

Exeunt.

Enter ORMADES, *disguis'd.*

ORMADES: Sure this must be the place Philotas meant;
For here alone I miss the noisie Croud;
This is the hour, and yet he is not come.
Methinks I wander like an out-law'd Slave.
Oh, when shall I have Peace?
By what strange Irony was wretched Man
Styl'd Monarch of the World, and made so vain,
To think all Pleasure was design'd for him?
That Nature's business was to make him happy;
And each substantial Form Created to obey?
Alas! how far from this, is our true State:
Vassals to Passion, that Lords it o'er our Souls,
And scorns the just Reproof of feeble Reason.
Slaves to the empty sounds of Fame and Honour:
Fantoms, which dazle with fantastick show;
But when persu'd with anxious fruitless care,
Like Shadows shrink from our deluded grasp:
Then loaded with the Fetters of fond Love;
Love! the great word which sums up all our woe;
The long continued Torment of our Lives.
Oh, Berenice, Berenice!

Enter PHILOTAS.

PHILOTAS: At last I've found you.
How fares my dearest Friend? Speak.

ORMADES: Forgive my Impatience; tell me first of Berenice:
Is she as blest as Woman can be made?
Pleas'd with the Ruins she has heap'd on me?
Speak; Does she Doat on the too happy King?
And is Ormades banish'd from her Memory?

PHILOTAS: Alas! she is a Sufferer like you;
And all the Pomp and Triumph of the Day
Cannot amuse her Grief.

ORMADES: Sure thou mistakest, for Berenice is Queen;
Love and Ambition both are made her Slaves!
She was design'd a Darling of the Gods:
And every Feature claims their tenderest Care
Where-e'er she moves; soft Peace and smiling Joy
Attend her happy steps, and Crown her wishes.

PHILOTAS: Forced to the Bed of loath'd Antiochus,
And made a fatal Sacrifice to State,
Whence shou'd her Pleasures rise?
All this long day I've waited by her side,
That I might find an opportunity
To tell her you had followed in disguise,
To obtain a parting look, a cold adieu;
And well I saw the anguish of her Soul,
Though much she strove to check the rising Sighs,
And hide the Tears that stole from her fair Eyes:
But when she heard her dear Ormades nam'd,
She scarce had Life to hear the Message out.

ORMADES: If any thing cou'd add to what I bear;
If there was any pain beyond despair,
This wou'd augment my Torture.

PHILOTAS: The Queen expects you at the Mask this Evening,
Where 'tis impossible you shou'd be known:
She'll send her Eunuch to see my Dress,
That he may find me out and bring me to her.

ORMADES: Now cou'd my Breast receive a thought of comfort;
The hopes of seeing Berenice wou'd give it:
But she is lost, and I am curs'd for ever!

PHILOTAS: See! the King and Queen.

ORMADES: Oh Berenice! shou'd I stand a nearer view,
My Passions now are swell'd to such a hight,
I might betray my self, and ruin thee.
Exit.

Enter ANTIOCHUS, BERENICE, IRENE, ARTENOR, SELEUCHUS,
GUARDS, *and* ATTENDANTS.

ANTIOCHUS: Why droops my Love amidst so many Pleasures?
Can nothing charm thy Mind, nor cheer thy Heart?
Hast thou no taste for Babylonian Mirth?
That whilst all view thee with rejoycing Eyes
Thou sighing, check'st their murmuring delight
With unexpected sadness.

BERENICE: I'm much indebted to the Peoples Love;
More to your tenderness and fond regard:
But do not let my Sadness interrupt;
Or their Diversion, or your Royal Peace;
For part of it is constant to my Nature;
The rest will wear insensibly away,
And unobserv'd be lost.

ANTIOCHUS: Pray Heaven it may, before I take Infection;
For something sits so heavy on my Heart,
I almost fear.

BERENICE: The Gods avert all Omens from your Majesty.

ANTIOCHUS (*embracing*): Thus let me thank thee for thy vertuous Prayers.
Thou Composition of unequal goodness:
But now retire my Life, and dress thy self,
In order for the Mask; the Night comes on:
Tis time we were preparing.

Leads her out, and Re-enters.

Thanks to the Gods, that have me in esteem;
They've made the best of Woman-kind my Queen.
Is there on earth another half so lovely?
So heavenly fair, and so exactly good?
Say, have you seen in any happy Court
Through all the various wanderings of Life,
A Form so excellent, a Soul so bright,
Beyond description, and above a Throne;
Unless 'twas rais'd on Jasper, deck'd with Stars,
Like those on which the Goddesses are plac'd.

PHILOTAS (*aside*): Oh, that I knew to dash this mighty Joy
With gnawing Grief, such as Ormades feels.

ARTENOR: But when I saw her in her Father's Court,
   There hung no heavy Cloud upon her Brow,
   All was Serene as Innocence or Peace.
   Now there's a sorrow settled in her Face,
   Which takes the place of many a native Charm.

   Aside, to SELEUCHUS

   Now is thy time, pursue him on this Subject.

ANTIOCHUS: She has lost a Father's dear Society.

SELEUCHUS: Has she not found a Royal tender Husband?

ANTIOCHUS: I cannot tell from whence her Sorrow springs:
   If you have heard another Cause, relate it.

SELEUCHUS: Princes Concerns are of the highest Nature;
   And all I heard was but imperfect Rumour.
   I beg your Majesty permit my Silence.

PHILOTAS (*aside*): Ha! I'm all surprise!
   A chill concern creeps through my trembling Veins;
   I fear some subtile Devil has betray'd us;
   And then what Power can save Ormades' Life?

ANTIOCHUS: Thou hast rais'd a Doubt which must have present ease;
   What is it thou canst mean?

SELEUCHUS: I heard a whisper, but it was no more,
   Among the Egyptian Lords,
   That Prince Ormades long has lov'd the Queen;
   And once had hopes he shou'd successful prove;
   If so, the Rage that now must rend his heart,
   May move her Royal Pity.

ANTIOCHUS: Pity's the Band that lets in Love by stealth;
   And first taught Falshood to relenting Nature.
   Pity! By all the Gods, it will corrupt her,
   And I shall curse the hour that joyn'd our hands.
   Philotas, know'st thou any thing of this?

PHILOTAS (*aside*): I am confus'd, and know not what to answer.

ANTIOCHUS: Why art thou mute? Thou art Ormades' Friend;
   I've met thee oft in Battle by his side:
   Each busied to defend the others Life,
   Where I had cause indeed to think he fought
   For Love as well as Fame: Say, was it so?

PHILOTAS: That Prince Ormades lov'd the beautious Princess
   Long e'er these happy Nuptials were design'd,
   I hope your Majesty will think no Crime?

ANTIOCHUS: 'Tis so! From this curs'd Source springs all her Grief;
   Her Sighs and Tears are for Ormades' Loss;
   And I obtain'd her on her Father's Oath:
   I cannot bear the thought.

ARTENOR (*aside*): It works as I cou'd wish.

ANTIOCHUS: How is my State in one short moment chang'd!
   But now, I thought my self a Demy-God.

SELEUCHUS: Wou'd I had died, e'er thus disturb'd your Peace.

ANTIOCHUS: Why am I thus concern'd? If she's unworthy,

I'll throw her from my Arms, and be at rest.
Oh! that my Rival was within my reach,
That happy Object of her secret wishes;
He soon shou'd prove my Rage!
Yet I'll be Calm; perhaps 'tis all Suspicion:
Ormades may have Lov'd without return.
I'll wait a little, to resolve my doubts;
But if I find her Heart another's prize,
My eager Love to endless Hate shall turn,
And load her life with Infamy and Scorn.

Exeunt.

ACT THREE

Enter LEODICE, *in a Masquing Habit,* CHILD, *and* CYPRE, *in Mourning.*

LEODICE: Wait near at hand; and when I call, appear,
  And strike his Eyes with sensible Remorse:
  And thou, the unhappy Off-spring of a slighted Mother!
  Plead my unhappy Cause, and move the King.

CHILD: Fear not your little Boy; My Royal Father
  Ne'er deny'd me any thing I ask'd him.

LEODICE: Oh! Why must thy unerring Innocence
  Suffer for Crimes unknown?
  Why must thy Parents' guilt fall on thy Head,
  And weigh thee down, before thou know'st to sin?
  My Infamy intail'd upon thy Name,
  Will make thee wish thou never hadst been born!

CHILD: I've done no Fault, and yet you make me cry.

LEODICE: Retire, dear pledge of an ill-fated Love,
  Or tender Pity will dissolve my Brain
  To everlasting Streams of flowing Tears.

Exit CHILD *and* CYPRE.

Now for my Task,
  In humble sorrow to relate my wrongs.
  This Dress will guard me from the least suspicion;
  And thus I shall have liberty to gaze
  On the curst Ravisher of all my Joys.
  Oh, that my Breath was mixt with baneful Pestilence,
  That I might blast and wrinkle her to Age;
  Or that my Curses had the power of Fate!
  Then she shou'd drink the dregs of my Despair,
  And swift Destruction overtake her Glories.

Exit.

ANTIOCHUS, BERENICE, IRENE, PHILOTAS, ARTENOR, SELEUCHUS, ORMADES, ARCHUS, *and several* LORDS *and* LADIES *in Masquerade. Enter* LEODICE.

LEODICE (*aside*): There stands the Queen: confusion to the Title!
  I know her by the sparkling Plume she wears;
  And there's the faithless King, unpunish'd yet,
  Though false to every God, as well as me;
  For 'twas by them he swore Eternal Faith.

ARTENOR *talks to* LEODICE, SELEUCHUS *to the* LADIES; PHILOTAS *and* ORMADES *directed to the* QUEEN *by the* EUNUCH, *who afterwards retires to* ARTENOR.

SELEUCHUS: How slight's the impression of all other Charms,
  When once the Heart hath felt Almighty Love?
  Nor Wit, nor Shape can draw the Lover's Thoughts
  From the dear Object of his Constant Flame.

ARTENOR (*aside to the* EUNUCH): What say'st thou?
  A Stranger, and in Tears at meeting! Ha!
  Observe him well, I'll make it worth thy Care.

A Dialogue, with Words by Mr Gildon, Sung between a BOY *and a* GIRL.

SHE: I Vow, I think I'm grown a Woman

Have Charms enough, enough to undo Man:
Besides, I'll add a thousand Graces
They ne'er will find in other Faces.
Where'er I come I'll raise Desire,
And light in e'ery Breast Loves Fire.
Here look brisk, and there look down;
On this I'll smile, on that I'll frown:
Gloat on this with Amorous Eye,
With looks severe that Fool deny.
With this I'll laugh with that I'll cry,
With this all languishing I'll die.
Thus from each Nymph I'll bear her Swain,
And every Beau shall fill my Train.

Enter a young Shepherd.

HE: Ah! Mirabella, Fair and Gay,
　　How oft I've wish'd this happy Day,
　　When I alone my Suit might move,
　　And tell you here how much I Love.
　　Ah! pity me, fair Mirabella.

SHE: What, Love from thee? Fough, filthy Fellow.
　　Is that a Dress, Is that a Mein,
　　With me in Publick to be seen.
　　No more of Love, oh, fie, fie, fie,

HE: Oh! pity me, or else I die.

SHE: You sawcy thing, why what care I?

HE: I'll force a Kiss if you're so shy.

SHE: Nay, pish, forbear; why what d'ye do Man?
　　You've nothing that can win a Woman.

HE: I've Love, my fair one,

SHE: But no Money;

HE: Enough to live on:

SHE: Peace, you Tony.
　　You've not enough to make you mine,
　　With Coach and Six, Sir, I must shine.
　　Sparkle in Box, and in the Ring,
　　Fough, be gone, thou filthy thing.

HE: Oh! Pity me:

SHE: Oh! No, no, no.
　　Be gone, I say, you are no Beau.

HE: No, I am Substance; He's but Shew.

Chorus
SHE: Be gone, I say, you are no Beau,

HE: No, I am Substance, He's but Shew.

A Dance; after which, as they are going out, LEODICE *kneels and holds the* KING's *Robe.*

LEODICE: Turn your All Gracious Eyes, Most Mighty Sovereign;
　　And for one moment listen to my Prayers:
　　Not as Partaker of these high Diversions
　　Came I here, but to intreat your Mercy.
　　'Mongst all that lately fill'd this Sacred Presence,

I guess there's none unfortunate but me;
And since a general Mirth inspires all,
Let not one Wretch be singled from its Influence:
None sure to Night can urge Complaints in vain,
When with a lavish Hand you scatter Joys
On all within your Reach.

ANTIOCHUS: What wou'd you? and it shall be granted;
(*Aside.*) Though perhaps I am not that Jove you think me.

LEODICE: I am descended from a Noble Family,
Whose bright Prosperity and rigid Vertue
Were of equal wonder. Impartial Death
Snatch'd my dear Parents from my heedless Youth.
'Ere half their Race was finish'd;
Who dying, left me for a lasting Pledge,
A Jewel of inestimable value,
And charg'd me to esteem it as my Life;
Then told me it included secret Power
To make me Bless'd, Belov'd, Admir'd and Happy;
That when I lost it, Misery wou'd ensue:
My Fame be blasted, and my Peace destroy'd.
I heard with due regard, and promis'd fair;
Swore to preserve it to my latest Hour:
And visiting the Silent, Sacred Urn,
Where afterwards their Pious Dust was laid,
Agen I often did renew my Vow.
Yet see
How fruitless my Resolves! how vain my Care!
In one ·unguarded hour came a Robber,
Who bore the Prize triumphantly away.
I wou'd have rais'd my Voice to loud Complaint,
But long he sooth'd my Rage, and flatter'd me to Peace,
'Till I believ'd the sad Predictions false.
But Oh, too lately I am undeceiv'd:
The Victor grown unmindful of my Wrongs,
Now treats me with ungenerous disdain,
And drives me like a Vagabond away;
The only shame of all my spotless Race,
Who from their happy Seats above look down,
And own my Sufferings greater than my Crime.
To you, Great Monarch, I appeal for Justice:
Oh save me, save me from approaching Ruine.
I love the Foe that has procur'd my Fall.
Let him restore me to his dear Embrace,
Return my Passion, and forget his Hate;
So may eternal joys reward your Aid,
And every God consent to what you wish.

ANTIOCHUS: Name me the Man, and he shall do thee Right,
By the Imperial Majesty of Kings;
By all that's great above, and just below,
I swear he shall.

LEODICE: A thousand Blessings on that welcome Oath.
(*Throws off her Disguise.*) See here Leodice.

ANTIOCHUS: Ha!

LEODICE: Whose Honour was the spoil of your Victorious Love,
'Gainst which no Heart's secure, no Vertue safe.

Happy in Innocence, and Chast Retirement
I spent the first soft Years of Blooming Youth:
And though an Orphan, stray'd not from my Duty,
'Till you remov'd the harmless Rural Scene;
And having heard how Fair I was, and Young,
Drew me to Court, and sully'd every Charm.
Thus Ruin'd, and made hateful to my self,
I wou'd have stole away and hid my Shame;
But then you seem'd to Love,
Pretended Grief, and counterfeited Passion;
And on your bended Knees implor'd my Stay;
Kiss'd every Murmer from my trembling Lips,
And drank the Tears that trickled from my Eyes:
Swore that the Crown shou'd to my Line descend;
And all with so much seeming Truth,
That I believed you wou'd be ever Constant,
And fondly let my Infamy be publick.
Now see how well an easie Heart's rewarded.

ANTIOCHUS: Why have you thus betray'd me to Dispute?
I wou'd have shun'd it and your Face for ever.

LEODICE: What have I done, that you shou'd hate me thus?
Be Just, and charge me with another Crime,
Besides my guilty Love of false Antiochus,
And I'll be patient, and deny I'm wrong'd.

ANTIOCHUS: What need I search for any other Faults?
I am in Love with Vertue, yours is lost.

LEODICE: Thus when Malicious Devils have seduc'd
And plung'd our poor unwary Souls in Sin,
Themselves with black Infernal Cruelty
Stand first Accusers of those Crimes they've urg'd.
If Vertue be the only thing you Love,
And has alone the power to keep you true;
Why does your Treacherous Sex take so much pains
To undermine the beautiful Foundation?
Oh! Let all fond believing Maids by me be warn'd,
And hate as I do, base ungenerous Man;
Whom if you trust, you're sure to be betray'd.
Fly from their power, laugh at their Complaint;
Disdain their Love, and baffle their Designs;
So you may scape my Sufferings, and my Faults.

ANTIOCHUS: Proceed, and let your Hate transcend that Love
Which once I priz'd, but cannot now return:
Forsake the Court, and you'll be soon at ease.
Farewel (*Going.*)

LEODICE: Stay, I conjure you; if you go, I die.
(*Draws a dagger.*) See, I'm prepar'd; and well you know, I dare.
Oh, that I cou'd return thy Barbarous Hate!
But 'tis in vain I wish, in vain I strive.
My Rage is feign'd, and I am still Leodice;
That Foolish, Doating, Lost, Abandon'd Wretch!
Still you are dearer to my soul than Peace;
Than Life; or pleasing Dreams of what I was.
Oh! look upon me, kneeling at your Feet:
Think in this Posture what I might have gain'd
Once, all that you cou'd grant; then hear me now,

Fallen to mean desires: I'll ask like what I am.
Revoke my Banishment, and let me stay
In some unminded Corner of the Court;
Confine me if you please, with Iron Bars,
To see you through the Melancholly Grates,
At distance as you pass, is all I ask.
And see, here's one to joyn in the Petition.

Goes to the Door, and brings in the CHILD *and* CYPRE.

ANTIOCHUS: I feel my Heart relent, and melt to Pity.
What shall I do to guard my yielding Soul?

CHILD: Long live my Royal Father.
See on his aking Knees your little Son,
Prays to the Gods you always may be Prosperous.

ANTIOCHUS: Sweet Innocence!

CHILD: Dear Father, for you still are so:
Though now they tell me, I must call you King.
What have I done to anger you?
You never send to bring me to your sight,
Nor take me in your Arms now I am come,
As you were us'd to do.

ANTIOCHUS: (*takes him in his Arms*): Rise kneeling Cherub.
Thus I restore thee to Paternal Smiles.

CHILD: But if you let my Mother and I go,
As she has told me that you say we must;
To be a-cold all Night, alone all Day;
Indeed you do not care if we were dead.

ANTIOCHUS: Fear not, my Boy; thy Mother goes not,
But where smiling Plenty waits her coming:
And thou, my well drawn Image, shalt stay here.

LEODICE: Wou'd you then? Cou'd you rob me of my All?
My only Comfort Rigid Fate has left me.
Him can you think to separate from my Breast,
Whose lovely Being I so hardly purchas'd?
But he will not desert his Mother so.

CHILD: No; I wou'd sooner die, if I knew how,
Than stay when you are gone:
But I'll kneel down agen, and hang about his Knees,
'Till he has promis'd we shall both stay here.

ANTIOCHUS: By all thy Mothers Wrongs I am o'ercome;
And you shall stay, though 'tis to my Destruction.
Can'st thou forgive a faithless perjur'd King?
If so, forbear to weep, and haste to thy Apartment.
Anon, when all retire to needful rest,
I'll come Conducted by thy faithful Brother;
Where every Minute that I stay with thee,
We'll rob the Queen of whole Ages of Love.

LEODICE: My Heart was sunk into such deep despair,
I scarce can raise it to a thought of Joy.
With trembling Doubts, and various hopes and Fears,
Confus'd Belief, and frantick wild Delight,
It flutters in my Breast, not yet at ease.

ANTIOCHUS: Let not disquiet longer vex thy Mind.

By Heaven, I swear thou'rt dear to me as ever.
Go then, and dress thy Face in Bridal Smiles;
For Love renew'd, is sweet as when begun.

LEODICE: It is, those tender Words have pierc'd my Soul,
And let in Transport with the charming Sound:
Oh! I shall long 'till the wish'd hour arrives;
And fondly chide old Time's dull, lazy pace:
Mistake each little noise for your approach;
And starting, make Addresses to a Shade.
Farewel, you will not fail?

ANTIOCHUS: Not for the World.

[*Exit* LEODICE, CHILD *and* CYPRE.]

This lucky Meeting has restor'd my Peace.
Now let the Queen prefer my Egyptian Rival;
I shall not grutch the Heart which I neglect;
He is not here to violate my Bed:
A hopeless Flame shall vex her anxious hours,
Whilst I am bless'd with all that Love can wish,
In My Leodice's fond faithful Arms.
With eager Passion, and soft Transport prest,
Of endless Truth, and boundless Joys possest.

[*Exit.*]

Enter BERENICE, IRENE, *and Train.*

BERENICE: Must everlasting hurry be my Fate?
When in my Father's Court, I had some ease;
Here I am haunted with eternal noise:
See, I intreat you'd leave me for a while,
And sure a Queen may hope to be oblig'd.

[*Exeunt Train.*]

Only do thou, my dear Irene, stay,
And help to calm the Tempest of my Mind.

IRENE: To Love so well, and to be Lov'd agen;
And thus to Lose, and to be Lost for ever,
Is more than Stoick Vertue cou'd sustain.

BERENICE: I've seen Ormades; nor is this the worst:
I have consented to a Private Meeting.
He swore to die this Night, if I refus'd.
What shall I do? Advise thy wretched Mistress.

IRENE: Alas, I'm at a loss.

BERENICE: Nothing but dire Confusion fills my Breast;
Yet in this Chaos of distracted thought,
Something is forming worthy of my Care.
What, if concealing my unhappy Love,
I meet him with a chilling proud indifference,
And justifie the Malice of my Stars?
Who knows but Heaven may prosper my Design,
And teach me to destroy his hopeless Flame?
It shall be try'd.
I'll lay by all this softness of my Temper;
Affect a haughty Coldness in my Eyes,
'Till he believe Ambition has betray'd me.
As yet I have but seen him in a Crowd,

Where I was forc'd to hide the pain I felt.
I am resolv'd, and he shall never know it.
If thus I give him Peace,
I'll willingly embrace an Age of Misery;
Where, like the Damn'd, it will augment my Torture,
To think how more than bless'd I might have been,
Now curs'd for ever.
All Ills, but such as mine, may hope redress.
There's none compleatly wretched but a Wife,
And she must bear the tedious Curse for Life.

[*Exeunt.*]

ACT FOUR

Enter BERENICE *and* IRENE.

IRENE: The important hour approaches,
  And the King's absence favours your Design.

BERENICE: A heavy Damp sits on my trembling Heart;
  I fear some fatal Consequence attends.
  Oh, my Ormades!
  The best, though most unfortunate of Men.

IRENE: All Egypt lately wonder'd at his Actions.
  Fame had no leasure but to sound his Praise:
  Still he was foremost in the bloody Field,
  And Fought, and Conquer'd like a Demi-God.

BERENICE: Yet no unpleasing roughness wrong'd his Temper;
  That was commiserate as pitying Angels.
  A Thousand thousand other Charms he has;
  All lost to Berenice, whose Royal Father,
  For Wisdom and for Mercy most Renown'd,
  To save the Lives of millions that must fall,
  Whilst horrid War presents the ghastly Scene,
  Propos'd a Peace to his half Conquer'd Foes,
  And gave his Child to bind the fatal Contract.
  'Till then Ormades was design'd his Son;
  Whose Merit plac'd him next my Father's Soul:
  Yet we conceal'd our growing Loves with Care,
  Lest Envy might oppose, and ruin all:
  But still we waited with impatient wishes,
  When the good King shou'd give us to each other.
  Instead of that, O bane to all my Joys,
  A solemn Oath is to Antiochus past,
  Unknown to me, that I shou'd be his Bride,
  And all denyal, all intreaties vain.

IRENE: Is this, ye Powers, the Reward we meet
  For Vertuous Love, for Innocence and Truth?

BERENICE: Oh! I have lost all that was Great and Good,
  Generous, Kind and True in my Ormades,
  His faithful Heart ne'er knew a Thought of Falshood:
  No injur'd Woman charg'd her Wrongs on him.
  Antiochus comes pall'd with other Love,
  And a forsaken Mistress loudly rag'd;
  The News reach'd Egypt, but alas too late.

IRENE: Leodice, I've heard the Story told.

BERENICE: Ormades no such guilty Actions knew:
  His Love was pure, his Fame and Honour white;
  Yet I must drive him from my sight for ever.
  No more his Eloquence must bless my Ears,
  No more his matchless Form delight my Eyes;
  No more his Vertue charm my wondring Soul.
  I am another's, and 'tis almost a Sin,
  Barely to think and talk of his Perfections.
  Antiochus is only mine;
  And he alone shou'd be to Berenice dear,
  And so he shall, in spight of Inclination.
  I'll teach my stubborn Tongue to know its Duty,
  To call on him, my dear Antiochus.

Enter ANTIOCHUS.

ANTIOCHUS: Oh, that transporting Voice!
(*Aside.*) Now where are my Suspicions? Lost, by Heaven!
Not one dare rise to face the charming Excellence.

BERENICE (*aside*): Assist ye Powers to hide my pale Confusion;
For ebbing Blood flies from my fainting heart,
And leaves each Joynt shivering with cold surprise.

ANTIOCHUS (*aside*): And cou'd I think to wrong such Innocence?
Now by the Gods, it must not, cannot be.
Leodice must fall, 'tis so decreed:
This minute shall destroy her towering hopes,
And set her free from fruitless Expectation.
(*To the* QUEEN.) Agen I leave thee for one fleeting moment;
At my return I'll ask Ten thousand Pardons,
And make thy tender heart a full amends.

Exit.

BERENICE: What Power has conscious Guilt?
Fixt like a Statue all this time I stood,
Unable to return a Word or Look:
But let us after him, my dear Irene;
Some Stratagem shall free me for one hour:
The Prince expects me, and I dare not fail,
Lest his rash Hand shou'd do some fatal Deed.
Oh, Antiochus, forgive me this, and I offend no more.

Exeunt.
Enter ARTENOR *and* SELEUCHUS.

ARTENOR: All's lost, my Friend; Curse on my feeble Plots:
The doating King is Berenice's Slave.
Soon as return'd, forgetful of his Promise,
He doom'd Leodice to gloomy Night;
Sent her a barbarous unexpected Message,
Strictly confining her to her Appartment:
Whence if the wretched Prisoner dares remove,
Eternal Banishment must be her Fate.

SELEUCHUS: What can retrieve a Lover's Heart when lost?
(*Aside.*) I find as yet I am but half a Villain;
This turn has eas'd my Heart, which fear'd for Berenice.

ARTENOR: Here comes my Last, my only glympse of Hope;
My faithful Spy on the unthinking Queen:
Unusual haste attends his eager Steps;
Something of moment seems to bring him hither.

Enter ARCHUS.

Say: What Discovery? What News?

ARCHUS: Such as perhaps you'll find it hard to credit.
Ormades was the Stranger I observ'd
So full of fond concern for blasted Love;
He has followed in disguise to Babylon,
Assisted by Philotas, long his Friend;
In whose Apartment, they this very Hour
Wait with impatience for the Queen's approach;
Whither Irene and my self attend her,
None else being Trusted with the dangerous Secret.

ARTENOR: Now, what Reward can pay thy Diligence,
Thou best and truest of Egyptian Race?
But give thy boundless Hopes their ample Scope,
Wish all that Interest and Ambition can:
Leodice shall rise, and give thee more.

ARCHUS: I must be gone; the Queen by this is ready:
Under the Notion of Religious Rites
Perform'd in Private to Egyptian Gods,
She gains with ease the unsuspected Hour.
At my return expect a full Account of what has pass'd.
Exit.

ARTENOR: There Eunuch, I'll spare thy needless trouble.
Thus, let the Mischief be as deep as Hell,
The Gods and Heaven still dwell upon the Tongue;
And strong Devotion Cloaks the black Design.

SELEUCHUS: Who wou'd have thought such seeming Innocence
Shou'd hide so unexcusable a Falshood?
When last I gaz'd on her Inchanting Beauty,
Such was her powerful Influence o're my Soul,
I felt my Heart inlarg'd, my Temper chang'd;
My Love refin'd from every gross Desire.
I cou'd have Lov'd, methought, through endless Ages,
Even at that submissive awful Distance;
And never wish'd a more substantial Joy.

ARTENOR: Awake from this unmanly Lethargy!
Thou see'st her False; unworthy thy Concern.
Let us away to Alarm Antiochus:
He must be Witness to the Dark Cabal.
This shall confirm his weak imperfect Doubts,
And fix his Heart Leodice's for ever.

Exeunt.
Enter BERENICE, IRENE, *and* ARCHUS.

BERENICE: My Courage fails me, and I dare not go!
Some Power Divine restrains my heedless Steps,
And I can move no farther.

ARCHUS: Pardon your Slave, if he presumes to say,
This ominous Fear which startles your Resolves,
Is only the effect of timerous Nature.

IRENE: I dare not urge my Royal Mistress on,
Lest the Event should contradict my Hopes.

BERENICE: What can I do? Advise me, dear Irene.

IRENE: Too well I know,
'Till you have took your everlasting leave,
Soft Peace will be a Stranger to your Breast.

BERENICE: And can'st thou think I shall have quiet then?
Alas, thou talk'st like those that know not Love!
Shou'd I succeed, and cure his hopeless Passion,
Where is my Ease, since I must still Love on?
Or shou'd I fail, which I have cause to fear,
And he persist in unrewarded Truth;
So much I feel his Suffering in my own,
That Pity, Gratitude, and Silent Love
Will burst my tender Heart.

IRENE: Oh, wretched State of unoffending Innocence.

BERENICE: I come, Ormades, but I come the Queen;
With guiltless Fraud, I mean to heal thy Grief:
'Tis a hard Task; but I was born to Suffer.

Exeunt.
ORMADES *Lying on a Couch;* PHILOTAS *sitting by him, soft Musick Playing.*

PHILOTAS: I grow uneasy,
And wish this busie parting Hour was pass'd.

ORMADES: These gentle Strains have charm'd my swelling Griefs,
And lull'd my Soul to a Prophetick Trance.
Just now, soft Slumber, Clos'd my yielding Eyes;
And straight methought, I mounted Light as Air,
And rang'd with wonder thro' the Starry Orbs;
No Weight, no Pain, no Grief oppress'd me there:
Nothing but pure Etherial Love remain'd,
Quite disingag'd from Passion and Dispair.
Oh Happy State, of immaterial beings!
No fatal Marriage can dissolve your Peace;
Exempt from Jealousy, and fierce desire
From hopes and fears, and unsuccessful Love.
You walk at large, with most Extatick Bliss,
The endless Circle of returning Joy.

Enter BERENICE, IRENE, *and* ARCHUS.

BERENICE: My sinking Heart, wou'd shun the Glorious Trial:
(*Aside.*) Be still thou Coward.

ORMADES (*kneeling*): See at your Royal Feet, a heap of Ruins
Thrown out by Fate from all the joys of Life:
Doom'd to the gloomy Mansion of the Grave;
There, in oblivion to be hid for ever.
Yet wandering like a discontented Ghost,
'Till I had leave to Sigh my last adieu;
And View once more the beauteous Heaven I've lost.

BERENICE (*aside*): Aid me ye Powers, for his dispair has Charms.
(*To him.*) Ormades Rise,
And know, I come timely to end your folly,
To Chide the Rashness that has brought you hither,
Within the reach of my Antiochus.
He has heard you Lov'd; and shou'd you be discover'd,
What cou'd secure your Person from his Rage?
Nor is my Fame in less unlucky danger.
How wou'd malicious Tongues, that feast on Censure,
Condemn this parly, shou'd it e'er be known.

ORMADES: My Life! It is not worth my least regard:
Since you were lost, it has a burthen prov'd;
Nor need you fear aspersion;
My Death will witness to your purity.

BERENICE: Wrong not your Reason, by indulging Madness;
This Love and Constancy are empty Notions,
Fantastick Traces in Romantick Brains.
Regard me, Prince; be wise by my Example,
And from your self seek your own Happiness:
You'll find, without me, you may still be Bless'd.
My Heart was once of this soft tender Mould,

And then Ormades was its only wish,
'Till great Ambition call'd, whose awful Voice
None but the dull unthinking disobey.
'Tis true, at first I made a doubtful pause:
But Reason soon directed me to choose;
And all the busie flattering Dreams of Love
In vain oppos'd the bright unerring Guide.
With blushing Joy I took the dazlling Crown,
Which joyn'd to that my Ancestors have worn,
With grace my Off-spring with Superior Majesty.
Let Fame and Conquest charm your Manly Breast,
And Shining Glory raise you from Dispair.
The dusty Field, and the shrill Trumpet's sound
Shou'd be at once your Business and your Sport:
For Amorous Sighs, and triffling Woman's Smiles,
Are things below a Heroe.

ORMADES: Prodigious change! Such difference have I found
Between the Princess and the Queen,
I scarce can think them one.
The first was mild and gentle as soft Peace;
The last with awful Greatness speaks an Amazon:
Yet do not think, because your Heart is free,
Captivity a Jest, or fond Chimera.
For I must drag the Chains that hold me yours
'Till Death release the Slave.
In vain you mind me of neglected Fame.
I'm lost too far to listen to her Call;
Yet I have Courted and persu'd her close,
But 'twas to raise my self to your regard.
Now I have done, since Berenice is lost;
Let the vain World contend for worthless Lawrels.

BERENICE: You nourish your Distemper, but take care,
For if you wou'd persuade my doubting Heart,
Berenice has influence on your Soul,
I charge you shake off this effeminate weakness:
I wou'd not blush to hear your Story told.

ORMADES: Nor shall you need; by all that's Great you shall
Unravel all my Life to budding Childhood
And charge it with a Baseness if you can;
And now I'll bravely fall the Prince I've liv'd,
True to my Love, and Master of my Honour.

BERENICE: Touch not your Life, as you regard the Queen;
I wou'd not have a Murder to account.

ORMADES: There is no other way to give me ease,
And quit this guilty weakness of my Nature.

BERENICE: Remember that you came to take your leave;
My dear Antiochus expects me back,
And little Dreams how far I have transgress'd.

ORMADES: And can you term it breach of Duty then,
To hear a wretched Lover Mourn a-while?
Oh! Seek not to augment my killing Torture
By pitiless Disdain and cruel Scorn:
But shew some small remorse for your own sake,
That I may think you are not turn'd to Stone.

BERENICE: Let this suffice; I wish your Peace,
And as you value mine, I here Conjure you
Not to touch your Life; therefore be sure you live.

ORMADES: Hard Injunction; but I'll try, since it is your Command,
And now adieu:
May all the Happiness which I have lost,
Even all I once expected,
By smiling Angels with officious Care
Be Scatter'd round your Throne,
And that no single Thought may cross your Joy;
Ne'er let the Wretch Ormades trick your Memory;
But from this Hour be forgot as if he ne're had been.
Once more adieu, a long, a long adieu.

BERENICE (*aside*): Support me, Heaven, or I sink with Grief,
Which wanting vent, will bend me to the Earth:
Yet I will struggle with this Heart of mine,
And bring it off, if Possible, with Glory.
Hold out one Minute longer,
And let me but pronounce the dismal Word:
When he is gone, thou shalt indulge thy self
In boundless Grief, and mad unequal'd Rage
Set all the Sluces to wild Sorrow free,
And ne'er regard whate're Constructions pass.

[*At the Door.*]

ARTENOR: Within: Who opens? Here's the King wou'd enter.

BERENICE: The King, and Artenor, then I'm betray'd.

PHILOTAS: Confusion! What curst Devil has done this?
What shall we do? The Prince my dearest Friend.

IRENE: The Queen, my Royal Mistress; Oh! we are lost.

ANTIOCHUS (*without*): Will no body obey? Break down the Door,
I'll learn the cause of this Security.

BERENICE: Why shou'd my Innocence submit to Fear?
And when I am clear'd, what can offend the King?

The Door broke open, Enter ANTIOCHUS, ARTENOR, SELEUCHUS,
GUARDS, *and* ATTENDANTS.

ANTIOCHUS: By the Infernal Powers she is a Sorceress,
And there her Minion stands:
But swiftest Thunder to the Centre strike me
If they escape my Vengeance.

BERENICE: Suppress your Rage, Till you have heard me speak;
(*Kneeling.*) He is not guilty, nor have I been false.

ANTIOCHUS: How dost thou dare to wish I would believe thee,
Thou matchless Cozener of the World and me?
With what Assurance canst thou tell the Cause,
Of meeting here in private with Ormades?

ORMADES: Gods! Am I still, and Berenice upbraided?
Turn thou Imperial Charger of Bright Vertue,
And wreak on me the Malice of thy Nature;
But do not urge the Powers to thy Destruction,
By wronging her unspotted Innocence.

ANTIOCHUS: Fear not I shall neglect thee, daring Prince;

For I have Rage sufficient for you all,
And thou shalt have a double share,
Who cam'st thus far to force it from my Justice.
Guards take him Prisoner.

BERENICE: Oh, hold!
A long extended Life of Grief and Infamy
Be my wretched Portion;
And not one Soul believe my Innocence,
Or pity my Distress, if he deserves this Usage.

ORMADES: Sue not for me, that will inrage him more;
But be remorseless as you were just now,
Re-act your Scorn, and prove your Innocence.
Your Faith to him, and Cruelty to me.

ANTIOCHUS: Furies and Hell! They wou'd delude me on
'Till I believ'd I was not wrong'd at all.

ORMADES: I fear not Death, nor do I wish for Mercy:
Had Berenice been kind, I had valued Life;
But now decree whate'er your Rage thinks fit,
Without a murmur I'll submit to Fate.

ARTENOR (*to* ANTIOCHUS): If all was fair, Why was not you acquainted
With this dark Mid-night Scene?
And plac'd to hear? So you had known the Truth.

BERENICE: Let those whose Vertue stands in need of Art,
Flie to such mean Designs to inhance their Merit;
Mine needs no Gloss; for Heaven and these can tell
How unblamable I stand,
Thy swelling Malice, and thy Master's Rage.

PHILOTAS: I've lost all Patience;
Here, Royal Sir, take this Sword
And plunge it deep in my Life's dearest Blood,
That dying I may speak their Innocence,
And force your Judgment to receive the Truth.

ORMADES (*interposing*): Oh! Do not take his offer;
Vex me with lingering Deaths a tedious Age,
Or sink me instantly to endless Night;
But spare his Life, and take the Queen to Mercy.

ANTIOCHUS: His Life's a Triffle, much below my Anger;
But all the deadliest, most contracted Plagues
Light on me,
If thou escape, or if I pardon her.

IRENE: Oh, cruel Resolution!

ANTIOCHUS (*to the* GUARDS): Draw, and by thousand Wounds let out his hated
Life.

PHILOTAS: Nay, then 'tis time to oppose; by Heaven, who stirs,
(*Drawing.*) Shall pay his Life a forfeit for his Courage.

ANTIOCHUS: 'Tis false, young Hector; Take him Prisoner there.

The GUARDS *seize him, he struggles, and is dis-arm'd.*

PHILOTAS: Curse on my feeble Arm,
That cou'd not keep my Sword to save my Friend.

ORMADES: Since you will urge my Fate, it shall be so;

But my own Hands must execute your Will!
Not those Plebeian Slaves, whose Wounds wou'd give
Dishonour to my Memory: (*Stabs himself.*) Thus I excuse their Service.

PHILOTAS: Oh! Hold! What have you done?

BERENICE: Oh, Fatal Night! Oh, miserable Berenice.

ORMADES: Death was my wish;
And now you cannot doubt my dying words.
By the Eternal Gods who wait my coming,
Your Queen is Chaste as purest Vestals are:
Nor in one Look transgress'd her Love to you;
Then take her to your Arms,
Tho 'tis a sight my Love wou'd once have shun'd.
Seek to appease her much wrong'd Innocence,
And let my Blood suffice to free my Friend.

PHILOTAS: Freedom and Chains to me are equal now.

ANTIOCHUS: Can it be possible. (*To the* QUEEN.) Hast thou not been false?

BERENICE: To him I have, but oh, to thee most true.

ANTIOCHUS: Then be restor'd to what thou wast before.

BERENICE: Restor'd to thee! To thy loath'd Arms!
Stand off thou Tyrant! I detest thee now.
See where my dear Ormades bleeding lies,
The untimely Sacrifice to thy curst Jealousie.

ORMADES: She loves me still.
Oh, Death! Thou art not half so welcome now.

BERENICE: He waited here but for a last adieu:
And though I Lov'd him more than now I can Hate thee,
I counterfeited Coldness and Disdain,
To put an end to this successless Passion.
The Task was finish'd;
And had you staid but one blest minute longer,
He had been gone, never to have returned,
Within the reach of thy inhuman Power.

ANTIOCHUS: Then I, it seems, shar'd nothing of your Love;
But all your Heart was parted with before.

BERENICE: It was; Oh, my Ormades!

ORMADES: Why did I live to hear these tender words?
I shou'd have died in Peace, and thought it gain:
But oh, to have an Interest in thy Soul,
And thus to lose it in Eternal Darkness,
Is worse than all I have endur'd already.

PHILOTAS: How wan he looks! How alter'd from himself!

ORMADES: Farewel thou faithful Friend, whom long I've Lov'd;
(*To the* QUEEN.) And thou the dearest Object of my Soul,
Who parts with less reluctance from its Body,
Farewel, Fate summons me away:
I wou'd have liv'd and stab'd the Cruel Tyrant;
Have broke through all that barr'd thee from my Arms;
But 'twill not be.
Now my Eyes dazle, and my Heart grows cold;
Sound is far off, and I am lost in everlasting Shade. (*Dies.*)

BERENICE: He's gone! And do I live? By Heaven, I will not (*Snatches his dagger.*)

IRENE: Help, e're it be too late.

BERENICE: Forbear this Insolence.

ANTIOCHUS: Why do I shake? He has but done me Right:
Yet Soft Concern steals gently o're my Spirits
In spight of what she owns.
Then rise, and leave this Place,
Cease to Lament my Rival in my sight,
And I'll forget what's past, and Love agen.

BERENICE: Cease to lament! Not till I cease to live:
Here will I stay, and with my Tears imbalm him.
Oh, if thou canst afford me any Favour,
Take from my Eyes an Object they abhor;
And place thy Love on any thing but me.

ANTIOCHUS: This Cuts off all Remorse: Guards seise the Queen,
And take that hated Object from my sight. (*They carry off the Body.*)
Who thus contemns my Love, shall feel my Justice.
Leodice shall now be made my Queen;
That faithful tender Beauty loves me still:
This Hour I'll flie to her forsaken Bed,
And in her Arms laugh at thy scornful Folly.

BERENICE: With Joy I give thee back both Crown and Title.
Oh! That I cou'd with the same ease resign
The endless Sorrows they have heap'd on me.

ANTIOCHUS: Seleuchus, To thy Charge I give her up,
'Till she is call'd to answer for her Falshood.

Exit.
BERENICE *led off by* SELEUCHUS *and* GUARDS. ARTENOR, IRENE, *and*
ARCHUS *follow.*

PHILOTAS: Curst Disappointment, and inevitable Death
Persue thee close, thou unbelieving Tyrant:
His Presence swell'd my Breast with Manly Rage;
But now the rising Flood of tenderest Friendship
Drowns my Eyes: Oh, my Friend!
Thou art at rest, set free from painful Life,
Whilst I am Rack'd with lingering Dispair;
Curst with a Being I'd be glad to lose.

Exit.

ACT FIVE

LEODICE's *Apartment.*
Enter LEODICE *and* CYPRE.

LEODICE: Agen deluded; Oh my credulous Heart!
How coud'st thou hope the faithless King's return?
As well thou might'st expect old hoary Time
To turn his Flight, and bring to Morrow back:
The swiftest Streams to stop their raging Course;
All the impossibilities of Nature
Will sooner be accomplish'd; sooner far
Than Perjur'd Man return to cancel'd Faith.

CYPRE: Do not Dispair, he may again be yours:
He knows the powerful Influence of your Eyes,
And by confining you, betrays his Fear.

LEODICE: No! 'Tis his Caution, lest the Queen's disturb'd;
I am a Prisoner to secure her peace.
Oh! For Revenge, and I shall die with pleasure.
Why am I still, if that be my desire,
Wasting my Time in idle Sorrow here?
Rouse up thy Rage, Leodice, and think
What daring Act may satisfie thy Wrongs;
Call all thy Courage to assist thy Will:
Bravely perform, or die in the Attempt.

CYPRE: Alas! Your Foes are guarded from your Power;
And all the Mischiefs you wou'd hurl on them,
Will bound with double Rancour back on you.

LEODICE: 'Tis false; they are Mortal, and shall feel my Rage;
Shall know what 'tis to wrong the undaunted Heart.
Look on me well, and read it in my Face,
Which glows with ripening Vengeance hot as Flames.
Now, by the Gods, I will persue the Work.
Antiochus shall wish he had been true:
Repent the Injuries he has done my Love.
Nor shall they drag Leodice to shame
When the great blow is given:
No; I'll secure my Person from their Out-rage:
Cypre, go to my Closet, where thou wilt find
A Viol seal'd with Death, bring it me here.

CYPRE: I dare not stir, so much I fear the consequence:
Forgive your Hand-maid, who 'till now has never disobey'd.

LEODICE: Nor must you this Command; for do not think
I have but one single Death within my Grasp.
(*Shews a Dagger.*) See here, and learn how well I am resolv'd.
But I have thought, and will not trace the dismal Shades alone:
No, I'll descend in pomp, in glorious Pomp,
And a young Queen shall grace my Royal Train:
She has obscur'd my Brightness for a while,
But she shall find my Star has the Ascendant,
And that to Night she must attend Leodice;
So Fate and I decree. Fetch me the Viol then,
And spare the trouble of a third Command.

CYPRE: Oh, that I durst refuse!

Exit.

LEODICE: Now clasp her in thy Arms, perfideous King.
  There! Press her close; 'twill be thy last Embrace.
  Regard her with those Transports once I gave;
  And on her Beauties gaze thy Soul away:
  For never more her Charms will fire thy Heart.
  How will it please my Eyes to see him rowl,
  Wild with Dispair along the bloody Pavement,
  Cursing his feeble Gods,
  That cou'd not rescue her from my Revenge.
  I feel my Soul enlarg'd, and all its softness lost.
  I've talk'd my self into convenient Fury,
  And shall act things beyond belief.

Re-enter CYPRE *with a Viol.*

Bring me some Wine, I'll temper it;
'Twill give me the more leisure to be pleas'd:

Exit CYPRE.

For shou'd the Poyson operate too fast,
  I shall be robb'd of half the Joys I expect:
  The full delight which Vengeance can afford
  To one so brave, and so abus'd as I.

Re-enter CYPRE *with two Bowls.*

Alas! Thy Diligence has over-done;
  I shall not need to renew the fatal Draught.

CYPRE: I did not think you wou'd;
  But on my knees implore I may partake:
  You have·often told me that you lov'd me well.
  Oh! shew it now, and let me share your Fate.

LEODICE: Generous Maid, why shou'dst thou die?
  Thou hast deserv'd much better of Leodice;
  Yet take thy wish. (*Divides the Poyson.*)
  Thy Friendship is so true, thy Love so entire,
  That I may want thee in the other World.

CYPRE: Now I rejoyce I shall not stay behind.

LEODICE: Oh, hold! Give me the Bowl; I had forgot my Child.
  Thou must survive to guard his Innocence,
  For sure my Brother will not live disgrac'd:
  And here I yield thee up a Mothers Right:
  Be tender of his Youth, and Heaven Reward thee.

Drinks and sets down the Bowls.
Enter ANTIOCHUS.

LEODICE: Ha! What makes him here at this important minute!

ANTIOCHUS: See, I am come according to my Word;
  Or rather to my Love, for that has brought me.
  Why does the Lovely Fair One look so Cold?
  Why flies she not into my Longing Arms,
  To seal the welcome of returning Love?

LEODICE (*aside*): Such Words, such Looks, such exquisite Deceit:
  Who cou'd distrust, that has not been betray'd?
  (*To him.*) Your Majesty is come most unexpected.
  Was not a Messenger in haste dispatch'd
  To bid me quit the Hopes of so high favour?

ANTIOCHUS: There was, but I repented soon;
And grew impatient till I Crown'd thy Truth.
(*Aside.*) I'll not relate what Accidents have past,
'Till I have done what's worthy of my Change,
Lest she shou'd think Revenge my only Motive.

LEODICE: Such fleeting kindness merits small Esteem;
When next you go, you'll treat me as before.
This trifling fit of goodness, like the last,
Will meanly end in aggravating Scorn.

ANTIOCHUS: Prithee forbear reproach,
Which the more Just, the harder to be borne.
Let not severe Reflections on the past,
Nor idle Fears of what's behind in Fate
Disturb our present Hours.
Wou'dst thou have Love? why, I am nothing else.
Come then, and meet my Flames with equal Rapture;
And be the dear soft Charmer thou wast wont.

LEODICE (*aside*): What shall I do? Cold Death invades my Heart:
And my faint Limbs refuse their kind support.
Nay, cou'd they bear me to the hated Queen,
My trembling Hands want strength to act their Vengeance.
Then must I fall unpitied, and alone,
And leave the King to bless my Rivals Arms?
To waste a long Luxurious Life with her,
Forgetful of my Wrongs? I cannot bear it;
No, that wou'd torture me agen hereafter:
He must go with me, there's no other way
To keep him safe from Berenice's Charms.
(*To him.*) And will you then forever be thus kind?
Swear that you will, and this shall bind your Oath;
This pleasing Draught compos'd of various Herbs.

Takes up the Bowl.

All Sacred to the Beautious Queen of Love;
Mingled with wondrous Art, and made to Charm,
By the strange Power of Mystick Words and Prayers:
This if you drink, will keep you ever mine,
I had it ready for your wish'd approach,
Before you sent the Cruel Fatal Message;
Then take the Bowl, and prove its kind effects.

Gives him the Bowl.

(*Aside.*) Now if he drinks, I shall at last be blest,
And undisturb'd sleep in my silent Tomb.
Nor restless Love, nor raging Jealousie,
Nor wild Ambition, nor unjust Revenge
Will these Tormentors with Antiochus die.

ANTIOCHUS: I've thought, and am resolv'd to shew my Love;
I'll drink the Philter, and secure thy Peace. (*Drinks.*)
This to our Mutual,

LEODICE: Everlasting Love.

ANTIOCHUS: Now let us Love and Revel in Delight:
Do thou forget the Sufferings that are past,
And I'll be Arm'd against approaching Fate.
Th' Infernal Powers are working some dire Mischief;

For as I cross'd the Court, a hollow Voice
In mournful Accent cry'd, Antiochus must fall!
I heard, and knew it was no humane sound.

LEODICE: And did it not alarm you?
Suppose the Hand of Fate,
Just on th' inevitable point of Death,
How wou'd you bear the knowledge?

ANTIOCHUS: The thought of Death unusually affects me:
Name it no more, it pierc'd me cold as Ice.
Why dost thou start, and rowl thy charming Eyes
With such disorder'd motion?

LEODICE: The Queen.

ANTIOCHUS: Forget her.

LEODICE: I shall, but not in thy perfidious Arms.

ANTIOCHUS: Wilt thou not then be kind? What dost thou mean?

LEODICE: I mean to die, and in the peaceful Grave
Forget both Sin and Shame:
My guilty Love, and thy unjust Disdain.
Nor must you stay behind to live anothers;
Now you are mine, and Berenice shall not part us.
This Hour concludes thy Falshood and my Fear,
Thanks to th' Immortal Draught.

ANTIOCHUS: Ha! What hast thou given me? Speak.

LEODICE: A wondrous Cordial for distemper'd Minds,
Whose Sovereign Vertue can relieve the Heart
From raging pains of unsuccessful Love,
And free the labouring Brain from frivolous Care;
Lull busie States-Men to eternal Rest;
Ease weary Monarchs of th' Imperial Load;
And the forsaken Mistress of vain Grief.

ANTIOCHUS: Am I then Poyson'd? barbarous Woman!

LEODICE: Inconstant Monarch, what cou'd I do less?
Was I not scorn'd when Banish'd? Now a Prisoner.
I Lov'd you, and was treated ill.
In private, and by stealth oblig'd;
But openly Dejected and Disgrac'd.
Yet think not 'twas Revenge alone that sway'd;
I too have drunk my Fate, and cannot live.

ANTIOCHUS: It works; a thousand pointed Torments rend my Heart.
What, must I die alone? My Guards, who waits there?

Enter the GUARDS, SELEUCHUS, *several* LORDS.

To fall thus meanly by a Womans Hand,
And add to History such a shameful Tale:
That Thought exceeds the Poyson.

LEODICE: Think not your Death ignoble from my Hand,
For I am much Superior to my Sex;
And all their timerous Weaknesses disown.
See! I had Courage to attend your Fate,
And bear you Company through the horrid Vault
Of never ending Darkness;
What my proud Rival durst not have design'd.

ANTIOCHUS: Alas! I had forsworn her Bed for ever,
And came prepar'd to satisfie thy Wishes.
I meant the Crown should on thy Son devolve,
And lasting Truth reward thy Sorrows past.
The Queen had injur'd me beyond forgiveness,
And to Leodice I flew for Peace;
But thy rash Hand has put an end to all.

LEODICE: What do I hear! Oh! Raging blind impatience,
To overthrough such generous Designs:
But why was not my fatal Hand with-held?
Shook with pale Horror and Convulsive Fear,
Why dropt it not the black misguided Bowl?
Where were the Gods that have regard to Kings?
All lost in Negligence and sloathful Ease?
Thunder and Lightning shou'd have warn'd you hence;
Not the Voice of one unheeded Demon.

ANTIOCHUS: Methinks I see my Glorious Ancestors
That Grac'd the Ancient House from whence I sprung,
From the high Arch look down with shame upon me.
Hide all your blushing Heads you Reverend Shades,
And let me plunge into profound Oblivion;
Forgetting and forgot by Human Race. (*Falls.*)

LEODICE: Oh! Do not go and leave me here behind;
Stay but one moment and I shall be ready.
I feel the deadly Influence disperse
Through every Atom of my Tortur'd Flesh;
But I have something still to do.
Thus on my Knees I beg you wou'd forgive me:
Remember Love was the unhappy Cause:
And do not shun me in the other World.

ANTIOCHUS: I do forgive thee, but can stay no longer. (*Dies.*)

LEODICE: He's gone, he's gone, yet I am curst with Life;
My stubborn Nature will not yield to Death,
'Till he is lost in the unbounded space.
Oh! That some gentle Ghost, whom soft Compassion
Has drawn to view, and to lament our Fall,
Wou'd yet be kind, and wait a moment longer,
To guide me through the unknown Paths below;
The gloomy Tracts which new-born Souls persue,
'Till I can find my dear Antiochus.
Oh! I cou'd Curse my Fate for ling'ring thus.
Malicious Powers, how long will you detain me?
Death is at hand, 'tis well, I feel him here:
Welcome thou kind reliever of the Wretched,
Met by the Brave, and only shun'd by Cowards. (*Dies.*)

SELEUCHUS: Still Providence is waking for the Innocent.
Now Berenice, thou art no longer Prisoner:
This dismal Scene prepares thy Glorious Triumph.
Remove the Bodies to some Bed of State,
And wait me to your Queen.

Exeunt.

The Palace. BERENICE *sitting at a Table Reading: Enter* ARTENOR *with a Dagger in one Hand, and Poyson in the other.*

ARTENOR: Two Queens there cannot be, then one must fall;

And Destiny has thrown the Lot on Berenice:
I dare not trust Seleuchus with her Fate;
He Loves, and may assist her to escape:
So her Great Father might renew the War,
And force Antiochus to take her back.

BERENICE *seeing him, rises and comes forward.*

BERENICE: Welcome, thou surly Minister of Death:
Why dost thou tread with Caution in thy Steps?
I am prepar'd, and meet thee with a Smile.

ARTENOR: The Great Antiochus has sent you these;
You guess the fatal meaning.

BERENICE: There's Mercy in the Choice,
And I'll receive it gratefully:

Going towards ARTENOR, *starts back.*

Feeble Resolution; I dare not:
The Womanish fit returns upon my Soul,
And Death appears in all its fancy'd horrors.
I wou'd not Live; Then why this strange Confusion?
To die is but to sleep, and yet I fear:
Poor Coward, Nature, how art thou perplext?

Takes the Dagger and Poyson.

This pointed Steel wou'd soon dispatch the Work;
Had I but skill to guide it to my Heart;
But my poor shaking Hands, untaught in Murder,
May easily mistake the Purple way.
This cannot fail; sure Death attends the Draught:
But I may linger long in raging Tortures,
'Till I grow mad, and curse the Holy Powers;
Sullying in Death my whole Lifes Innocence.

ARTENOR (*aside*): I'll wait no longer, lest some unseen Chance
Shou'd snatch her from my Power;
Though 'tis the dead of Night when all shou'd rest:
A Lover may be waking to prevent me.
(*To her.*) Not yet determin'd? Then accept my Judgment;
This is the easiest, and the speediest way:

Snatches her Dagger, but as he is going to Stab her,
Enter SELEUCHUS, IRENE, PHILOTAS, *and* ARCHUS.

SELEUCHUS: Perfidious Villain. (*Stabs him.*)
Was Awful Majesty become thy Prey?

BERENICE: My Friends, are you made Prisoners too?

IRENE: No; we are free, and come to wait on you
To Liberty and Peace.

PHILOTAS: This best of Men has brought you Life and Empire:
He Lov'd you; and with that Ambitious Wretch
Contriv'd your Fall, to further his Design;
'Till mov'd by Suffering Vertue to Repent,
He soon resolv'd to come and set you free,
Asking no more than to be thought your Friend.

BERENICE: That Title wear forever:
To give me Friends and Liberty, and prove 'em,
Merits Reward larger than I can pay.

SELEUCHUS (*shewing* ARCHUS): Here is another Mourning Criminal
  Who sues with me for Pardon.

BERENICE: With you he is forgiven.

SELEUCHUS (*going to* ARTENOR): Why didst thou lift thy Arm against the
Innocent?

ARTENOR: Thou know'st the Cause.
  I'm going, and the Gods alone know whither:
  I am griev'd I fell by thee, the Man I lov'd.

SELEUCHUS: I mourn thy Fate; forgive my hasty Rage:
  For when thou'st heard what I have to declare,
  On any Terms thou wou'dst not wish to live.
  The King is poyson'd by Leodice,
  Who died her self by the same violent means.
  Her little Helpless Son is made a Prisoner
  'Till Philadelphus, who must be appeas'd
  For all the Wrongs his Daughter has receiv'd,
  Pronounce his Fate.

ARTENOR: Enough; Farwel curst Life,
  Vain Ambition, and unsuccessful Policy. (*Dies.*)

BERENICE: Antiochus dead!
  Instead of a kind Mistress's tender Arms,
  Press'd in the cold Embraces of pale Death:
  Then Artenor alone persu'd my Life,
  Unknowing of his Sisters Lost Estate.

PHILOTAS: And justly he's rewarded.

BERENICE: Now I'm again a Queen; you think me such:
  But herè I quit the gaudy empty Title:
  I wore the Pageantry but a few Days,
  And I am happy to resign the Load.
  Back to my Native Country I'll retire,
  And lay my Crown at my Great Father's Feet.

ALL: We'll All attend you thither.

BERENICE: 'Tis well; my Royal Father will Reward you
  For all the Faithful Care you take of me.
  Soon as I've gain'd his Blessing, I'll withdraw,
  And seek some lonely unfrequented Shade;
  There to lament Ormades's Cruel Fate:
  Thither, my dear Irene, thou must go
  And prove the kind Companion of my Life.

IRENE: To the Worlds utmost Limits I would wander,
  To follow you in Power or Distress.

BERENICE: I know thou wou'dst do more than I deserve;
  For I am guilty, Oh, yet Sacred Powers!
  By you I swore to be Ormades's Bride:
  Yet when my Father gave me to another,
  And bound the Contract with a solemn Oath,
  I chose to live a false perfidious wretch,
  Rather than fix the Perjury on him:
  'Twas a hard Case: yet I am justly punish'd.
  I had no right to swear; there was my Crime.
  Then let all those that shall these Mischiefs hear;
  To shun our Fate, wisely our Crimes forbear:
  For Heaven its severest Justice shows
  On lawless Love, and violated Vows.

EPILOGUE

Writ by a Friend.

LEODICE: This Story, on my Conscience, can't be true;
  For Constancy is so like Wedlock, few
  Would e'en a seeming Husband's Love persue.
  To hate and leave that dowdy lawful Life,
  Is here the great Prerogative of Wife.
  A well bred Writer, let whate'er betide,
  Had plac'd th' Elopement on the Woman's side:
  This of my Sexes, Privilege bereaves me;
  And I must Murder him because he leaves me.
  Much the fond Tale more probable were made,
  If I had Poyson'd him because he stay'd.
  Let no rude Husband after this grow Nice,
  Nor fear his Wife should follow my Device:
  Revenge more just our British Ladies find;
  A Husband's Wrongs are always paid in kind:
  Mens Stratagems but small Advantage get,
  And injur'd Women seldom die in Debt.

BIBLIOGRAPHY

Ashton, John. *Social Life in the Reign of Queen Anne.* 2 vols. London, 1882.
Astell, Mary. *A Serious Proposal to the Ladies for the Advancement of Their True and Greatest Interest. Part 1.* 4th ed. London, 1694. *Part 2. Wherein a method is Offer'd, for the Improvement of their Minds.* London, 1697. Both parts printed together, 1701.
Avery, Emmett, L. *The London Stage 1700–1729: A Critical Introduction.* Carbondale: Southern Illinois University Press, 1968.
Barbour, Paula Louise. *A Critical Edition of Mary Pix's* The Spanish Wives *(1696), with Introduction and Notes.* Diss. Yale University, 1975. Ann Arbor: UMI, 1976, 76-13,695.
Berquist, G. William, ed. *Three Centuries of English and American Plays.* (Microcard.) New York: Hafner, 1963.
Bevan, Bryan. 'Queen Anne 1665–1714.' *Contemporary Review* 205 (1964): 432–435.
Birch, Thomas. 'An Account of the Life of the Author.' In *The Works of Mrs. Catherine* [Trotter] *Cockburn, Theological, Moral, Dramatic, and Poetical.* Ed. Thomas Birch. 2 vols. London, 1751. i-xlviii.
Bowyer, John Wilson. *The Celebrated Mrs. Centlivre.* 1952. New York: Greenwood, 1968.
Boyer, Abel. *The History of the Life and Reign of Queen Anne.* London, 1722.
Centlivre, Susanna. *The Artifice.* London, 1722.
  The Basset-Table. London, 1706.
  The Beau's Duel; or, A Soldier for the Ladies. London, 1702.
  A Bickerstaff's Burying; or, Work for the Upholders. London, 1710.
  A Bold Stroke for a Wife. Ed. Thalia Stathas. Lincoln: University of Nebraska Press, 1968.
  The Busie Body. London, 1709.
  The Cruel Gift. London, 1717.
  The Dramatic Works of the Celebrated Mrs. Centlivre, with a New Account of Her Life. 3 vols. 1760–61. London, 1872. New York: AMS Press, 1968.
  The Gamester. London, 1705.
  Love's Contrivance; or, Le Medecin Malgre Lui. London, 1703.
  The Man's Bewitched; or The Devil to Do About Her. London, 1709.
  Mar-Plot; or, the Second Part of the Busy Body. London, 1710.
  The Perjur'd Husband; or, the Adventures in Venice. London, 1700.
  The Perplex'd Lovers. London, 1712.
  The Platonick Lady. London, 1706.
  The Stolen Heiress; or, the Salamanca Doctor Outplotted. London, 1702.
  The Wonder: A Woman Keeps a Secret. London, 1714.
Cibber, Colley. *An Apology for the Life of Colley Cibber.* Ed. B.R.S. Fone. Ann Arbor: University of Michigan Press, 1968.
Clark, Constance. *The Female Wits: Catherine Trotter, Delariviere Manley, and Mary Pix – Three Women Playwrights Who Made Their Debuts in the London Season of 1695–96.* Diss. City University of New York, 1984. Ann Arbor: UMI, 1984. 8409389.
[Cockburn], Catharine Trotter. *Agnes de Castro.* London, 1696.
  Fatal Friendship. London, 1698.
  Love at a Loss, or Most Votes Carry It. London, 1701.
  Olinda's Adventures; or, the Amours of a Young Lady. 1693, 1718. Los Angeles: William A. Clark Memorial Library, UCLA, 1969.
  The Plays of Mary Pix and Catharine Trotter. Ed. Edna Steeves. New York: Garland, 1982.
  The Revolution of Sweden. London, 1706.
  The Unhappy Penitent. London, 1701.
  The Works of Mrs. Catharine [Trotter] *Cockburn, Theological, Moral, Dramatic, and Poetical.* Ed. Thomas Birch. 2 vols. London, 1751.
Cotton, Nancy. *Women Playwrights in England c. 1363–1750.* Lewisburg, PA:

Bucknell University Press, 1980.
Davys, Mary. *The Northern Heiress; or The Humours of York*. London, 1716.
The Works of Mrs. Davys. 2 vols. London, 1725.
Day, Robert Adams. 'Muses in the Mud: The Female Wits Anthropologically
Considered.' *Womens Studies* 7 (1980): 61–74.
Faderman, Lillian. *Surpassing the Love of Men: Romantic Friendship and Love
Between Women from the Renaissance to the Present*. NY: William Morrow, 1981.
Ferguson, Moira, ed. *First Feminists: British Women Writers 1578–1799*.
Bloomington: Indiana University Press, 1985.
Gagen, Jean. *The New Woman: her Emergence in English Drama 1600–1730*. NY:
Twayne, 1954.
Goreau, Angeline. 'Aphra Behn: A Scandal to Modesty.' In *Feminist Theorists:
Three Centuries of Key Women Thinkers*. Ed. Dale Spender. New York: Pantheon,
1983. 8–27.
Gosse, Edmund. 'Catharine Trotter, the Precursor of the Bluestockings.' *Transactions
of the Royal Society of Literature* 2nd series 34 (1916): 87–118.
Green, David. *Queen Anne*. London: Collins, 1970.
Sarah, Duchess of Marlborough. New York: Scribner, 1967.
Gregg, Edward Queen Anne. London: Routledge, 1980.
[Holt], Jane Wiseman. *Antiochus the Great: or, the Fatal Relapse*. London, 1702.
Hook, Lucyle. Introduction. *The Female Wits; or, The Triumvirate of Poets at
Rehearsal*. Los Angeles: William Andrews Clark Memorial Library, UCLA, 1967.
i–xvi.
Hughes, Leo. *The Drama's Patrons: A Study of the Eighteenth-Century London
Audience*. Austin: University of Texas Press, 1971.
Hume, Robert D. 'Marital Discord in English Comedy from Dryden to Fielding.'
Modern Philology (February 1977): 248–272.
Kendall, Kathryn. 'From Lesbian Heroine to Devoted Wife: or, What the Stage
Would Allow.' *Journal of Homosexuality* 12 (May 1986) 9–22.
*Theatre, Society, and Women Playwrights in London From 1695 Through the
Queen Anne Era*. Diss. University of Texas, 1986. Ann Arbor: UMI, 1986.
8618505.
The London Stage, 1660–1800. Ed. Emmett L. Avery, et al. 11 vols. Carbondale:
Southern Illinois University Press, 196068.
Manley, [Mary] Delariviere. *Almyna; or, The Arabian Vow*. London, 1707.
The Lost Lover; or, The Jealous Husband. London, 1696.
Lucius, the First Christian King of Britain. London, 1717.
The Novels of Mary Delariviere Manley. Ed. Patricia Köster. 2 vols. Gainesville,
FL: Scholars' Facsimiles and Reprints, 1971.
The Royal Mischief. London, 1696. [Included in Fidelis Morgan's anthology, *The
Female Wits (Virago, 1980).]*
McBurney, William H. '*Mrs. Mary Davys*': Forerunner of Fielding.' *PMLA* 74
(1959): 348–55.
Milhous, Judith. *Thomas Betterton and the Management of Lincoln's Inn Fields
1695–1720*. Carbondale: Southern Illinois University Press, 1979.
Morgan, Fidelis. *The Female Wits: Women Playwrights on the London Stage 1660–
1720*. London: Virago, 1981.
Perry, Ruth. 'The Veil of Chastity: Mary Astell's Feminism.' In *Sexuality in
Eighteenth-century Britain*, Edited by Paul-Gabriel Bouce. Manchester:
Manchester University Press, 1982.
Pix, Mary Griffith. *The Conquest of Spain*. London, 1705.
The Czar of Muscovy. London, 1701.
The Deceiver Deceiv'd. London, 1698.
The Different Widows; Or, Intrigue All-A-Mode. London, 1703.
The Double Distress. London, 1701.
The False Friend, Or, the Fate of Disobedience. London, 1699.
Ibrahim, The Thirteenth Emperour of the Turks. London, 1696.
The Inhumane Cardinal. London, 1696.

The Innocent Mistress. London, 1697.
The Plays of Mary Pix and Catharine Trotter. 2 vols. New York: Garland, 1982.
Queen Catharine, or, The Ruines of Love. London, 1698.
† *She Ventures and He Wins.* London, 1696.
The Spanish Wives. London, 1696.
† *Zelmane: or, The Corinthian Queen.* London, 1705.
Rogers, Katharine M. *Feminism in Eighteenth-century England.* Urbana: University of Illinois Press, 1982.
Smith, Dane Farnsworth. *Plays About the Theatre in England.* London: Oxford University Press, 1936.
Smith, Hilda L. *Reason's Disciples: Seventeenth-century English Feminists.* Urbana: University of Illinois Press, 1982.
Snyder, Henry L. 'New Light on Mrs. Manley.' *Philological Quarterly* 52 (1973): 767–70.
Spender, Dale, ed. *Feminist Theorists: Three Centuries of Key Women Thinkers.* NY: Pantheon, 1983.
Women of Ideas and What Men Have Done to Them from Aphra Behn to Adrienne Rich. London: Routledge, 1982.
Stathas, Thalia. 'A Critical Edition of Three Plays by Susanna Centlivre.' Diss. Stanford, 1965.
Steeves, Edna L., ed. *The Plays of Mary Pix and Catharine Trotter.* 2 vols. New York: Garland, 1982.
Stefanson, Donald H. 'The Works of Mary Davys: A Critical Edition.' 2 vols. Diss. University of Iowa, 1971.
Suwannabha, Sumitra. 'The Feminine Eye: Augustan Society as Seen by Selected Women Dramatists of the Restoration and Early Eighteenth Century.' Diss. Indiana University, 1973.
ten Hoor, Henry. 'A Re-examination of Susanna Centlivre as a Comic Dramatist.' Diss. University of Michigan, 1963.
Trotter, Catharine. See Cockburn.
Wilson, John Harold. *All the King's Ladies: Actresses of the Restoration.* Chicago: University of Chicago Press, 1958.
Winton, Calhoun. 'Sentimentalism and Theater Reform in the Early Eighteenth Century.' In *Quick Springs of Sense: Studies in the Eighteenth Century.* Ed. Larry S. Champion. Athens, Georgia: University of Georgia Press, 1974. 31–42.
Wiseman, Jane. See Holt.

† The authorship of these plays is in question.